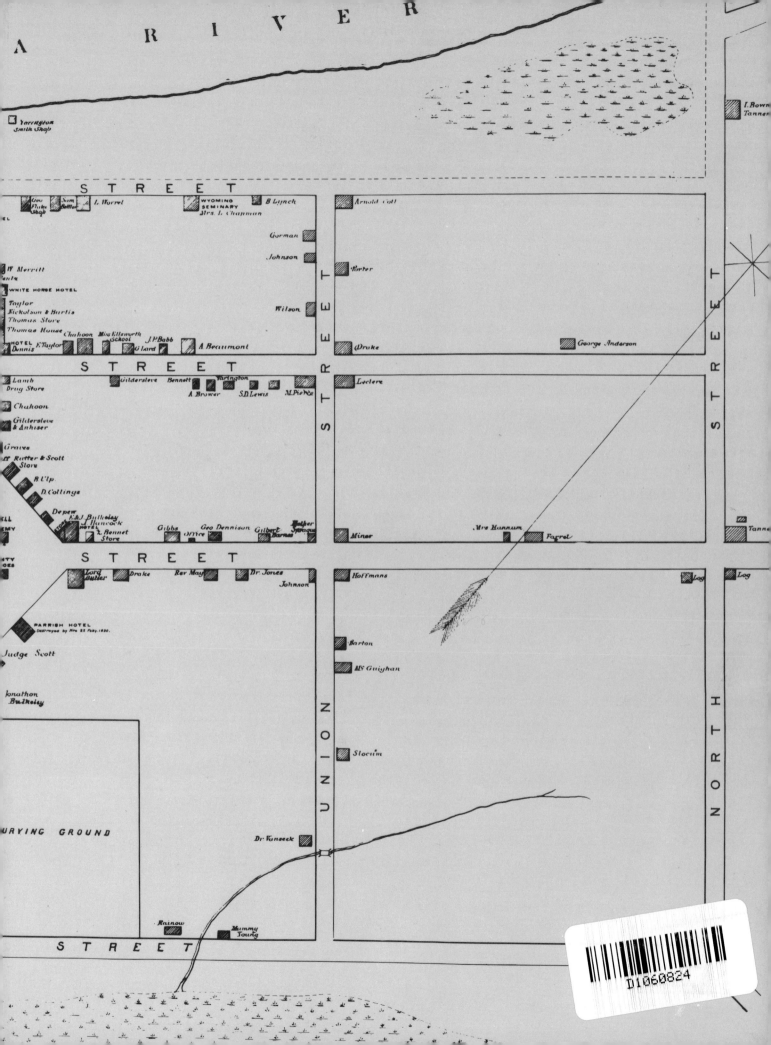

THE WYOMING VALLEY
AN AMERICAN PORTRAIT

Edward F. Hanlon

THE
WYOMING
VALLEY

AN AMERICAN PORTRAIT

EDWARD F. HANLON

PICTURE RESEARCH BY JOHN BECK

"PARTNERS IN PROGRESS"
BY DAVID PHILLIPS

SPONSORED BY
THE GREATER WILKES-BARRE CHAMBER OF COMMERCE

WINDSOR PUBLICATIONS
WOODLAND HILLS, CALIFORNIA

Windsor Publications, Inc.
History Books Division

Publisher: John M. Phillips
Editorial Director: Lissa Sanders
Production Supervisor: Katherine Cooper
Senior Picture Editor: Teri Davis Greenberg
Senior Corporate History Editor: Karen Story
Marketing Director: Ellen Kettenbeil
Production Manager: James Burke
Design Director: Alexander D'Anca
Art Production Manager: Dee Cooper
Typesetting Manager: E. Beryl Myers
Proofreading Manager: Doris R. Malkin

Staff for *An American Portrait*
Editor: F. Jill Charboneau
Picture Editor: Kevin Cavanaugh
Assistant Editors: Todd Ackerman, Leslie King
Editorial Assistants: Susan Block, Phyllis Gray, Judith Hunter,
   Patricia Morris, Susan Wells
Sales Manager: William Koons
Sales Representative: Glenn Edwards
Production Artists: Beth Bowman, Colleen Maggart
Typographer: Barbara Neiman
Proofreaders: Jeff Leckrone, Kaylene Ohman

Designer: John Fish

Previous page: *This painting of Wilkes-Barre in the 1840s is the work of an unknown artist. The panorama shows the city (population about 2,000) looking toward the southwest, probably from the top of Redoubt Hill. Left of center, the one clearly discernible street is North Franklin. To the right, a covered wooden bridge carries Market Street from Wilkes-Barre to Kingston. Courtesy, Eugene S. Farley Library, Wilkes College, and D. Leonard Corgan Library, King's College; Edward Welles, Jr., Collection*

Library of Congress Cataloging in Publication Data

Hanlon, Edward F., 1938-
   The Wyoming Valley.

   "Sponsored by the Greater Wilkes-Barre Chamber of
Commerce."
   Bibliography: p.
   Includes index.
   1. Wyoming Valley (Pa.) — History. 2. Wyoming
Valley (Pa.) — Description and travel. 3. Wyoming
Valley (Pa.) — Industries. I. Phillips, David (David G.)
II. Greater Wilkes-Barre Chamber of Commerce.
III. Title.
F157.W9H18   1983   974.8'32   83-12360
ISBN 0-89781-073-2

CONTENTS

TO MY STUDENTS
PAST, PRESENT, AND FUTURE

Although collieries tended to be dirty and to spread their dirt over the surrounding landscape, their unusual architecture and their dynamism made them as fascinating as they were repellent. Alice Marea (Welsh) Jenkins captured some of this ambivalence in "Spotlight," which depicts the Woodward Colliery of the Glen Alden Coal Company in 1957, two years before the Knox disaster brought subsurface mining to an end. Courtesy, D. Leonard Corgan Library, King's College; Edward Welles, Jr., Collection

FOREWORD

How easy it is to think of history as something that happened to the people in another place! Even for people like me—who have grown with the 20th century and seen much history made (and I like to think I made a little myself)—it is somehow hard to remember that our lives and our experiences in our own Valley are as much a part of history as events in Washington or Philadelphia or places halfway around the globe.

I was especially delighted to read in *The Wyoming Valley: An American Portrait* that our Valley is a microcosm of American history—partly because its history exemplifies the whole American experience in so many ways and partly because so many events of national significance have happened here.

For many of us, for example, the Susquehanna is first and foremost the source of terrible disaster in 1972. But how many of us—hurrying across the Breslau Bridge or the Market Street Bridge or the Fort Jenkins Bridge—ever pause, however briefly and however infrequently, to think about the river and the Valley? How many of us recall that a mighty army once camped along our Susquehanna's banks? How many of us know that a ditch—a little canal four feet deep and 40 feet wide and 18 miles long (built for $234,070.17)—first brought prosperity to the Valley from Nanticoke to the mouth of the Lackawanna in Pittston?

From the day we enter kindergarten, we are told over and over again that America is a *melting pot*, that we give, in George Washington's words "to bigotry no sanction, to persecution no assistance"; but we soon learn that some of us are Protestants, some Jews, some Catholics, some Poles, some Welsh, some Slovaks, some Irish, some Italian, and on and on. Yet Dr. Hanlon shows clearly how America is not so much a melting pot as it is a *welding shop*, of which our Valley is a superb example—a place where the chunks and chips of the old have been annealed into something brighter and stronger.

How I love to visit the annual folk festival each autumn. There, under the great roof of the vast Kingston Armory, I see the people of my Valley coming together to celebrate at once their different backgrounds and their common heritage. We have endured so much, we Valley folk, including the decline of our major industry and the devastation of a dreadful flood. But we have learned so much too—the troubles that hurt us have also brought us together. The ethnic and religious differences that once separated us have now become the wellspring of a diversity that paradoxically brings us together.

This is the message I take from *The Wyoming Valley*. Despite the depressions and the disruptions of our past, we have learned much and accomplished much. We can stride into the future confident that we will achieve still more.

Daniel J. Flood

ACKNOWLEDGMENTS

Long before the author became associated with this project, Mr. John Sheehan, executive director of the Greater Wilkes-Barre Chamber of Commerce, Mrs. Margaret E. Craft, acting director of the Wyoming Historical and Geological Society, Attorney F. Charles Petrillo, chairman of the Society's Ways and Means Committee, and Ms. F. Jill Charboneau, senior editor at Windsor Publications, saw a need for an illustrated local history and contacted me to prepare the manuscript. Throughout the months which have followed that contact, they have all been most helpful in responding to my requests for assistance. They have allowed me to pursue my work with independence. I acknowledge their assistance and am grateful for their confidence.

Without the help of the librarians of Wyoming Valley this work would not have been possible. Mrs. Margaret Craft and her staff at the Bishop Memorial Library of the Wyoming Historical and Geological Society were invaluable throughout my research. Ms. Judith Tierney, special collections librarian at King's College, was especially helpful in sharing the collection under her care and in responding to many requests for assistance. Mr. Joseph Lusksic of College Misericordia, and Sr. Sylvia Connell, R.S.M., archivist of the Sisters of Mercy, also provided generous assistance.

Ms. Mary Theresa Stemmer of King's College's Center for Independent Learning typed the manuscript with accuracy and retyped it with good humor. Ms. Marisue Elias, a student at King's, proved a diligent and effective research assistant.

Ms. Gloria Galante of King's College went through every sentence of the manuscript, providing invaluable suggestions, corrections, and criticisms. Without her patient, thorough, and encouraging collaboration, the work would not have appeared in this form.

Finally, the text of the book would have been incomplete without the illustrations and captions that have been collected by Mr. John Beck of The Bookmakers Incorporated, of Wilkes-Barre. Most important, I have found that Mr. Beck has the skills of an artist, the talents of a fine researcher and editor, and the patience of a good friend. I am especially grateful to him for his enrichment of the manuscript.

Special thanks for illustration assistance is due to the following: the staff of the Wyoming Historical and Geological Society (director Burt Logan, curator Joseph Sgromo, and—again—librarian Margaret Craft); the staff of the D. Leonard Corgan Library (director Terrence Mech, audiovisual director Karl Burke, and—again—reference and special collection librarian Judith Tierney); William Gladish and Michael F. Conner of Bohlin Powell Larkin Cywinski; Herbert F. Godfrey of the Wilkes-Barre Redevelopment Authority; Michael J. Lewis III, who shared his knowledge of the history of Wilkes-Barre architecture; F. Charles Petrillo who shared his knowledge of canals and river traffic as well as his superb postcard collection; Thomas Hartz of Meban Offsett, whose skill with a line camera recaptured the luster and legibility of stained and faded maps and drawings; and Ed Mengak and his Professional Photographic Services staff, who restored as much as could be found in many old photos and postcards, both black and white and color.

To these people, and to many others who have helped me, I express my deep gratitude. I am, of course, responsible for any errors of fact that remain and for all the judgment in the work.

King's College
15 January 1983

Edith (Merrel) Keller painted "Public Square Looking up East Market Street" in 1957, but her picture shows that scene as it would have appeared around 1940. The red brick building in the center with its tower and high flagpole is Wilkes-Barre City Hall, designed by W.W. Neuer in the early 1880s, which has now lost the tower and all its other roof ornaments. Courtesy, D. Leonard Corgan Library, King's College; Edward Welles, Jr., Collection

"From the Market Street Bridge," painted around 1950 by Charles Burrott Zimmerman, shows the Wilkes-Barre skyline almost as it appears today. The great sign atop the bank now says "United Penn Bank" (same bank, different name), and the bridge has been disfigured with overhead lane-use indicators. Courtesy, D. Leonard Corgan Library, King's College; Edward Welles, Jr., Collection

INTRODUCTION

The title of this work, *The Wyoming Valley: An American Portrait*, contains a statement of its subject, theme, and method of presentation. It deals with the Wyoming Valley of northeastern Pennsylvania, from Pittston on the north to Plymouth and Nanticoke on the south, on both sides of the Susquehanna River. While it does deal with the land itself, the coal that lies under it, and the river that flows through—and occasionally over—it, it emphasizes the people who have dwelt on that land. From the first Indians who came here, seeking refuge from white intruders on their homes in Maryland, to the present residents, seeking to build a community for the 21st century, the peoples of Wyoming Valley have had to struggle with the elements and with one another to bring a unity out of diversity.

They have come here from many places. At first, they came from Connecticut and southern Pennsylvania, then from Britain and Ireland, then from Germany and Italy, and finally from the Russian and Austro-Hungarian empires. With diverse ethnic and religious backgrounds, they have faced and solved problems, endured and triumphed over poverty, and created wealth and security. The story of their failures and victories—their ordinary activities and extraordinary accomplishments as farmers, millers, miners, factory workers, business and professional people, artists and students—is the subject of this work.

Their activities, however, are considered only in the context of national history. The Wyoming Valley can be seen as a center of American history, a place where nationally important developments have occurred, and a place which accurately and effectively reflected major themes in American history. Thus, its local history derives its importance from its relation to a broader picture, the development of the United States. This theme should help readers and students come to a clearer understanding of American history through the use of local examples.

Finally, the work is a portrait—accenting art more than science, clarity more than depth. It is meant for general readers rather than professional scholars. The bibliography indicates the availability of scholarly work on the subject and also indicates the great gaps. Perhaps this book will stimulate others to conduct the studies needed for a thorough and deep understanding of the region's history. But, in any case, this book does not claim to be more than it is.

A portrait is not a complete picture. Many important features of local history have received little or no consideration. The transportation systems, journalism and other forms of communication, banking, the fine arts, sports, and other types of entertainment have received scant emphasis. This has resulted from limitations of space rather than from a judgment that such subjects were insignificant.

The author wishes to acknowledge his deep attachment to and respect for the people of Wyoming Valley. He has spent all but five of his years here, surrounded by the natural beauty and the man-made ugliness of the region, studying in the local schools and libraries, worshipping in the local churches, reveling in the diversity of the local communities, teaching in three local colleges. While aware of the regions's problems, he sees it as a place well worth the work needed to improve it. It is his hope that this book will not only bring pleasure to his fellow citizens, but will provide them with inspiration and ideas to follow the example of their predecessors in solving problems and transcending manifold difficulties.

The Wyoming Valley Battle Monument, erected in the 1840s, received the following dedication in 1878, "This monument commemorative of these events, and in memory of the actors in them, has been erected over the bones of the slain by their descendants and others who gratefully appreciated the services and sacrifices of their patriot ancestors." Courtesy, Wyoming Historical and Geological Society (WHGS)

Dial Rock (also known as Campbell's Ledge), rising from the east bank of the Susquehanna just north of the mouth of the Lackawanna, is traditionally the northern portal of the Valley. For the earliest travelers, who most frequently used the river, this was their first sight of "Wiomink." This oil painting by Charles B. Zimmerman is called "Dial Rock— October." Courtesy, D. Leonard Corgan Library, King's College; Edward Welles, Jr., Collection

Chapter One

A
SECOND
FRONTIER

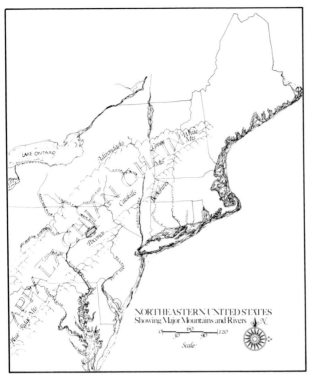

NORTHEASTERN UNITED STATES
Showing Major Mountains and Rivers

Left: *The principal barrier to inland migration for settlers from the Eastern seaboard was the vast chain of the Appalachian Mountains that rise in New Hampshire and extend southward to central Georgia. The Indians' "Long-reach River" (the Susquehanna), with its branches and tributaries, drains much of south central New York and eastern Pennsylvania. Settlers from Connecticut had to cross the Housatonic, the Hudson, and the Delaware to reach the Wyoming Valley. Courtesy, The Bookmakers, Incorporated, copyright 1983*

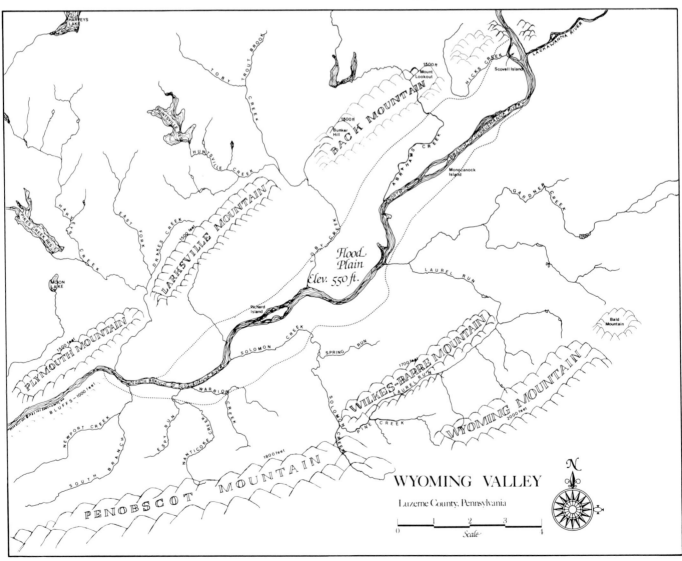

WYOMING VALLEY

Luzerne County, Pennsylvania

To understand any part of American history, including that of Wyoming Valley, it is wise to look first to the land itself. The geography of the New World profoundly influenced, if not determined, the attitudes and institutions of Europeans who settled here. The mountains, plains, rivers, and lakes received peoples from similar European backgrounds but changed them so profoundly that the ultimate product was a distinctly American culture.

Whether they walked from Connecticut in the first years, sailed from Britain and Ireland and the Germanies in the middle of the 19th century, or came by steamship from Italy or the Austro-Hungarian and Russian empires in the later decades, it was the geography of the Wyoming Valley that would alter their lives. The land itself would make the Valley folk different from their cousins in Europe—and from those in other parts of the United States.

The first great physical fact of eastern North America is the Appalachian chain of mountains. With such pleasant names as the Berkshires, the Catskills, the Adirondacks, the Poconos, and the Blue Ridge mountains, this continental range descends from the coast of Maine—where it seems to rush into the sea—to the backwoods of Georgia several hundred miles from the coast. These mountains, which formed the natural western boundary of British North America, seemed impenetrable to all but the Indians, the scouts, and the most daring traders.

The great rivers that sprang from these mountains and poured into the Atlantic became America's first highways. Some short, shallow waterways moved lazily from the base of the mountains to the sea. Other rivers—like the Hudson, the Delaware, and the Potomac—had cut through the mountains in ages past to provide hundreds of miles of banks for farming and easy access to the coast.

Of America's eastern rivers none was longer or potentially more important than the one the Indians accurately described as the "Long-reach River"—Susquehanna. Its north branch began near modern Cooperstown, New York. It flowed erratically, sometimes north but usually south, sometimes east and sometimes west, bending, twisting, sometimes rapidly but most often gently, for 444 miles. The Chemung joined it near Binghamton, New York, providing an opening to the Finger Lakes and the Great Lakes. Its west branch joined it at Sunbury and opened most of central Pennsylvania and upper New York. The Juniata poured into the Susquehanna north of Harrisburg, creating a "road" into the rolling hills of southern Pennsylvania. The Long-reach River flowed through the rich land of central Maryland till it entered Chesapeake Bay at Havre de Grace. Thus the river was part of an intra-continental waterway that drained colonial America's breadbasket.

From the point where the Lackawanna River joined the Susquehanna near modern Pittston, downriver to a gap in the mountains south of Nanticoke, lay an area the Indians simply described as *Wyomink*, meaning the expansive plain. Early visitors described this piece of real estate as an "august and stupendous work of creation." It extended for 16 miles along the river and "contained several good Islands, good large Meadows on both sides about four miles to the east mountain and three to the west." Its soil was found to be "deep, strong, fat black, and fine, exceedingly kind, and warm."

Unknown to the Indians and the first settlers, a second river flowed through Wyoming Valley: an underground river, a river of coal. This began at what would become Forest City in Susquehanna County and passed through Lackawanna County, underlying the entire Wyoming Valley and ending slightly to the south in Shickshinny. Never more than six miles wide and often many hundreds of feet deep, this river contained almost pure carbon—the finest anthracite in the world. One day it would

Facing page bottom: *Bounded on two sides by low mountains and to the north and south by bluffs where the Susquehanna River enters and leaves, the Wyoming Valley has remained basically unchanged since the last Ice Age. Today, dikes protect the most densely settled parts of the flood plain from the river's periodic rampages. A large measure of the Valley's charm comes from the brooding, friendly quality of the surrounding mountains. Courtesy, The Bookmakers, Incorporated, copyright 1983*

bring wealth and work, benefits and pain.

Despite a river filled with fish, flats ripe for planting, and hills teeming with game, the rich Wyoming Valley had not been the ancestral home of any Indian peoples. Aside from traveling groups who used the river banks as rest stations, this land was uninhabited until the first English settlers came to Virginia in 1607. The settlements there and especially those in Maryland upset the native Americans' way of life and made them look to Wyoming Valley as a haven.

When the whites settled near the Chesapeake Bay, the Susquehannock Indians were already firmly established on the lower parts of the river from which they took their name. As more and more whites

came, the Indians moved further north. They settled in the Wyoming Valley and there encountered another enemy, the Iroquois. Grouped into a confederation of five nations and dominating the region now known as upper New York, these highly organized tribes wanted to maintain their monopoly on the valuable fur trade with the English. They waged war on the Susquehannocks and in 1675 (seven years before William Penn received his charter) defeated them. With this victory they claimed the Wyoming Valley and the headwaters of the Susquehanna as their own lands. These claims based on conquest were recognized as valid both by English and colonial governments and by other Indians. The Iroquois, nonetheless, felt keenly that the Valley had to be occupied—and by

Campbell's Ledge (also known as Dial Rock) rises sharply from the eastern bank of the Susquehanna just to the north of the mouth of the Lackawanna River. Traditionally the northern portal of Wyoming Valley, it looks much the same today as it did to the early settlers and explorers. Courtesy, Ace Hoffman Studios

friendly forces. Since they could not afford to dispatch their own tribesmen to settle here, they made it a refugee camp for displaced Indians of the East Coast.

At the invitation of the Iroquois, Shawnees came to Wyoming as early as 1701, and some stayed till the 1740s. They planted the flatlands near modern Plymouth until they moved on, first north and then west. The Conoy or Piscataway Indians came originally from the mouth of the Potomac in Chesapeake Bay and later from around Washington D.C. Their close relatives, the Nanticokes, came from the eastern shore of Maryland in 1748 and stayed five years, leaving behind their name and traces of their residence to delight 20th century archaeologists. The Tuscaroras from North Carolina spent some time near Pittston before joining the Iroquois as the sixth nation of the confederation.

Of all the tribes to reside here, none better demonstrate the crises between Indian and white relations than the Lenni Lenape or Delaware Indians. This great tribe once dominated the area from Delaware Bay to Manhattan, but contact with the whites ruptured their society. Their population shrank with exposure to diseases such as measles and smallpox for which they had no natural resistance. They saw the benefits the white man derived from guns—for hunting and defense—and soon became dependent on him for this technology. Many also became dependent on the distilled spirits, especially rum, which whites had introduced. Some converted to Christianity, but others tried valiantly to maintain their own traditions. From their number emerged a truly remarkable man—Teedyuscung, self-proclaimed "King of the Delawares." In 1754 he led a few of his people to Wyoming, where he tried to preserve the Valley as an Indian sanctuary.

To achieve this, Teedyuscung needed to balance the needs of his increasingly dependent people with the demands of the powerful Iroquois; to placate his allies in Pennsylvania on whom he relied for protection and rum; and to ward off the French who threatened to advance into Pennsylvania. These gigantic tasks were complicated by the fact that Teedyuscung was an alcoholic. At vital points in his life the endlessly talented King would be incapacitated by his disease. He found his life further complicated when still another group showed interest in his Valley—the members of the Susquehannah Company of Connecticut.

To contemporary Americans the presence of Connecticut Yankees in Wyoming Valley in the mid-18th century seems strange, especially considering the terrain that separates Connecticut from the Susquehanna. To reach this area the New England Puritans had to cross the heavily forested mountains which separate the two regions. Admittedly, established Indian trails eased the problem, but still the difficulty posed by geography was enormous. Colonists had to ford first the Hudson with its Palisades and then the Delaware. That they were willing to do so shows the value of the Valley. That they also felt justified requires some explanation.

Connecticut had begun as an outgrowth of Massachusetts. Towns in the Connecticut Valley and on the southern coast of New England seemed to grow almost spontaneously in the early colonial period. It was not until 1662 that the leaders of these settlements secured from King Charles II a charter that legally justified their existence. This charter described the boundaries vaguely—the western border was to be the "South Sea."

Two years later when Britain defeated the Netherlands, a Dutch colony immediately west of Connecticut was part of the peace settlement. This acquisition the generous, if grandiose, Charles II turned over to his brother James, Duke of York (later King James II). Thus New York and Connecticut claimed the same lands. They settled their differences in

1683 when Connecticut accepted the modern dividing line between the two.

In the meantime Charles II had made still another grant—in 1681 he bestowed on his young friend William Penn a territory bounded on the east by the Delaware River and on the north by the 43rd parallel. Clearly the Wyoming Valley fell within this parcel; and, by English law, it belonged to William Penn.

For 70 years after Penn received his charter, his claims to Wyoming remained unexercised and basically uncontested. Because the Iroquois held the land by right of conquest, and because various tribes resided there periodically, this was clearly Indian land. The Penns consistently respected Indian titles and prohibited white settlements unless and until the lands had been purchased from the native Americans. Even as late as the 1750s Pennsylvanians felt no need to expand into the fertile, strategic Valley.

A need for expansion had, however, arisen in Connecticut. In the generation between 1730 and 1753, its population tripled. Soil exhaustion, especially in eastern Connecticut, and dreams of recovering the "lost" western lands of the province led to the formation on July 18, 1753, of the Susquehannah Company. This joint stock company hoped to form a New Connecticut by taking and cultivating the lands beyond New York, which would then be shared by the members of the company.

These Yankees looked to Wyoming Valley as the best spot to begin their venture. At the Albany Congress of July 1754 they tried to buy the land from the Iroquois. The Confederation had been willing to sell vast tracts west of the Susquehanna to their friends from Pennsylvania, but "as to Wyomink and Shamokin (Sunbury) and the Land continuous there to on the Sasquehannah, We (the Iroquois) reserve them for our hunting ground and for the Residence of Such (Indians) as in this time of War shall remove from the French and chuse to live there."

Despite this definitive statement, an agent of the Susquehannah

Among the few whites to visit the Valley before it was settled was Count Zinzendorf, a Moravian missionary who attempted to convert the Shawnees during a three-week stay in the fall of 1742. Zinzendorf did not encounter any Delawares, who must have arrived in the Valley shortly after his departure. Courtesy, Wyoming Historical and Geological Society (WHGS)

Teedyuscung, king of the Delawares, showed considerable diplomatic skill in protecting his tribal interests against the Pennsylvanians, the Iroquois, and the French. The Connecticut settlers defeated him only through treachery. The details in this old drawing suggest that it may be an actual likeness. Notice the knife worn in the headdress just above the right ear. (WHGS)

Company, John Henry Lydius, began to secure signatures from various Indians on a deed conveying the coveted land to his company. This sharp character used rum to induce compliance. Most of the signatures were obtained singly, over a period of weeks. More important, the signatories had no right to transfer the land. That right only belonged to the Onondaga Council of the Iroquois, which repudiated the treaty and transfer at once. In addition, Pennsylvania's agents denounced it as fraudulent and illegal; and the British Board of Trade, governing agency for all the colonies, denied its validity. Even the opponents of the Susquehannah Company in Connecticut argued against it. On this dubious deed, however, the company based its claim for future settlement and began to take steps to exercise the newly "purchased" rights.

The company sent surveyors to Wyoming in June 1755. They encountered opposition from the Delawares led by Teedyuscung. After charting the land they returned to New England with glowing reports of its potential. Despite the fact that Britain was waging war with France and her Indian allies (1754-1763), the Yankees gave some attention to the new plantation. They cut a road through the mountains and over the rivers, completing it in September 1762. They built a few log houses, a sawmill, and a gristmill. Despite the opposition of the Indians, the protests of the Pennsylvanians, and the discouragement of the royal government, the intrepid Connecticutters proceeded.

Teedyuscung complained to the proprietary governor in Philadelphia that as many as 150 men with "all sorts of tools as well for Building as for Husbandry" had settled on his land. The governor sympathized but did not act. Finally, the Indians took things into their

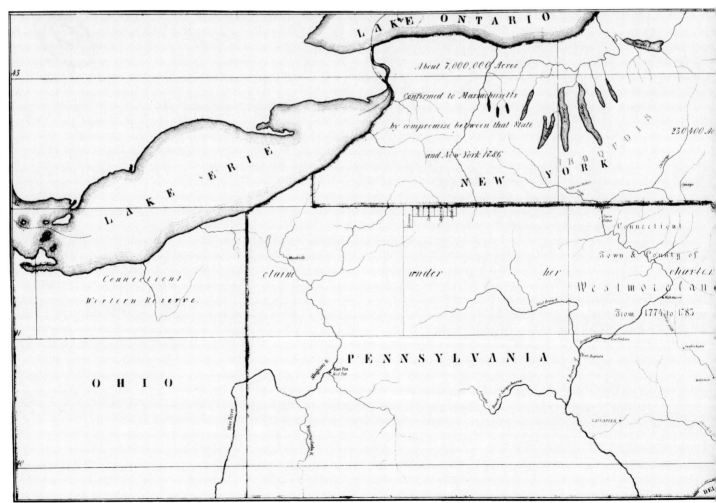

own hands and harried the intruders out of the Valley in 1762. The victory was to be short-lived.

On April 19, 1763, Teedyuscung retired to the cabin that had been built for him by his friends, the Pennsylvanians. There, on the river's east bank near the beginning of Old River Road, he fell into a drunken stupor. A person or persons unknown approached the shelter and set it afire with the King of the Delawares in it. Within hours all the Indian homes in the Valley had burned to ashes. Anthony F.C. Wallace, Teedyuscung's biographer, concludes that ''There does not seem to be much room for doubt that the Susquehanna Company was behind the murder of Teedyuscung and the remarkable simultaneous firing of the houses at Wyoming.''

With this enemy gone, settlers moved into the vacant Valley with apparent impunity. They built and planted through the spring and summer; but on October 15, 1763, Delaware Indians, led by Teedyuscung's son ''Captain'' Bull, returned to avenge their king. In the Valley's second massacre in a year, red men slew whites—killing about 20 and scattering the rest into the wilderness.

During the next six years the members of the Susquehannah Company prudently remained east of the Hudson. The governor of Pennsylvania sent a few people to settle in Wyoming and protect the region from all others. But the landlust of the Yankees was not to be stayed. The company selected 40 men to repair to Wyoming before February 1, 1769. These 40 would be granted a ''township'' to divide among themselves. They would be followed by another 200 settlers who would share four additional ''townships.''

Facing page, top: *Despite the royal charter granting all of Pennsylvania to them, the Penn family clearly understood that the resident Indians did not recognize the right of the king of England to give away tribal land. The Penns accordingly were meticulous in purchasing each tract on which they proposed to settle from the Indians themselves. This map shows early purchases of land to the south of the Wyoming Valley.*

Left: *Several books have been devoted to Connecticut's disputed claim to the northern half of Pennsylvania. The boundary between New York and Connecticut was determined in 1683, but land-hungry Connecticut settlers insisted that their claim resumed to the west of the Delaware River. They called the northeastern corner of the state Westmoreland County, a name that survives in only a few places— notably the Westmoreland Club in downtown Wilkes-Barre. This map was published early in the 19th century. (WHGS)*

When the first 40 arrived, under the leadership of Major John Durkee, they were arrested by Pennsylvanians and sent to trial at Easton. The matter was unresolvable legally because no one agreed about the jurisdiction of any court to settle the question. Those who had been arrested soon returned to the Valley where they were joined by their associates. Skirmishes broke out between the members of the Susquehannah Company and the Pennsylvanians. This first Yankee Pennamite War would go on from 1769 to 1775.

To forestall anarchy during this war, a virtual martial law prevailed from 1769 till 1773. A "Settlers Committee," headed by Colonel Zebulon Butler, tried to maintain law, order, and morality, as well as defend the townships from the raiders from Pennsylvania. Wilkes-Barre invited the Reverend Jacob Johnson from Groton, Connecticut, to minister to spiritual needs. The citizens gradually developed rules for self-government to replace military rule. They laid out plans for their townships to provide for equitable distribution of the land and to raise revenue. They built log cabins, sawmills, gristmills, and stockades. The first phase of the Yankee-Pennamite War came to an end in 1775 with a Connecticut victory at Rampart Rocks at the southern end of the Valley.

The Wyoming settlements during this time of war show something

Although the Wyoming Valley ultimately became a part of Pennsylvania, the names that the Connecticut settlers gave to the five original townships have persisted over the years. The unusual but alliterative name of Forty Fort derives quite simply from the 40 settlers who arrived under Major John Durkee in 1769 and built the fort. Although only a few hundred people were involved, the First Yankee-Pennamite War ranged from one end of the Valley to the other; a moment-by-moment account of its history is confusing beyond belief. Courtesy, The Bookmakers, Incorporated, copyright 1983

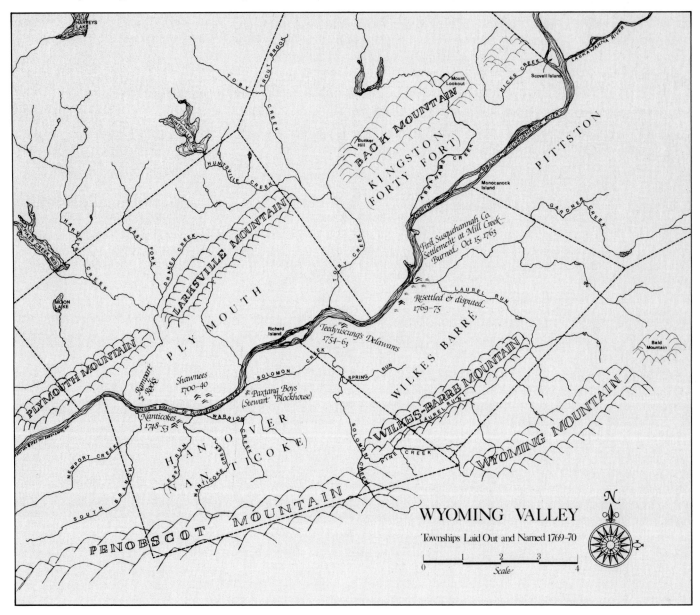

WYOMING VALLEY

Townships Laid Out and Named 1769-70

about the thinking of the colonists on the eve of the American Revolution. In naming their townships Plymouth (after a major British port), Kingston (after the monarchy itself), and Hanover (after the ruling family), these Yankees showed that they thought of themselves as good Englishmen away from home. The other names they chose are even more revealing. William Pitt, the prime minister for whom Pittston was named, had not only led Britain through the recent war with France but also defended the rights of the colonists to participate in decision-making affecting their own futures. Colonel Isaac Barré had served with General James Wolfe, who died in Barré's arms during the siege of Quebec. He won the affection of Americans by his defense of their rights in Parliament. Another member of Parliament, John Wilkes, one of the greatest scoundrels of the 18th century, hardly seemed the type of man Christians would seek to honor. But he too had defended self-rule in America. His politics, rather than his conduct, won him a place of honor in America.

In honoring contemporary politicians the settlers showed their need for allies in London. They also needed allies at home. They knew enough to make friends with their enemies' enemies. They invited a group of Scotch-Irish Presbyterians from western Pennsylvania to join them here. The Paxtang Boys, led by Lazurus Stewart, who had already alienated the government in Philadelphia, felt estranged from any loyalty to the English crown. They had developed a reputation as intrepid Indian fighters and as political radicals. They settled in Hanover Township, casting their lot with the frontiersmen from New England. These allies added a revolutionary element to the local population.

A question naturally arises about the significance of these developments in the broad picture of American history. Why did the

Above left: *Son of a wealthy brewer, John Wilkes became at various times in his eventful life lord mayor of London, a prisoner for debt, and a member of Parliament. He was known as a champion of liberty, a demagogue, a scoundrel, and a wit. He died in poverty. (WHGS)*

Above right: *Isaac Barré's ancestors were French, but his family migrated to Ireland, and young Isaac studied at Trinity College. The high point of his military career was the siege of Quebec, where he became acquainted with John Durkee, the man who is generally credited with the naming of Wilkes-Barre. Barré served in Parliament for 40 years, and he nearly always took positions favorable to the Americans. (WHGS)*

development of a few miles of riverbank by a few hundred pioneers cause such conflict? Until the Connecticut settlement at Wyoming, almost all English American colonies resulted from up-river migrations—growth that was necessarily quite limited and reasonably easy to control. By cutting a road across the mountains these Yankees blazed a trail heretofore unthinkable. Before this, America had to exist east of the mountains. If this colony succeeded, others could be planted throughout the west.

Although such a possibility delighted land-hungry speculators, it terrified both the Indians and the British. The Indians, from their first contacts with the whites, had learned that coexistence was virtually impossible. They did take stands to defend their lands; but while they might win battles, they always lost the wars. Their only real hope was escape, and until the settlement of Wyoming, the mountains gave them a refuge.

Britain had recognized this in the Proclamation of 1763, which prohibited white settlement west of the crest of the Appalachians. The English wanted the great plains to be an Indian preserve. Although the settlement at Wyoming did not violate the proclamation, it did prove that trans-Appalachian settlements were possible.

On the eve of the American Revolution there were many trouble spots in the 13 colonies. None, not even Boston after its Tea Party, was more troubled than Wyoming Valley. None raised more significant questions about the future of America than this second frontier.

Facing page: *John Wilkes was a prominent fixture of 18th-century London. His feuds were legendary, and his enemies included poets, playwrights, philosophers, and painters, as well as politicians. It is said—to his credit—that he was so full of wit and good humor that even his enemies enjoyed his company. The great caricaturist William Hogarth immortalized Wilkes's more devilish qualities. (WHGS)*

Below: *This drawing was made around 1900 and based on an earlier picture, now lost. It shows the blockhouse built by Lazarus Stewart and his Paxtang boys in what is now Hanover. Other fortified cabins built by the first settlers were undoubtedly quite similar.*

This Victorian lithograph shows the myth of the Battle of Wyoming more than the battle itself. The settlers (including an old man), armed with farm implements, face certain death at the hands of heavily armed invaders. The Indians tortured many of their prisoners to death and looted the Valley; these actions invited the lethal reprisals of the following year. (WHGS)

Chapter Two

IN
WARS
AND
PEACE

Despite the impression often created by our early schooling, the American Revolution was not a simple struggle between good and evil, between patriots and Tories. For those who lived through it, it was a soul-searing and terribly complex conflict. Long after the the Revolutionary War, John Adams estimated that the Tories "had seduced and deluded nearly one-third of the people of the colonies," and other historians have estimated that one-third of Americans supported the patriots, and the other one-third didn't care. Raised as good Englishmen, Americans were loyal to the Crown and expected to be accorded the rights guaranteed by the English Bill of Rights. Few thought of themselves primarily as Americans—they thought of themselves as New Yorkers or Georgians or Marylanders.

The American people were also divided along class lines. Farmers who worked small parcels of land wanted to direct their own futures, but the elite believed that the right to rule belonged to them. The Revolution resulted, as Carl Becker wrote in *The History of Political Parties in the Province of New York,* "from two general movements; the contest for home rule and independence, and the democratization of American politics and society."

These issues would all be extremely important in Wyoming Valley. Conflicting claims on their loyalty troubled its 2,500 residents in 1775.

Fort Wyoming was typical of the frontier fortifications at the time of the Revolution. Log buildings were built around a rectangular courtyard, with the remainder of the perimeter secured by stout log fences. The only windows faced inward onto the courtyard. Essential stores were protected by the buildings. In times of danger, settlers from the surrounding area moved inside for protection. Fort Wyoming stood along the river near the present intersection of West South and West River streets in modern Wilkes-Barre. General Sullivan's army assembled at Fort Wyoming in July 1779.

Throughout the first year of the war, their dispute with Pennsylvania overshadowed events of Lexington, Concord, and Bunker Hill in distant Massachusetts. After they had defeated the Pennsylvanians at Rampart Rocks in December 1775 and exiled their opponents, however, local citizens were able to look to the national questions.

Most of the Yankees in the Valley supported the American side, in part because their seizure of the land here had followed American tradition, not English law. Local land distribution had been democratic and a democratic government had developed, so that the main thrust of the revolutionary movement seemed to correspond to the practices and impulses of the local settlers. Still, some Connecticut Yankees, unable to cut their loyalty to England, joined the Tory movement.

On the other hand, many Pennsylvanians interested in the Valley favored the British side. Certainly the Penn claims would be supported by an English court; and those who based their hopes in the Valley on the proprietary position would clearly be better off if the Revolution failed. The linkage of Pennsylvania's cause in the Valley with that of the Crown was so close that the Yankees falsely labeled all their opponents "Tories." Pennsylvania had its own share of revolutionaries who would struggle to control Wyoming after the defeat of the British.

For the Iroquois, who still claimed the Susquehanna, the war between two white groups at once posed a dilemma and presented an opportunity. If they chose the winning side, they might regain at least a portion of what they had lost. At the very least, the English promised them control of the lands west of the Appalachians. The Americans hoped to gain those lands in order to plant new settlements on the other side of the mountains similar to and patterned after settlement in the Wyoming Valley.

Thus, gradually, the sides were drawn. On April 15, 1776, in response to a petition from Wilkes-Barre, the Continental Congress asked the residents of Wyoming to suspend their fight with Pennsylvania. The local folk agreed, and Yankee-Pennamite hostilities ceased for the remainder of the Revolution. Valley residents built powder mills to arm themselves, erected stockades for shelter, and raised troops to join George Washington. Eventually three companies joined the Continental army. One, led by Lieutenant Colonel Zebulon Butler, formed in Connecticut. Two others, led by Major Robert Durkee and Major Samuel Ransom, organized here and marched off to join Washington, camping at Morristown, New Jersey, on New Year's Day 1777.

At home the American Revolution proceeded as a social movement. Democratic practices had become commonplace—major decisions, including the election of officers for the militia, resulted from the votes of the majority. Moreover, in establishing Presbyterian churches in Wilkes-Barre and Plymouth the locals abandoned the Connecticut practice of using tax monies for the support of the church. The American practice of separating church and state began here quite early.

Organizing themselves as "Westmoreland County of the State of Connecticut," the Yankees hastily erected a courthouse and a jail on the diamond they cut out of the best land in Wilkes-Barre (Public Square). They also built 10 "forts"—crude wooden stockades about 12 feet high to surround their homes and stores of goods. As they tried to carry out their daily lives in peace, they became increasingly aware of the pressing reality of the war.

Some signs of that war took the form of isolated problems involving Indians which occurred as early as August 1776 and continued through 1777. The Iroquois, who had not yet officially sided with Britain, continued to plead with the local population not to blame the Six Nations for the actions of individuals. They wrote almost pathetically, "Brothers, we

A native of Salem, Massachusetts, and a graduate of Harvard College, Timothy Pickering fought in the Revolutionary War from the opening gunfire at Lexington to the very end. By that time, he was quartermaster general, reporting to Washington. When he came to the Valley to settle conflicting land claims, he acquired sizable holdings of his own in the region. He resided in Wilkes-Barre from 1786 to 1792 but departed to accept cabinet posts in the administration of both Washington and John Adams. (WHGS)

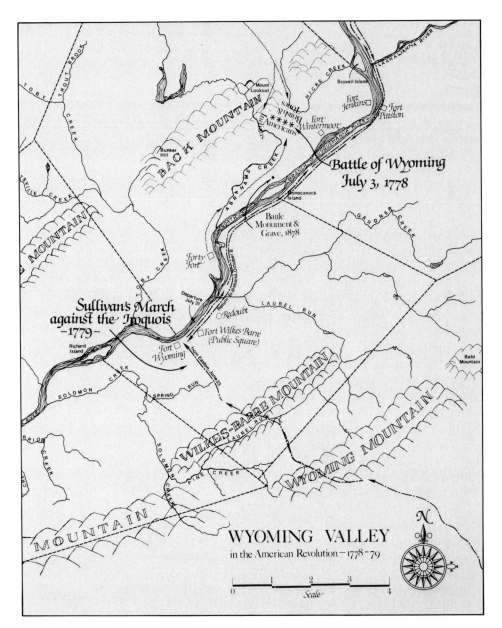

WYOMING VALLEY
in the American Revolution—1778–79

During most of the American Revolution, the Wyoming Valley was safely distant from conflict. In July 1778, however, a band of British, Tories, and Indians swept down from the north to defeat a small garrison of ill-trained Americans in the Valley. After the battle, the British lost control of their native allies, who brutally plundered the settlements. In retaliation, Washington sent General John (Black Jack) Sullivan to the Valley the following year to destroy forever the power of the Six Nations of the Iroquois. Courtesy, The Bookmakers, Incorporated, copyright 1983

do not want to hurt you. We are your friends. We hope you are our friends and won't hurt us. . . ." Indian leaders came through Wilkes-Barre in January 1777, en route to a peace conference with the patriots at Easton. They were received here civilly, but cautiously.

After the British appointed General Sir Guy Carleton to direct the western war, however, the Iroquois decided to join forces with Great Britain. Thus the Valley became a focal point of military strategy. By 1778 its 3,000 residents constituted the largest population center on the Susquehanna. If this stronghold of American patriotism could be eliminated, Britain might dominate the frontier. By the spring of 1778 the residents of Wyoming found themselves at the center of America's future. They were justifiably frightened.

General Carleton commissioned Major John Butler to organize a force of British and Tory soldiers, known as Butler's Rangers, to secure the West. This force included some former Valley residents and worked with the Indians favorable to Britain. Butler looked to Wyoming Valley as his first important conquest. His scouting parties alarmed the inhabitants, who now petitioned the Congress to release the two Westmoreland companies to return to the defense of their homes and of the West. These requests finally won the endorsement of Colonel Timothy Pickering, at

the time one of Washington's chief military aides. Pickering urged the release of the "very much reduced" companies led by Durkee and Ransom. On June 23, 1778, the Continental Congress ordered that the companies unite and return; but they would not reach home in time to forestall Butler's Rangers and their Indian allies.

John Butler's forces came down the river on June 30, 1778. Oscar Jewell Harvey in his *History of Wilkes-Barre* estimated that they numbered about 250 British and Tories, about 350 Senecas (one of the Six Nations of the Iroquois), and about 100 "miscellaneous" Indians, including a few "squaws." Local Tories helped the invading army secure the surrender of Wintermoot's Fort, a small stockade on the west side of the river south of Pittston, which then became John Butler's headquarters.

By the third of July most of the Valley's inhabitants had gathered in Forty Fort (named for the first 40 settlers) under Colonel Nathan Denison or in Fort Wilkes-Barre under Colonel Zebulon Butler. The British commander demanded the unconditional surrender of all the forts, arms, ammunitions, and stores of the Valley. He also demanded that all Continental officers and soldiers be handed over as prisoners of war. He promised to protect the safety and property of those who surrendered. He threatened to attack in full force if his offer were refused.

On the morning of July 3, Zebulon Butler traveled from Wilkes-Barre to Forty Fort to consult with the leaders there and assess the situation. In the fort itself were 375 men capable of bearing arms, including some teenagers too young to join the Continental army and others too old to bear arms. Still others—like Butler, Ransom, and Durkee—were officers and men on leave from Washington's army, then relatively inactive. In the face of the danger posed by Major John Butler, his rangers, and the Indians, well-seasoned soldiers urged caution and even surrender to the vastly superior force of the enemy. But other men, including the leader of the Paxtang Boys, Lazurus Stewart—demonstrating that uncommon bravery is no substitute for common sense—urged, and even demanded conflict. Their arguments won the debate and lost their lives. Zebulon Butler, to salvage what he could, tried to organize his untrained forces for military action and led them out of the protecting fort to find and destroy their enemy.

As shown in this old drawing, Forty Fort, from which the tiny army of settlers marched to battle, was little more than a rude, windowless stockade. In the event of an attack or an Indian raid, settlers could take shelter here. Other fortifications along the Valley were quite similar. (WHGS)

They marched about three miles to the north and drew up their battle line on a plain near the present Fourth Street in Wyoming. The British and Tories faced the patriots while the Indians surreptitiously infiltrated the area between the river and the American position. The shooting, initiated by the Americans, lasted about 30 minutes as the chaos so common in battle devastated American discipline: British guns, aided by Indian spears and tomahawks, turned the battle into a rout. Almost 100 Americans and about 80 of the enemy died in that half hour. Wounded Yankees tried to flee, but many of them were captured and killed—including Samuel Ransom and Robert Durkee. Colonels Butler and Denison led some men back to the safety of Forty Fort. During the night the residents watched the fires and listened to the screams of 16 or 18 of their comrades whom the Indians tortured to death.

The next day Major John Butler renewed his demand for unconditional surrender. Colonel Denison delayed while Zebulon Butler and other Continental soldiers and officers fled the Valley. In the late afternoon of July 4, 1778, Denison surrendered the whole Wyoming Valley at Forty Fort. John Butler first ordered the summary execution of a British deserter caught at Forty Fort; after that he sought to save the lives of his vanquished foes. The Indians—perhaps remembering the destruction of the Indian village at Wyoming 15 years earlier—systematically burned the buildings of the settlements and looted whatever tangible property they could carry. Although this action violated the terms of surrender, it followed the practices of 18th century frontier warfare. The defeated Americans—men, women, and children—were sent into exile, moving to havens to the south. Butler's Rangers and the Indians returned to the north. The Valley was once again a no-man's-land.

The battle and massacre of Wyoming shocked the new nation. Stories of atrocities (magnified beyond their horrible reality) added to the myths of British perfidy, Tory viciousness, and Indian savagery. The defeat of patriot forces at Wyoming galvanized the American determination to rid America of all three enemies. General Washington, who had begun his military career fighting the Indians on the western Pennsylvania frontier, had to wait almost nine months before addressing the problem directly. In early spring 1779 he ordered General John Sullivan to lead an army of 3,500 Continental troops to punish the Iroquois. He advised Sullivan that "the immediate objects are the total destruction and devastation of their settlements, and the capture of as many prisoners of every age and sex as possible." In this message Washington really began the official Indian policy of the United States. The nation did not treat the Indians as soldiers to be defeated in battle but as a people to be uprooted and displaced.

Sullivan reached the repopulated Wilkes-Barre on June 23, 1779, almost a year after the battle. He tarried for more than a month, awaiting cumbersome supplies and more men to tote them. He finally moved upriver, eventually marching to the Genesee River in upper New York. By the time he returned to Wilkes-Barre on October 8 he had burned 40 Indian towns, ripped up thousands of their fields, and destroyed 160,000 bushels of corn. Sullivan proudly stated that "we have not left a single settlement or field of corn. . . . (n)or is there even the appearance of an Indian on this side of the Niagara." The dead of Wyoming had been revenged by a savagery at least as great as the savagery visited on them.

As victory became more likely and the war moved into the South, soldiers campaigned for home rule and politicians sought to decide who would rule at home. Most states, including Pennsylvania, drew up new constitutions based on exaggeratedly democratic principles. Connecticut, in many ways the most democratic of colonies, simply used its colonial form of government. All states considered themselves sovereign entities

New Hampshire native Major General John Sullivan commanded the army Washington sent to avenge the Wyoming Massacre and destroy, if possible, the Six Nations of the Iroquois. His expeditionary force of 3,500 men built a road from Easton to Wilkes-Barre (a path still followed by modern highways). The army camped along the river for more than a month while the expedition's boats and supplies were prepared. When the army returned to disband in October 1779, the Iroquois had been driven beyond the Niagara. Sketch by Stanislaus Wojtowicz III

When Daniel Perkins and his family returned to the Valley, they built this house (at first just the section to the left) in Wyoming not far from the site of the battle. Like other ordinary settlers, the Perkins family were farmers who depended on the land for their livelihood. Their house was unusual only in surviving pretty much unchanged into the 20th century. (WHGS)

that had entered a loose confederation.

The Articles of Confederation, our first attempt at a national constitution, preserved the reality of state sovereignty and local self-determination. Thus, the issue of the disputed settlement of Wyoming Valley presented a problem. If states were sovereign, who would decide disputes between them? If local populations ruled themselves, under whose laws would they rule?

The ninth article addressed the question of decision-making. It provided that those states party to a dispute should establish a court or board of arbitration with authority to make "final and conclusive" judgments on that issue. Connecticut and Pennsylvania agreed to submit their dispute to just such a court. It met at Trenton, New Jersey, in November and December 1782, after the last battle of the Revolutionary War but before the Peace of Paris had been signed. The court unanimously ruled that "the State of Connecticut has no right to the Lands in Controversy . . . [and that these lands] do by Right belong to the State of Pennsylvania."

This clear judgment heartened all supporters of constitutional government. The Marquis de La Fayette predicted that this precedent, the first under the Articles of Confederation, would eventually be cited in settling disputes among the sovereign states of Europe. Thomas Jefferson felt the decision proved the articles provided a satisfactory form of government for a great nation. Everyone seemed happy—except, of course, the Connecticut settlers.

They accepted the fact that they lived in Pennsylvania. They felt strongly that they had a right to remain on the land they had cleared and farmed, for which they had fought and for which so many of their relatives had died. The Trenton court had dealt not with land ownership, but only with the sovereignty of Pennsylvania in the region. When Pennsylvania denied citizenship to the Yankees, refusing them the right to vote in Pennsylvania's elections, they found a new champion in Colonel John Franklin, a survivor of the Battle of Wyoming, who now proposed

Left: *Colonel John Franklin, a big man of enormous strength, had little formal education but great acumen and personal charm. He and his followers attempted to solve the Yankee-Pennamite conflict by creating a new state out of northeastern Pennsylvania and southern New York. He was actually brought to trial for high treason against the Commonwealth of Pennsylvania in 1788, but charges were dropped when he abandoned his plan. Franklin Street in Wilkes-Barre was named in his honor. Sketch by Stanislaus Wojtowicz III*

Below: *In order to exercise its right to the Wyoming Valley, Pennsylvania created a new county (carved out of the ill-defined northern reaches of Northumberland County) with its seat in Wilkes-Barre. This action gave Wyoming Valley residents some measure of autonomy. The new county was named for the Chevalier de la Luzerne, who had been French minister to the United States from 1779 to 1784. (WHGS)*

the creation of a 14th state with its center at Wilkes-Barre. Although Franklin was willing to continue to fight anyone who challenged his position, Pennsylvania—having won in the courts—was not prepared to lose Wyoming again. Declaring the region part of the newly established Luzerne County, Pennsylvania sent men to claim the lands. Conflict again came to the Valley, the second Yankee-Pennamite War. It was waged for four months in 1784 and, like so many wars, decided nothing.

In the midst of the conflict, Pennsylvania sent one of its newest citizens, Colonel Timothy Pickering, to the region to study the situation and make recommendations for a settlement. Pickering proposed the land remain part of Pennsylvania but that Yankees who held title to lands before the Trenton decision be recognized as rightful owners. Pennsylvanians with competing claims (most of whom had never lived in the Valley) would be compensated with public lands in the western parts of the state.

The Yankees accepted this approach. After initial agreement, however, the Pennsylvania legislature disavowed the urgings of Pickering—its own agent. Legal disputes about land ownership continued for decades but in the end the approach suggested by Pickering largely prevailed.

In the generation between Teedyuscung's murder in 1763 and Washington's inauguration in 1789, the Wyoming Valley was the site of nationally important events. Twice its homes were totally destroyed. Three times its population was sent into exile. Here Indians massacred whites, and from here whites left to annihilate Indian civilization east of the Appalachians. Twice the peoples of Connecticut and Pennsylvania went to war to defend their claims. And finally they settled their problem in the courts. It was a bloody epoch, and by 1789 the people of Wyoming had many reasons to pray for their chance to farm this good earth in peace.

When he came to Wilkes-Barre, Pickering built this handsome house in the second block of South Main Street. When he left, he sold the property to General William Ross, whose family owned it into the 20th century. Judge William Sterling Ross was born and died in the same room. Although the oldest house in the Valley and of considerable historical interest, the building was demolished in 1931. R.E. Smith made this drawing in 1898. (WHGS)

In 1928, as part of the Valley's sesquicentennial celebration, the living room of the Pickering-Ross house was furnished with authentic items of the revolutionary period. The chandelier, wallpaper, and coal-burning grate are all later than Pickering's time. Four of the pictures on the mantelpiece can be identified: left, Phoebe Haight Butler, Zebulon's third wife; center, two portraits of Pickering; and right, Lord Butler, Zebulon's son. (WHGS)

The Reverend Jacob Johnson built this house shortly after his return to the Valley in 1781. The white house stood near the corner of Union and River streets. When it was photographed in 1885, H. Ingham lived there. The church that Johnson hoped to build was still a dream at the time of his death. (WHGS)

Chapter Three

A COMMUNITY IN TRANSITION

Wilkes-Barre's Public Square as it appeared early in the 19th century was drawn from memory in 1866 by C.I.A. Chapman. The Academy is to the left; the courthouse and Old Ship Zion Church are in the center. The stagecoach heading down South Main Street will probably turn left onto Northampton Street and labor up over Wilkes-Barre Mountain on the Easton Turnpike (the Sullivan Trail). (WHGS)

The frontier played so important a role in developing the attitudes and institutions of early America that it has been elevated almost to the status of myth: a romantic place where a man depended only on himself, his family, and the Almighty to produce the good life. The frontier did exist—but it was real, not ideal. It took enormous labor to carve a field from a forest and to make that field yield food. It took heroic struggle to live at the edge of civilization, away from the comforts of home. The Indians knew no alternative, but white settlers did. Knowing that it took great talent simply to survive, they wanted more than the simple, rude life of the wilderness. Men and women went to the frontier to make comfortable lives for themselves and a prosperous one for their children. They mastered improvisation and invention simply to solve problems. In the half-century from 1789 till 1840, the Wyoming Valley would change from a rude settlement to a center of commercial agriculture, a hub of transportation, a nursery for industry, a seat of simple culture, and a home of deep but divided religious feelings.

That transition was not easy. At the time, great world events were also changing the little communities on the Susquehanna. The French Revolution that began on the King's Tennis Court at Versailles in 1789 and ended at the fields of Waterloo in 1815 affected Wilkes-Barre and its environs. The Wars of the French Revolution diverted thousands of European peasants from their fields and created a prosperous world market for agricultural goods. The farmers of Wyoming Valley jumped at the chance to provide some of those goods and to share in the national prosperity based on commercial agriculture stimulated by the European wars.

The acceptance of a new American Constitution in 1789, the third fundamental form of government in 14 years, created a new political climate; and within this new framework both the Commonwealth of Pennsylvania and its new citizens in Luzerne County created new political institutions in the wilderness. They expected that these institutions would provide a settled future.

Valley folk participated in these changes on all levels. In 1789 Pennsylvania decided that the state, too, needed a new constitution; and the settlers at Wyoming were entitled to send a delegate to the state convention. They chose Colonel Timothy Pickering, who had come to the Valley to mediate the Yankee-Pennamite dispute and had earned sufficient respect in his adopted home to be considered a worthy representative by both old and new settlers. (He had also acquired large land-holdings in the Valley and built an impressive home on South Main Street in Wilkes-Barre.) While serving the state, he met his old military chief, President George Washington. Pickering accepted a number of assignments from

Washington, serving first as the president's representative to the Seneca tribe, then as Postmaster General of the United States, and eventually as Secretary of State under both Washington and John Adams. He used the diplomatic experience he had gained here to keep the new nation out of the wars between the lion that was France and the shark that was Britain.

While this great Pennsylvanian was moving on, so was his chief adversary in the Pennamite Wars. Colonel John Franklin hated to face the reality that the Wyoming Valley was a permanent part of Pennsylvania. Perhaps he hated to face permanence in any form. He served for a brief time as sheriff of Luzerne County, as a leader of the local militia, and, for a long while, as delegate to the Pennsylvania legislature. But Franklin was a perpetual frontiersman; and the Valley, which had been so important a part of his life, was becoming too tame for his restless spirit. Franklin eventually moved north, blazing new trails, fighting new enemies, and founding new settlements.

While Pickering and Franklin had brilliant careers that flashed for a time around Wilkes-Barre, a more typical transition figure was Nathan Denison. Born in Connecticut in 1740, he was a fourth-generation American. One of the first 40 settlers, he had significant experience with farming and fighting before the region's ties to Pennsylvania were settled. Denison commanded Forty Fort at the time of the Battle of Wyoming, surrendered the fort to Major John Butler, witnessed the destruction of the Valley, and led the survivors into the wilderness. He returned to build his career, at first living in a simple cabin and ekeing out an existence from the soil. In 1789, when he and his wife Betsy (Sill) were expecting the sixth of their seven children, they began to plan a new home for their growing family. They wanted something appropriate for the judge of Luzerne County and a former official of two states. They wanted something to aid their primary occupation as farmers that would also accommodate a more comfortable and diverse future. Denison's home in Forty Fort still stands on the street named for him. Modeled on the finest homes of Eastern Connecticut, it reflects his respect for the past, his busy present, and his hope for the future as a commercial farmer of the 19th century.

Above: *The kitchen of Nathan Denison's house was the focus of much family activity. Meat and fish were salted, smoked, or otherwise cured. Textiles were spun and woven. Breads and pastries were baked. The enormous chimney contains a fireplace for general cooking and heating and an oven for baking.*

Left: *Nathan Denison's house, built in 1790, resembles Connecticut houses of the period rather than other Pennsylvania buildings. Built around a massive central chimney that accommodated eight fireplaces, the house is therefore almost square. Here Judge Denison and his wife Betsy raised seven children and went about their various agrarian and protoindustrial activities. Undoubtedly there were barns and other outbuildings that have not survived. The house is now a museum. Courtesy, Wilkes-Barre Citizens' Voice*

Although the typical frontier farmer in the 18th and 19th centuries cleared a reasonably small parcel of land (the average in the Valley was 30 acres) and tried to raise a large variety of crops to support his family and feed his livestock, for men like Nathan Denison subsistence farming was merely the first stage. Denison went on to clear many more acres than his family needed for food in order to be a seller of foods rather than simply a consumer.

His home reflects his family's role as transition figures. It contains spinning wheels like those used by the women to produce linen, woolen, and cotton thread. Obviously the family had first claim on such products; but the Denisons and others produced for sale. A textile industry, depending mostly on female laborers, developed here early in the 19th century. By 1810 the 259 looms in Wyoming Valley produced more than 50,000 yards of cloth, most of it for sale outside the Valley. Carding and fulling machines reduced the amount of labor needed to produce salable cloth, leading to the development of an extensive textile industry in the region.

Denison's house also shows the interest of the transition farmers in another occupation important in the Valley's early commercial life. He had a distillery to produce whiskey from the fine rye grains that grew so well here. Rye itself was a bulky item to ship great distances, but whiskey traveled more easily and found handier markets. This important commercial item presented both problems and opportunities for early American settlements.

The problems resulted from the abuse of alcohol and the disorderly and antisocial conduct related to that activity. As early as 1772, the town meeting decided to restrict the sale of liquor to a few licensed "Publick-

Another prosperous farmer, Luke Swetland, built a house about a mile from Denison's in 1797. Unlike Denison, Swetland followed a more conventional Pennsylvania plan, with chimneys at either end of a long rectangle. Like the Denison House, the Swetland Homestead is now a museum, but it still retains the accretions of five generations that have been stripped away from the Denison House in the name of authentic historical mummification. Photo by Bill Manganiello

houses''. This measure was ineffective—in a single month in 1790, 18 persons pleaded guilty to selling liquor without a license. The local courts found that 10 percent of the cases heard around 1800 dealt with the illegal sale or abuse of alcohol.

Clearly whiskey-making produced problems; it also produced opportunities. As America became more populous and more prosperous, whiskey could be sold for significant profit. Secretary of the Treasury Alexander Hamilton recognized this in 1792, and made a tax on whiskey a major source of revenue for the new federal government. Whiskey-producing frontiersmen in western Pennsylvania so objected to this impost that in 1794 they began the Whiskey Rebellion against the new government. But the commercial farmers of Wyoming Valley—perhaps eager to eliminate the competition from the west—supported the government. They raised a company of local men to put down the rebels. Though the local men never saw action in the rebellion, the government eventually succeeded in establishing itself as an effective taxer of spirits.

Denison's house shows signs of another activity that some hoped would lead to commerce. Its proximity to Abrahams Creek assured him of more than an adequate supply of fresh, safe water and made fishing easy. The role of fishing in the early commerce of the Valley seems strange to those who think of the Susquehanna as a polluted stream. Until the building of the canals, which interfered with access to the spawning grounds, the river teemed with fish of many varieties, none more important than the shad. This ocean-going fish, the largest member of the herring family found in America, normally grows 18 to 24 inches long. The mature shad come to fresh waters, including the Susquehanna, only to spawn. Each spring hundreds of thousands of fasting fish, the

The first public building to be completed in Wilkes-Barre in the 19th century was neither a church nor a school nor a court but a jail—built in 1802. Although the engraver of this old print seems to have attempted to make the building look formidable, it was made of wood, as were all other buildings in the Valley at the time. The jail stood at the corner of modern Washington and Market streets. Excavations at the site in the late 1970s uncovered the stone arches of forbidding subterranean dungeons.

Jacob Cist, a Philadelphia-born German-American, married Matthias Hollenback's daughter Sarah on August 25, 1807. The following year he settled in Wilkes-Barre, where he opened a store on River Street near his father-in-law's warehouse. Cist's store was also the post office because Cist was the postmaster. Cist was an artist of some repute, known especially for his detailed scientific drawings of insects. This view was drawn by G.W. Leach, Jr. (WHGS)

Although the Susquehanna is a scant quarter-mile in breadth at Wilkes-Barre, the river caused an impediment to travel that ferries could only partly reduce. The first of four bridges to span the river at Market Street opened in 1818 and collapsed the following year. The next bridge lasted until 1826 when a gale demolished it. Matthias Hollenback's warehouse can be seen in the foreground of the only surviving picture of the original bridge. (WHGS)

females laden with roe comparable to fine caviar, fought their way upstream, thus providing ample opportunity for the locals to catch them with nets, even buckets. The fish provided food in the spring, and some residents hoped to develop a commercial fishing industry, but to do so needed salt. Without a readily available local supply of salt, these entrepreneurs could not commercialize fishing. Although the Denisons salted and smoked as much as they could for personal use, they never made a business of fishing.

The most important potential industry was, therefore, agriculture. When Denison began to build his home only 10 percent of the land of the Valley had been cleared. The cleared lands produced good yields of wheat, flax, rye, oats, buckwheat, corn, and hay—even without fertilizer. As the prosperity triggered by the wars of the French Revolution continued, land became increasingly valuable and more intensively farmed. The Wyoming Valley was becoming a center of commercial agriculture.

Now the towns needed reliable facilities to store and transport goods, and adventuresome farmer-businessmen such as Matthias Hollenback, a German-American who came to the Valley with the Paxtang Boys, responded. He built docks and warehouses along the east bank

of the river between Northampton and Market streets and a general store on Public Square. An active speculator in lands both in the Valley and to the north, Hollenback became the first successful merchant of the settlement in transition. Although he would play roles in the transportation, agricultural, political, cultural, and religious life of the community, he was primarily a merchant.

Goods left Hollenback's docks on flat-bottom boats called arks, Durham boats, even flat-bottom sailboats. Opportunity dictated adaptation of old forms to maximize the flatboat as a transporter of goods. As the 19th century progressed, far-sighted Pennsylvanians, unwilling to see the Valley's produce move to Baltimore, tried to divert trade to Philadelphia. If nature had separated the rivers, men could unite them.

As early as the 1770s, public funds had been used to improve the river system of Pennsylvania by building canals. When New York built the Erie Canal in 1825, Pennsylvania already had an extensive but not comprehensive system of canals. Private and public investments led to

The Susquehanna ark was an ingeniously efficient means of moving cargo. An ark was built at the point of embarkation and then filled with coal, lumber, grain, or any other bulky commodity. Once filled, the ark went only one way—downstream. Upon reaching its destination, the ark was unloaded and dismantled for the lumber that it contained. Because the river is so shallow, arks could be used only during the period of high water caused by the spring thaw. Unfortunately this amounted to only about 12 days a year. Courtesy, F. Charles Petrillo

the great improvement of this system. By 1828 a 55-mile two-ditch canal with eight locks connected Nanticoke with Sunbury; and by 1834 this system had been extended to Pittston—opening the entire Valley to an integrated transportation system available to deep-draft boats. Had water transportation not quickly been outstripped by the "newfangled" railroad, the Wyoming Valley would have remained a center of the national transportation system.

In the opening decades of the 19th century, however, the railroad and related industrial developments were still in the future; and the Valley had entered a stage of political, cultural, and religious transition. Few areas of the United States had more difficulty in establishing permanent political institutions than did the area settled as Westmoreland County, Connecticut, and developed as Luzerne County, Pennsylvania.

Nathan Denison's life illustrates the problem of changing political jurisdiction. When he came to Forty Fort, he thought of himself as an Englishman living in the newest part of Connecticut. He served as judge of Westmoreland County in the colonial period and as a legislator in the

A stone lock of the North Branch Canal, completed in 1828, still stands in West Nanticoke. The vertical channels held the timbers (traces of which remain) that held the lock's plank lining in position. When the canal was extended to Pittston in the 1830s, politics pushed it to the east side of the Susquehanna, and canal boats had to be towed across the river above a shallow dam. In Hanover, the canal followed Solomons Creek inland before curving to a path just east of Back Street in Wilkes-Barre. Courtesy, Ace Hoffman Studios

Assembly of the sovereign state of Connecticut during the period of the Articles of Confederation. With the Trenton Decree of 1782, he became a Pennsylvanian; and for three years, he served on the supreme executive council of that sovereign state. With the adoption of the United States Constitution in 1789 and the Pennsylvania Constitution of 1790, he became a citizen of two new entities. The pragmatic Denison bobbed in the changing political seas. He accepted an appointment as judge of common pleas of Luzerne County, a position he held till his death in 1809.

On the local scene, a new generation used the processes of direct democracy to take the Valley into the future. Colonel Zebulon Butler's son, Lord, was elected sheriff of Luzerne County and sought to build a courthouse and jail on Public Square in Wilkes-Barre. Town meetings provided the bases of local governments. The local communities used participatory democracy to solve their political problems. Wilkes-Barre became a borough in 1806, but the government provided almost no public services for the citizenry. Policing, law enforcement, and education

Above: *Lord Butler is one of the few Valley residents of the period whose portrait has survived. Son of the Revolutionary War hero Zebulon Butler, Lord became Wilkes-Barre's first postmaster in 1794 and later Luzerne County sheriff. He was instrumental in the building of both the jail and the courthouse. As an entrepreneur, he sent the first ark of coal downriver in 1813. (WHGS)*

Above left: *The new courthouse was begun in 1801 and completed in 1804. In an age when a block and tackle and a team of workhorses constituted heavy equipment, "raising" a building meant the arduous task of hauling the structural timbers—posts, beams, and rooftrees—into position. The volunteers who assembled to raise the courthouse consumed 32.5 gallons of whiskey in the course of their labors. This drawing was made in 1896 by G.W. Leach, Jr. (WHGS)*

were regarded as personal responsibilities. Almost no qualification for public office was deemed necessary besides polling more votes than the opponent. The problem-solving, wealth-producing citizens of Luzerne County had no fancy name for their system of government which like Topsy just "growed and growed." Political analysts of later generations would give it a label—Jacksonian Democracy. In the Wyoming Valley, however, the practice was a way of life before Andrew Jackson became a national figure in 1815 and long before he became President in 1829.

The practical democrats of Wyoming Valley saw to it that their children learned to "read, write, and cipher." Parents conducted most of this instruction in the home and a simple literacy was quite common. In 1807 private citizens established the Wilkes-Barre Academy in the remodeled building that had served as the first courthouse. The Academy provided a reasonably sophisticated curriculum to prepare sons of successful local men for college. Since the sons of ordinary farmers did not attend the Academy because their labor was needed at home, the Academy's service to the affluent helped create a class system within the local democracy.

Two Valley boys demonstrate the diversity and the quality of service among local residents of the second generation and illustrate the developing class differences. George Catlin was born in Wilkes-Barre in 1796, the fifth of 14 children. In 1787 his father Putnam Catlin, who had come from Connecticut, was one of the first four lawyers to be admitted to practice law in Luzerne County. His mother, the former Polly Sutton, had been only eight years old when she witnessed the surrender of Forty Fort. In his parents' home, George Catlin learned the "three R's," delighted in his parents' tales of the romantic days of their youth, and received encouragement for his talents in drawing and painting. He had no formal education, though he did "read law" with a friend in Connecticut. He practiced law in Wilkes-Barre until he was 29.

At 29 Catlin abandoned his legal career to devote himself entirely to painting. His individual and group portraits barely enabled him to support himself; but his real interest was in "rescuing from oblivion the looks and customs of the vanishing races of native man in America." In his lifetime Catlin painted more than 600 portraits of Indians and filled vast notebooks with written descriptions of those peoples, preserving for posterity a way of life that was clearly threatened with extinction. More than any American painter of his era, he used painting to serve both history and anthropology. His writings provided an invaluable legacy for his century and ours. Despite his great accomplishment, this sophisticated child of the frontier died in poverty in 1872.

In his days as a lawyer in Wilkes-Barre, the keenly observant Catlin might have noticed Hendrick B. Wright who enrolled in the Wilkes-Barre Academy in 1824 at the age of 16. The lad was born in Plymouth, the first child of a Pennsylvania father and a Connecticut mother. Hendrick Wright attended the public schools that had recently been established to provide elementary education. At the Academy he discovered and developed his talents as an orator and an actor. From there he went brief-

After considerable remodeling the Wilkes-Barre Academy was housed in the old courthouse, which had been finished in 1791. This drawing, like others included here, was made by G(eorge) W(ashington) Leach, Jr. (1854-1925), a Wilkes-Barre native who maintained a studio in the Coal Exchange Building for many years and produced hundreds of portraits and landscapes. His drawings of old Wilkes-Barre are accurate renderings of early photographs that have faded beyond reproducible quality. (WHGS)

ly to Dickinson College, but returned to Wilkes-Barre to read law. Using his education in law, his skill as a speaker, and his talent as an actor, Wright became the region's first nationally important political leader. He served as the Chairman of the Democratic Convention of 1844 which nominated the Jacksonian James K. Polk and the Pennsylvanian George Dallas for President and Vice President. Always a proponent of democratic principles, he served four terms in the House of Representatives, championing the cause of the workingman in an industrializing society. As his native region moved from an agricultural base to an industrial one, Hendrick B. Wright shifted with it. His *Historical Sketches of Plymouth* (1873) show his willingness to correct the problems of the industrial future. This friend of the workingman—this consummate democrat—died both rich and revered.

Throughout this half-century, the community activity that most engulfed the local citizenry was neither the politics of Wright nor the painting of Catlin, neither the commerce of Hollenback nor even the

Old Ship Zion Church was named for an old ship, the Zion, that was dismantled for its timbers. Ordinary lumber was both plentiful and cheap, but the great foot-square lengths of oak or ash needed to frame a large building were always in short supply. Valley people chose a Connecticut architect who gave them a building reminiscent of colonial New England. Drawing by G.W. Leach, Jr., 1896. (WHGS)

farming of Denison. The most important part of most Valley inhabitants' lives was their relation to God. A French visitor to America during this era, Alexis de Tocqueville, noted that the Americans were the most religious and least church-going people he had ever seen or heard of. This was certainly true of the local community. The area had been settled by God-fearing men and women who thought of their move to this wilderness as a way of pursuing the glory of God. Almost all who came either from Connecticut or Pennsylvania adhered rigorously and vigorously to Protestant Christianity. As Calvinists, they believed in the predestination of humans to heaven or hell. They earnestly hoped that they had been included among the former. To demonstrate their "election," they sought to engage only in godly conduct, and they expected that God would show His favor by rewarding their work with prosperity. Thus, for these earnest saints, work that produced wealth demonstrated most clearly that they walked the right path.

In the earliest days they did not deem it possible to build a church, but they did deem it necessary to have the Word of God preached. The Reverend Jacob Johnson came from Groton, Connecticut, in 1773, bringing with him his large family and a slave. He quickly became one of the Valley's most respected (and richest) men. He lost a great deal in 1778; but in 1781 he returned to seek new prosperity and to bring back God's Word. Since the community had no church Johnson became an itinerant preacher. For more than a decade he cajoled and exhorted his congregation to build a central house of worship. But by the time he died in 1798, no church had been erected. In religion as much as in education and government, the frontiersmen kept their own counsel.

Finally in 1800 plans were made for a church to be raised on Public Square in Wilkes-Barre. This edifice, which became known as the Old Ship Zion Church, was to serve the whole Protestant community. As was usual on the frontier, denominational differences were not so deeply felt as to interfere with practical considerations. Presbyterians, Episcopalians, and Methodists used the plain, box-like building with its high-backed, locked pews. Roving ministers of various sects mounted the 10-foot pulpit and preached the Word to the faithful.

Old Forty Fort meetinghouse would be at home anywhere in New England. This tiny building (about 20'x35') probably survived because it stood away from the path of development. Had the North Branch Canal run up the west side of the river, today's history buffs might make pilgrimages to Old Ship Zion Church in quiet little Wilkes-Barre and remember the Forty Fort building only by a plaque set into the wall of an office building. (WHGS)

As prosperity increased, so did the opportunity to express sectarian differences. In 1817 a dispute over Christmas decorations of the Old Ship Zion Church (the Episcopalians put them up; the others considered them sacrilegious) caused the local Episcopalians to rethink their interdenominational participation. They waited until 1821 to sell their interest in the old church, and in 1824 moved into their new quarters at Saint Stephen's Church on South Franklin Street. Obviously their differences with their fellow Christians were not all that pressing. In the seven years between the Christmas spat and Bishop White's dedication of the new church, the Episcopalians continued to worship regularly, either in private homes or in the Old Ship Zion Church.

The Presbyterians and Methodists next came to disagreement. Beginning in 1818, the two congregations fell out over the order of worship in Old Ship Zion. The Methodists lost out to the more numerous Presbyterians and moved to a room in the courthouse. There they held services according to the Methodist style. They occasionally shared their quarters with Baptists and continued to meet there until the Presbyterians sold their interest in the old church and moved to a new wooden building on South Franklin Street in 1833. Fifteen years later, they built a brick church on this site, the modern Osterhout Library—the oldest public

Built in 1808, the meetinghouse at Forty Fort is still used as a church. Its plain interior shows what Old Ship Zion's was like. There is absolutely no ornamentation, and the only reference to Christianity is the cruciform paneling of the high pulpit. The locked pews were opened only for paying members of the congregation. Note the size of the supporting timbers. (WHGS)

structure in Wilkes-Barre. The Methodists then returned to the old church, but when they built a more spacious house of worship in 1849 Old Ship Zion was torn down and its timbers used to build a barn.

From the day Nathan Denison built his sturdy house in Forty Fort in 1790 to the day the Old Ship Zion was razed, the Wyoming Valley had gone through a transition that demonstrated a remarkable phase of American history. What began as an errand into the wilderness ended as a complex and developing community. The whole history of agrarian America flashed by in Wyoming Valley during that half-century. The vast majority of good Protestant, English-speaking Americans believed that they had produced a new Ship Zion by tilling the fertile soil. Their lives and their community would undergo enormous change as the economic emphasis changed from tilling the land to mining it.

The Baptist Church of 1847 (like the Methodist Church of 1848, which was almost its twin) reflected the classic revival style. Both buildings were extremely severe—with only the suggestion of Doric columns in the brickwork, and lintels and entablatures consisting of unrelieved horizontals. Charles Parrish's stable (on the right) was regularly flooded whenever the baptismal pool was filled. (WHGS)

Early coal breakers, like this one photographed in 1860, were smaller than the monstrous structures of the 20th century, but no coal breaker ever looked like anything else on this earth. The mineshaft, with its superstructure, pulleys, and great cables, is housed in the tall building at the top. Mine cars ran by gravity into the breaker, where the coal was crushed, freed from culm (slag), sorted, and washed as it moved downward, ultimately to chutes that fed into the open railroad cars (called gondolas) that carried it to market. (WHGS)

Chapter Four

BLACK MAGIC

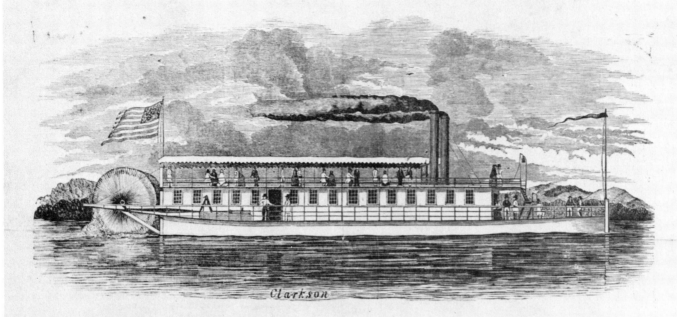

THE NEW STEAMER

Clarkson

WYOMING!

CAPT. G. CONVERSE,

Will leave this port for Wilkes-Barre, this day at 12 1-2 o'clock.   Fare one dollar.

In many ways the history of the United States is the history of unending, unprecedented, and usually rewarding work. The nation proclaims itself a "land of opportunity," which really means that almost all who came here, at whatever time, to whatever place, had an opportunity to work—often with the chance that their work could yield enough wealth for them to live in a reasonable degree of comfort. As the population of Western Europe began to swell in the mid-19th century, growing faster than the substructure of the European economies could accommodate, the lower classes found themselves without work at home. America provided them a seemingly unlimited opportunity to work.

A farming community like the Wyoming Valley, or like the United States as a whole, found that its ability to produce wealth was limited only by a shortage of labor. If the population increased by 50 percent per decade, there was still more work than workers, more land than people to farm it. Human and animal power alone could not produce enough energy to supply the goods and services demanded by inexhaustible appetites.

Water, especially rapidly falling water, could be put to work if it could be harnessed. One of the considerations that made the Wyoming Valley a desirable place to settle was the availability of that source of

The sternwheeler Wyoming *ushered in the era of regular riverboat travel in 1849 (although the first steamboat to reach Wilkes-Barre arrived in 1826). Steamboats would continue to chug up and down the natural waterways of the region for half a century, but they never became the important freight movers. Speedy (8 mile per hour) horse-drawn packet boats also carried passengers over the canal system.*

energy. Wheels placed in streams would move machines with fine results. Mills to grind flour from coarse grains, mills to saw boards from felled trees and move the looms that made cloth from thread, mills to do all sorts of work dotted the Valley, enabling the mill owners to benefit from the energy of falling water. Still there was not enough power available.

But around 1750 James Watt discovered a way to harness the energy of steam, and thus revolutionized the world of work. Water, one of nature's freest goods, could be used in steam engines to do almost any kind of work man desired. Within a half-century of Watt's discovery, steam power had been applied to thousands of tasks, none more important than transportation. In 1807 Robert Fulton demonstrated that steam could reliably propel a great mass over water, thereby rendering ancient forms of transportation obsolete. No longer would human muscles or uncertain wind provide energy to propel ships. Steam could do the work more efficiently and less expensively.

A steam engine, of course, required heat which was originally produced by burning wood. This renewable resource had become scarce in Europe, but in America it abounded. The introduction of so many steam engines, however, combined with the use of wood to build homes, ships, and factories as well as for fuel, threatened even America's abundant supply. The nation needed an alternative source of energy.

Industry followed the canal, and the railroads followed industry. By the time of the Civil War, canal traffic was at its heaviest although the waterways were used until 1881. The original South Street Bridge, left, carried street traffic over the canal and rail yards to the heights from which this photo was taken. The South Street Basin of the canal, to the right of the bridge, was a lumber depot. Courtesy, F. Charles Petrillo

Leach, del.
1896

From the earliest days of the Valley's occupation by whites it was known that a locally available substance—technically called *anthracite* and informally known as "stone" or "hard" coal—burned at a consistent heat over a long period. Hard coal was so accessible near the surface that ingenious farmers and blacksmiths had been chipping it away from the hills for years to heat their homes and fuel their forges. Although it provided good heat, it was virtually impossible to keep burning without a continuous forced draft.

In 1808 Judge Jesse Fell, a local innkeeper and political leader, solved this problem with a simple but revolutionary idea. By breaking the coal into reasonably small lumps and placing them on an open grate, to which he gradually added new coals while removing the falling ashes, he could keep a fire burning indefinitely. Fell's successful use of the open grate in his tavern at the corner of South Washington and Northampton streets led more local families to use the readily available coal to heat their homes and cook their food, and the practice spread to those urban centers where firewood was becoming scarce. (Fell's original fireplace and grate are still on duty in the restaurant that occupies the site today.)

It did not take Americans long to connect Watt's fundamental discovery, Fulton's application, and Fell's innovation. Coal could provide a safe, virtually inexhaustible form of energy to fuel the Industrial Revolution around the world. Though coal is found in many parts of the world, including Ireland's "peat," Poland's "brown" coal, and the bituminous or "soft" coal of Wales and Appalachia, the finest coal is

Judge Jesse Fell's tavern stood at what would become the corner of Northampton and Washington streets. Here Fell discovered how to keep an anthracite fire burning indefinitely without the use of a forced draft. The grate on which he demonstrated his technique on February 11, 1808, is part of the restaurant that now occupies the site. The tavern was drawn by G.W. Leach, Jr. (WHGS)

anthracite—almost pure carbon, almost totally combustible. It produces the highest degree of heat per ton, can be used in large furnaces or on open grates, and leaves little waste. An ideal home heating fuel, its availability speeded America's urbanization.

These "black diamonds" exist in only three separated fields of northeastern Pennsylvania. The first and largest of these underlies the entire Wyoming Valley and would profoundly and sadly change it.

The story of mining this coal is an almost continuous tragedy. The industry had no Rockefeller, no Carnegie, no J. P. Morgan to organize it. For the century from the 1830s to the 1930s, the anthracite industry experienced repeated booms and busts in which the market for anthracite grew regularly—to fuel railroads, to fire industries, to heat homes. It became almost as essential as food. But, as happened with the disorganized food producers of the United States, overproduction and other shortsighted business decisions pushed many coal producers to abusive practices. They exploited their workers; they ravaged the earth; and, more often than not, they failed in business.

The people who came through the mining experience with the greatest and most consistent gain were the holders of "mineral rights." It became the legal custom of Wyoming Valley landowners, many of them descendants of the original Connecticut Yankees, to sell parcels of land to individuals and corporations while retaining the rights to the ore beneath the land. The "mineral rights" allowed the original landowners and their successors to claim a fee or royalty for each ton of coal extracted. Many of

Judge Fell's grate as it stood in the original tavern. Being harder and purer than other coal, anthracite burns slowly; without a forced draft, large chunks of it will not burn at all. Fell crushed the coal to fragments no larger than golf balls and placed them on an open grate. With fresh coal added to the top and ashes falling through to the bottom, the fire would burn as long as it was stoked. (WHGS)

the first families of the Valley became quite rich through this practice and did so without risk or pain.

The mines themselves were often subsidiaries of railroad companies, usually those based in New York or Philadelphia. These corporations attracted some of America's most ambitious and callous men—but seldom its most talented. The entrepreneurial skills that made other industries great did not apply to the anthracite industry. Seeking to make a quick fortune, these men produced so much coal that they saturated the market, driving down the price. Rather than reduce production, they sought to cut costs—without regard to the needs of the workers, the future of the industry, or the condition of the earth itself. Most managers of the anthracite industry made the phrase "businesslike efficiency" a cruel joke.

Mine owners found that coal was available almost everywhere in the Valley, and deep shafts were sunk into the ground throughout the region. When a good seam of coal appeared, it was tunnelled through.

Working far below the surface, a miner sought and followed the veins of coal. His only source of light was the lamp attached to his helmet, his only tool a pick. This photograph communicates something of the claustrophobia inherent in mine work. (WHGS)

The workers followed the coal in its natural beds. Engineers directed the projects, and carpenters built support systems designed to keep the mines from collapsing. "Fire bosses" were responsible for monitoring the safety of the underground workings. All these men needed great knowledge and skill, and were usually well trained, often well-educated men who could command high wages. If they made mistakes, great capital investments would be lost—and therefore the managers "in the city" did not want this group of their employees to be dissatisfied. They received good pay, often lived in fine company houses, and had other benefits from their employment.

The actual extractors of the coal from the seams were, properly speaking, "miners." Because anthracite was so hard, it was necessary to chisel a small hole into the coal, fill it with dynamite, and blast out the coal. Miners were supposed to know just where to place the charges, just how much dynamite to use, and just how to detonate it, so that the coal would be accessible but the mine would neither collapse nor explode. The

Mine carpenters placed timbers and "collars" to shore up the caverns left when the coal had been extracted. The timbers, used in vast quantities, were simply logs. They needed no chemical treatment to prevent decay, because even bacteria avoided the dismal environment of the mines. (WHGS)

miners held a middle position in the industry's economic pyramid; they received less pay and benefits than the engineers and fire bosses, but considerably more than common laborers.

Once the miners had blasted the coal from a seam, many other unskilled laborers would chop lumps into portable pieces and load it into cars to be taken to the entrance of the mine. This back-breaking, mind-numbing work was the chore of the vast majority of mineworkers. With only the light shining from lamps in their hats, these men would chop and load till they reached their daily quota—often more than 32,000 pounds of coal per man per day. The "sixteen tons" made famous in song had its origin in the cruel reality of coal mining.

Carpenters, engineers, fire bosses, miners, and laborers lived in constant danger. They had an understandable concern with their own safety and they tried to make their work as hazard-free as possible. Nevertheless, accidents within the mines were frequent. Legs were crushed by falling coal; eyes were blinded by misplaced charges; hearing was impaired by the constant blasting. For much of this period the absentee owners had no real concern about such losses, unless capital equipment was endangered. A few small, locally-owned and operated mines had good safety records, but these were exceptional operations.

The first great mine disaster in the Wyoming Valley occurred at the Avondale Colliery near Plymouth on September 6, 1869. In that instance an outside fire caused the ventilation system of the mine to fail, leading to suffocation of 110 men and boys. The community contributed some

In time, subterranean roads were created as more and more anthracite was extracted. This is Road 249A. By the beginning of the 20th century, it is said, one could walk from Nanticoke to Pittston—the whole length of Wyoming Valley— without once leaving the mines. (WHGS)

Four thousand pounds of coal in a small subterranean car can develop considerable momentum should the car get out of control. The laborer in the center of this photograph has his left foot planted firmly on a brake bar to prevent this as his companions finish loading. Cars were hauled or pushed either by laborers or by the only other living creatures to inhabit the mines—mules.

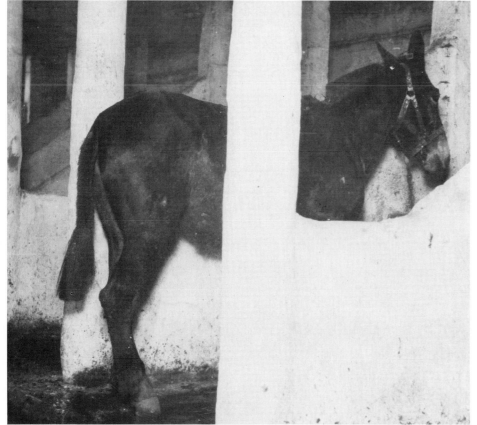

Mine mules were stabled below ground. They were brought to the surface only for veterinary treatment or—if they were too old, sick, or injured—to be destroyed.

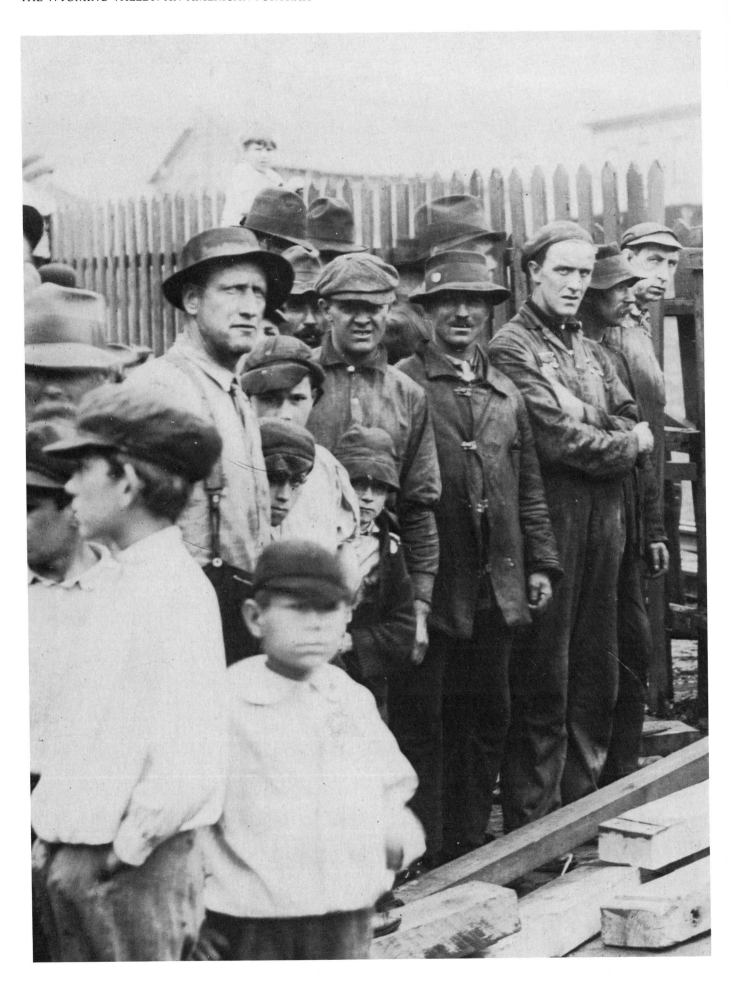

funds to help the widows and orphans bear their losses. But the owners responded by moving their expensive equipment away from the mine entrances.

Accidents occurred frequently, though not on the scale of the Avondale tragedy. If a man emerged safely from his 10 to 14 hours in the mine, he felt blessed. But no one spent even a day in the mines without suffering permanent physical damage. The coal dust within the mine did more than blacken the faces of the miners—it petrified their lungs. Men who worked in the mines did not live long. Anthracilacosis or "miners' asthma" was epidemic in the coal regions. Mining was a killing occupation, but the nation needed coal.

Once the coal came out of the earth in large cars, it had to be separated from the rock and slate that surrounded it. In the beginning this was done by hand, using simple machines. By the 1850s huge buildings called breakers were constructed near most mines, creating a new architectural form peculiar to the coal regions. The coal was moved from a mine to the top of a breaker by a long conveyor belt. Boys and men too weak to work in the mines drew the large pieces of slate out of this moving pile, allowing the coal to enter the breaker. There it moved through a variety of washes into different-sized funnels. The sized, washed coal would drop into waiting railroad cars called "gondolas" at the bottom of the breaker. The refuse of this process, called slag, was simply dumped over the green hills, changing the rare beauty of the landscape to lunar desolation.

Because railroads were needed to take the crushed coal from the breakers to the national markets, the connection between mining and railroading was intimate. Without readily available fuel, the railroads could not run; without a transportation system capable of moving the bulky coal to the cities, mining was pointless. For these reasons the earliest railroads in the nation were built in the coal region, and all railroad companies wanted to connect their lines to this area.

The geographical factors that made Wyoming Valley attractive to farmers and millers raised problems for railroaders, however. The low mountains that created the Valley severely slowed the trains, especially those hauling heavy loads. Railroad corporations decided to build their main north-south and east-west lines away from the Valley. They chose a pleasant village to the north, once called Slocam Hollow, then Harrison, and finally Scranton in honor of two leading businessmen, as their main junction. This decision, combined with the farsighted economic leadership of the Scranton brothers and others of the area, accounted for rapid growth into the largest city in the anthracite fields. In 1878 Scranton became the seat of a separate Lackawanna County, cut from Luzerne County.

While Scranton was developing at a very rapid rate, Wyoming Valley continued more slowly. Trains moved in and out of the community, symbolically at a slowed pace. The mountains that had protected the frontier community tended to isolate the industrial center.

The Wyoming Valley did grow, however, and not exclusively from natural population increases. The mine crews included a large number of immigrants to the Valley, starting with the Welsh and Irish in the 1830s. These Celtic peoples had experienced rapid population growth in their homelands. Led by able and strong young men, they began a significant migration to northeastern Pennsylvania.

The Welsh had certain distinct advantages over the Irish. They were British and Protestant; and some had experience in mining. In spite of these advantages they found hard and unsteady work, poor wages, and hateful working conditions. A Welsh scholar, Alan Conway, has recently published a collection of letters from emigrants written between 1817

Facing page: *Everyone in this photograph is an employee of the Kingston Coal Company. The men spent 10 to 14 hours a day underground hacking and loading coal for wages that would not support their families. For that reason, their sons went to work in the breakers at the age of seven or eight sorting slag from chutes of moving coal.*

In 1869, when this photograph was taken, the Nanticoke Breaker of the Susquehanna Coal Company fed its output into canal boats that took it south. The water seen here is the slack section of the river created by the Nanticoke dam. The chutes at the left were lowered to fill the boats. The mineshaft is under the scaffold at right. (WHGS)

Culm, or slag, is the by-product of coal mining. Culm consists of slate mixed with low-grade coal and sulphurous debris and mounded up into great dead hills. Neither the hardiest weeds nor even the persistent sumac will grow on a culm bank until decades of rain have washed away its poison. The water that drains from a culm bank is also poisonous. As the years went by, hundreds of thousands of tons of it turned parts of the Valley into lunar-like wastelands. (WHGS)

and 1872. In it, those who went to rural America wrote glorious accounts of the promise of American life. Those in the mine fields sent one message: "Stay in Wales! Difficult as conditions are there, it is worse in the American coalfields." But the people of Wales did not heed that advice. More and more came, lured by new companies starting mines.

Though these Welsh were Protestants, most did not follow Episcopal, Presbyterian, or Methodist ways. They started their own churches, chiefly Baptist and Congregationalist. Since the miners had neither the time nor the means to travel to distant churches, they built small congregations in the many new towns that sprang up in the Valley.

At the same time and for similar reasons as the Welsh, Irishmen

This panoramic photograph shows Wilkes-Barre in the early 1870s looking west from the heights to the east of the city. Small farms occupy the foreground; the railroad yards in the middle distance were created by draining a swamp. Beyond the railroad and the canal, Canal Street stretches from South Street (left) to Northampton (right). The tall spire to the right of center belongs to St. Mary's Church, built in 1872. (WHGS)

Emigrant miners from Wales and Ireland, like the other emigrants from Eastern Europe who would follow in later years, formed small congregations and built small churches to which they could walk from their homes. This one stood next to a railroad, probably in Pittston—but it could have been almost any denomination almost anywhere in the Valley.

moved to the region. When the Great Hunger hit Ireland between 1846 and 1851, the trickle became a deluge and both men and women migrated. Although two-thirds of these Irish knew English, they had no experience in mining. More important, they were not Protestants. As the first Catholic migrants to the communities on the Susquehanna, they had great difficulty being accepted into the mainstream of Valley life. There is little doubt that they would have been accepted as Protestants, but they steadfastly insisted on maintaining their separateness. Encouraged by the Bishop of Philadelphia, Francis P. Kenrick, they established a parish on the canal (Pennsylvania Boulevard) in Wilkes-Barre in 1842. Seven years later they moved to South Washington Street as St. Mary's of the

Coal companies built and
maintained housing—called
"patches"—for their employees.
Patches consisted of row upon row of
cheaply built shacks. Rents were not
low, and they were deducted from
laborers' pay envelopes, as were all
purchases made at the company
stores. The dwellings shown here
were two-family houses.

Immaculate Conception. Other "Irish" Catholic churches were established in Pittston (1853), Nanticoke and Plymouth (1872), and Sugar Notch (1879).

The Irish, Welsh, and native workers quickly learned that they were employed by corporations that sought profit in every conceivable way. The companies bought land surrounding the collieries and erected com-

pany houses in little patch towns from which their employees could walk to work. These shacks were rented out at profitable rates. A company often ran a store in the patch, selling food, household necessities, work clothes, and the tools required in the mines. The coal companies hired not only company doctors and nurses (charging each worker a fixed fee and determining the quality of medical care available) but also private policemen to protect their property and maintain law and order. (A typical mine worker might earn $30 per month, pay $4.50 rent for a small company house, $7.50 for food at the company store, and 50 cents for the company doctor. If he needed work implements or clothes, there was very little left for his family's needs.) Agents of the companies sought to direct local politics and education and to influence religion. The domination of the coal community by the coal companies was almost total. The great American historian Henry F. Pringle has compared the lot of the mine workers to that of the slaves of the South.

Mining was not the only industry to grow in the Valley. Older than the mines, the textile mills expanded, producing linen, cotton, woolen,

Life along River Street in the Wilkes-Barre of the 1860s became ever more gracious. The Phoenix Hotel was replaced by the grander and more luxurious Wyoming Valley House, built in 1863 by J.C. Sidney of Philadelphia, whose visitors often arrived by train. Diagonally across the street from the hotel stood the toll house that guarded the entrance to the bridge across the Susquehanna. (WHGS)

and silk materials as well as lace. Most workers in the mills were women and children.

The Wyoming Valley of the 1870s resembled the worst forms of "roaring capitalism." Their wages kept many workers on the brink of extinction. Yet despite this exploitation, the period did have some bright spots. The farming community continued to prosper and some cottage industries appeared, producing a variety of goods. The established churches sought to alleviate suffering. Education made significant advances with the establishment of Wyoming Seminary (1844) by the Methodists, St. Mary's School (1875) by the "Irish" Sisters of Mercy, and St. Ann's Academy (1877) by the "German" Sisters of Christian Charity. A Music Hall (1870) provided a gracious spot for those with enough wealth, knowledge, and leisure to enjoy the cultural life, and a General Hospital in Wilkes-Barre (1872) provided medical care.

On July third and fourth in 1878 the Valley paused to celebrate the centennial of the Battle of Wyoming. Kingston native General Henry Hoyt, a leader of the many Valley men who had served in the Civil War and shortly to be elected governor, invited President Rutherford B. Hayes to the plains of Wyoming. There, 100 years to the day after Nathan Denison surrendered to the British, the president of the United States greeted 100,000 natives, immigrants, and visitors. On that day the mines closed, the breakers stopped, the mills were quiet. On that day the Valley celebrated its past with genuine pride, and the misery of the present was suspended. But when the celebration ended, the misery continued.

Music Hall, Wilkes-Barre's first genuine theater, was built in about 1870 at the northeast corner of Market and River streets, site of the present Hotel Sterling. The architect, Isaac G. Perry, delighted in elaborate cornices and mansard roofs pierced with complicated gables. For some reason, the River Street elevation is much simpler than the Market Street facade. Music Hall stood for only a quarter-century, but some of Perry's simpler commercial buildings further along Market Street are in use today. (WHGS)

The second covered wooden bridge spanned the Susquehanna from 1824 to 1892. The bridgekeeper-toll collector's gatehouse stood at its eastern end. Tracks for a horse-drawn trolley were laid in 1866, and service from Wilkes-Barre to Kingston was inaugurated on June 25. The wooden gatehouse was replaced with a brick structure in 1885. R.E. Smith's drawing, dated 1897, is based on a photograph. (WHGS)

Regular steamboat service between Nanticoke and Pittston began in 1871. Here a boat heads upriver from the landing just south of the Market Street Bridge. The River Common overlooking a bend in the Susquehanna was a popular promenade. The mansion of William Conyngham in the background stood on the site of Fort Wyoming—a spot that commands an uninterrupted view up and down the river. The Dorothy Dickson Darte Center for the Performing Arts was built there in the 1960s. (WHGS)

Chapter Five

THE WELDING SHOP

When President Hayes came to the Valley to dedicate the Wyoming Monument on July 4, 1878, he saw a great mass of people united in their celebration of the values of the past—people who also shared a belief in the promise of America, for themselves and for their children. Had Hayes mingled with these people, he might have noted great diversity among the local folk.

Class division had arisen in the half-century between the beginning of the mining industry and the centennial. A virtual aristocracy, based on wealth, education, and culture, had descended from the first families of the Valley. With names like Dorrance, Hollenback, and Shoemaker, the grandchildren of the simple farmers of Connecticut and Pennsylvania

Above: *Exactly who was who among the bewhiskered dignitaries assembled to celebrate the centennial of the Battle of Wyoming is difficult to determine. President Rutherford B. Hayes is second from the left among those seated; standing third from the left (with muttonchop whiskers) is Senator Hendrick B. Wright near the end of his long career. The photo, by G.W. Leach, Jr., is taken from a stereopticon slide. (WHGS)*

Left: *In the summertime, the River Common was becoming increasingly gracious. This view shows the expanse from Market Street north. In the background is the new North Street Bridge, opened in 1887. The Susquehanna was also bridged at Shickshinny in 1860 and at Pittston in 1878. In 1892, the wooden bridge at Market Street was also replaced by a steel one. (WHGS)*

had acquired riches based on land and security based on education.

A significant middle class, consisting of educated and professional people, served themselves and the public more through the work of their minds than the work of their hands. Physicians, lawyers, teachers, ministers, engineers, merchants, owners of small service businesses, and the operators of small factories constituted a most respected segment of the population.

There was clearly a lower class in the Valley—tens of thousands of men, women, and children who lived in poverty without any guarantee of next week's food or shelter. No one approved of this poverty, but many, following the fashionable ideas of social Darwinism, considered it the natural state of the masses.

The population was also divided because many did not speak English well. Beginning in the 1840s German-speaking Protestants, Catholics, and Jews had come; by the next generation more than a dozen languages—English, Welsh, Irish, German, Italian, Polish, Slovak, Russian, Lithuanian, Greek, Ukrainian, Yiddish, Arabic, and Hungarian—would be heard on the streets of the old townships of Wilkes-Barre, Nanticoke (Hanover), Pittston, Plymouth, and Forty Fort (Kingston). Towns unknown to Nathan Denison—Swoyersville, Edwardsville, Pringle, Luzerne, Larksville, Ashley, Parsons, Miners Mills, Georgetown, Honey Pot, Glen Lyon, Wanamie, Sugar Notch, and many more—had become enclaves of one or more ethnic groups. To some the community once divided between Tories and patriots now seemed a virtual Babel.

Below: *The original Temple B'nai B'rith was built in the 1840s by John Henry Willis Hawkins. The first synagogue in the Valley, its congregation consisted primarily of German Jews. As more and more Jews arrived, especially from eastern Europe, small synagogues sprang up all over the Valley. Eventually, they consolidated into three congregations reflecting the three branches of modern Judaism.*

Left: *The Dr. Edwards Memorial Church at the corner of Main and Church streets in Edwardsville was built by a Welsh Presbyterian congregation. Dozens of similarly unadorned wooden churches can still be found all over the Valley. Locally owned and operated, the Kingston Coal Company showed greater concern for its workers' welfare than did operations based in Philadelphia or New York. The company maintained a free playground, used mainly by the children of its employees. (WHGS)*

Each of these patch towns, usually centered about a colliery, had its own stores, saloons, boarding houses, and—most importantly— churches. Although one Protestant church had served the whole community comfortably only 50 years earlier, non-Protestants constituted a significant portion of the population by the time of the centennial. Roman Catholics had a clear plurality, though they were deeply divided along ethnic lines. German Jews, organized in 1837, built Temple B'nai B'rith on South Washington Street in Wilkes-Barre in 1849. As more Russian, Polish, and Lithuanian Jews fled from Tsarist persecution, the number of synagogues increased steadily. Jews eventually split into orthodox, conservative, and reform factions, not so much on ethnic bases as on the degree of their adherence to forms of worship.

Left: *Immigrants eagerly sought any kind of knowledge that would be useful to them. Here, employees of the Kingston Coal Company in Edwardsville practice first aid. The company also provided courses in American history, civics, geography, and, of course, English. (WHGS)*

Right: *Since 1879, the Boston Store has broken new ground in merchandising in the Valley. In 1904, Fowler, Dick, & Walker proudly operated the first horseless delivery van in Wilkes-Barre. Other innovations over the years have included the first escalator and the first parking garage. The founders at first used a broom plant as their trademark. Later, they switched to a Scottish Tartan. (WHGS)*

Right bottom: *Floods, like this ice flood that occurred in 1875, were not uncommon. Most often they took place in March when spring rains conspired with melting snows. Ice jams were an added hazard when a particularly cold winter was followed by a swift thaw. The river might then deposit large chunks of ice all over the common. At normal low water the bridge stood 20 feet above the surface of the water. (WHGS)*

The process of Americanization, in fact, divided the local community profoundly. Some groups—Welsh, Scots, English, and Protestant Germans—sought and achieved integration into the dominant community. Others—most notably the Irish and German Catholics—rejected complete integration, seeking instead to hold to the European culture of their homeland. For many immigrants the struggle to maintain the old ways resembled the bigotry of the social Darwinists. A cultural war was waged in the Valley between the Americanizers and the traditionalists, and, in the end, both sides won because both sides lost.

To demonstrate this struggle, it might be helpful to look at a few of the ethnic groups. By 1878 the Welsh—the first to arrive in the Valley—had their own churches and through them maintained Welsh traditions such as the *Eisteddfod,* an annual celebration of Welsh folk music. In south Wilkes-Barre, in the Heights, in Edwardsville, in Plymouth, and in other spots in the Valley, the Welsh defended their culture and traditions. The St. David's Society (a social, cultural, and mutual aid organization) tried to preserve an ethnic consciousness. But within two generations, the Welsh language was gradually lost and Welsh-Americans found they could better serve their own interests by joining the dominant Anglo-Saxon community rather than by fighting it.

Scots never constituted a major ethnic group in the region, but the few who did settle achieved influence and success in almost every field they entered. Some, like William McLean and Gilbert McClintock, achieved preeminence in the law. Others, like George Fowler, Alexander Dick, and Gilbert Walker, entered the world of commerce. Backed by a group of Scot merchants in Boston in 1879, Fowler, Dick, and Walker began a diversified store in central Wilkes-Barre which they gratefully called The Boston Store. For more than 100 years this department store has held a central place in the commercial life of the Valley. In 1906, as the founders aged, they passed leadership on to the Scots-born Malcom Burnside. He and his family maintained control of this emporium until very recent times.

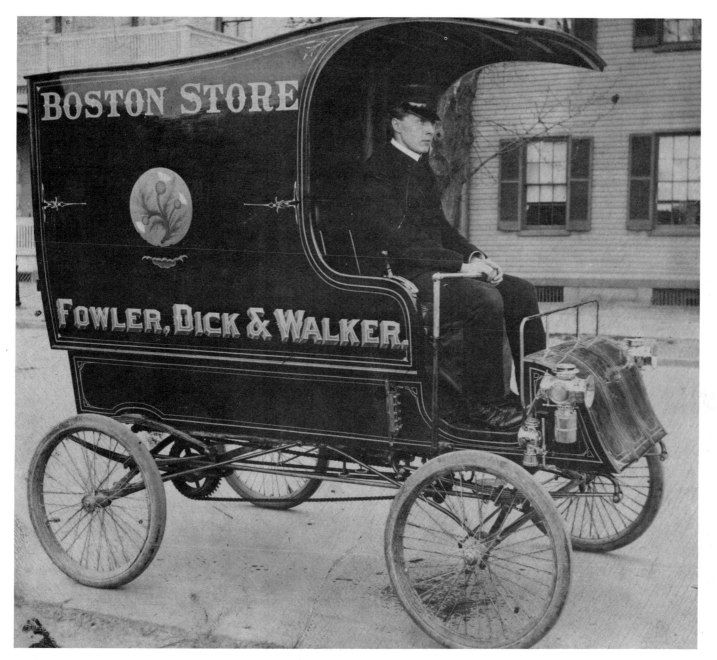

The growing city needed an expanded legal system. In 1856, a New York architect, J.C. Wells, was brought in to build a new county courthouse on Public Square on the site of the second courthouse, the original academy, and the Old Ship Zion Church. In 1875 Bruce Price was commissioned to add a third story and increase the Victorian ornamentation of Wells' simpler building. (WHGS)

Americans of English stock influenced local commerce and industry. At the same time that Fowler, Dick, and Walker began their department store, three clerks in a Watertown, New York, dry goods store decided to apply a novel approach to merchandising. Frank Woolworth, his brother Sumner, and Fred M. Kirby thought they could profit by providing the general public merchandise at fair prices while cutting out middlemen between producers and retailers and keeping their labor costs quite low. Using a sales device pioneered in Port Huron, Michigan, they planned to open stores offering all merchandise at a flat price—5 cents an item. Frank Woolworth opened his first store at Utica, New York, in 1879. Sumner Woolworth followed with a store in Scranton in 1880; and Fred Kirby, at the age of 23 and with the help of the Woolworth brothers, opened his first store in Wilkes-Barre in 1884. In the early years they introduced a second line of "expensive" merchandise for 10 cents. This alternative approach to merchandising—which revolutionized the world

The coming of streetcars condemned the riverboats to slow extinction. The Mayflower of Plymouth, *pictured here, sank in 1894. The ship was refloated and taken to Harveys Lake where it was allowed to rot rather than being rebuilt. In more spectacular departures, the* Hendrick B. Wright *was crushed by ice in 1881, and the* Susquehanna *blew up at the foot of the Market Street Bridge in 1883. Courtesy, F. Charles Petrillo*

of commerce—spawned 5-and-10-cent stores first throughout the United States and then throughout the world. By 1912, when 96 stores bore Kirby's name, he joined the Woolworth brothers and three other partners to combine their 596 stores into a single corporation, F.W. Woolworth and Company. The giant corporation opened a district office in Wilkes-Barre, but the local Woolworth store continued to use Kirby's name, as it still does today.

Kirby developed close relations with a group of outstanding English-American entrepreneurs such as Charles Parrish, William Conyngham, and Abram Nesbitt. This trio of self-made millionaires helped to bring to the Valley such diverse industries as the Hazard Wire Rope Company, the Vulcan Iron Works, the Sheldon Axle Company, the Wilkes-Barre Lace Manufacturing, the Dorranceton Silk Works, the Wyoming Cutlery Company, the Penn Tobacco Company, and the Wales Adding Machine Company. These major manufacturers employed men, women, and children, generating wealth for their owners, who reinvested in the local economy and shared some of their wealth through contributions to various causes, especially those connected to the major Protestant churches.

In 1912, Abram Nesbitt purchased the old home of Charles Dorrance in Kingston and added a wing to the back to provide a hospital for the West Side. Nesbitt and his son Abram G. Nesbitt continued to support their hospital. In 1927, the latter bequeathed the institution the funds necessary to replace the old house with a new building. (WHGS)

On August 17, 1890, a tornado swept through Wilkes-Barre, killing several people and destroying or damaging several hundred buildings in the space of 20 minutes. The twister scattered the proud tower of St. Mary's Church over the churchyard. The building, designed by E.F. Durang in 1872 in a restrained Italian baroque style, was less than 20 years old. For whatever reason, the spire was never replaced, and the entire surface of the building—except for the stonework—was later covered with stucco. (WHGS)

The early Irish population in the Valley were a hard working lot, with most of the men and boys employed in and around the mines and most of the women and girls working in mills or as maids. Their initial desperate poverty sparked an ambition to escape from it. The Irish gift of language and genius for organization helped many to find work as salesmen or to become small business owners, teachers, journalists, priests, and politicians. Many of the sons and daughters of the Irish immigrants

The German Catholics who organized the St. Conrad's Society built their hall in a distinctly Germanic style on the corner of South Washington and East South streets, diagonally across from St. Nicholas' Church. The society was named to honor Father Conrad Nagel, pastor of St. Nick's for more than 50 years. Today's St. Conrad's Hall is a few buildings'to the south, and the building on this site houses (among other businesses) Ell's Barber Shop. Courtesy, F. Charles Petrillo

Employees of the Hess-Goldsmith Silk Mill posed outside the factory around 1890. Because their husbands and fathers were underpaid as mineworkers, women of the Valley were eager to augment their families' incomes. Their readily available labor turned the Valley into a textile center.

worked their way into positions of authority, if not wealth. The Irish eventually came to dominate the Democratic Party and the Roman Catholic Church in the region, and to exercise significant power in the educational system. Their dogged unwillingness to accept second-class citizenship and their insistence on running the Church, the party, and the schools in an Irish-American way sometimes caused resentment in the Protestant community and from non-Irish Catholics.

The Germans who came to the Valley seemed to have an easier time blending into American life. Perhaps their experience with cultural and religious diversity in their homeland, or the liberal leadership provided by men exiled after the German revolution of 1848, may have provided support for their new life in a democracy. They did, however, establish German Lutheran and German Catholic churches, German schools, and the St. Conrad's Society, a self-help organization. Although some Germans worked in and around the mines, the vast majority found other occupations. German-Americans who owned the Duplan Silk Mill in Kingston and Hess-Goldsmith & Company in Wilkes-Barre and Kingston produced textiles. George Stegmeier brought his skills to make a fine lager beer which became nationally famous and gave employment to many of his old countrymen. Isaac Long and Justin Bergman, both German Jews, built successful emporiums bearing their names in central Wilkes-Barre.

All of these immigrant groups responded to industrialism by welding their old world values and institutions to their new world conditions. None of the ethnic groups was ever "melted down" so that it lost its distinguishing characteristics. Rather, each became branches added to the modern sculpture of contemporary American society through processes that seared and enriched both the old and the new Americas. In the cultural struggle, the national motto, *E pluribus unum*, would be sorely tested. Could the United States build a genuine unity out of this diversity? The events in Wyoming Valley in the 20th century would provide the answer.

In the early 1930s, Ell's Barber Shop needed three full-time barbers and a shoeshine boy. To the left, Adolph Ell is shaving an unidentified priest who leapt from his chair when the flashbulb for this photo went off; in the center, Dan McTague shaves William Kear, a popular local contractor; and in the rear, Eddie Ell is cutting the hair of William O. Sword, who would organize the Committee of One Hundred in 1955. Next to Eddie is Walter Ras, the shoeshine boy. Courtesy, Edward Ell and Robert Ell

Among the 1890 tornado's hapless
victims was this coal breaker.

APPROACHING HUNT

The turn of the century marked many changes. The North Branch Canal, which had brought Wilkes-Barre its initial prosperity, closed in 1881; and in five years, no trace of it remained in the city but the aqueduct over Mill Creek, which became a railroad bridge and survives to this day. At Hunlocks to the south, canal and railroad went side by side until 1901. Even today,. a cyclist may encounter a stretch of canal lying quietly retired in the sun, dreaming perhaps of boats and mules and the torches that lit their way by night. Courtesy, F. Charles Petrillo

On the days when the colliery was in operation, miners traveled down in an open-cage elevator. Equipped with a kerosene-burning helmet torch, each miner also carried a lunch bucket. The cold drink on the top of the bucket helped to keep the rest of the bucket cool in the mine.

Chapter Six

THE LABORER IS WORTHY

Left: *On the perimeter of the square opposite the courthouse stood a symbol of prosperity—the First National Bank. Like many other commercial and domestic buildings of the 1860s and 1870s, the bank is the work of Isaac G. Perry (1822-1904). The facade comprises three sets of colonnades surmounted by a massive and intricate cornice supported by equally massive brackets. Above this, the mansard roof is pierced by three gables surmounted by another cornice. (WHGS)*

Right: *Unlike many of the coal operations, the Kingston Coal Company was locally owned and operated. The company was more concerned about its workers' welfare than operators headquartered in New York or Philadelphia. Interested in documenting its own activities, the company left a large number of excellent photographs taken in the early years of the century. Here the company's home office is decked out either for the Armistice (1918) or the Sesquicentennial (1928). (WHGS)*

Of all the events in the Valley, none was more important than the settlement of the Anthracite Strike of 1902. National processes started at that time began to make it possible for working-class people to achieve economic security in the United States.

Before 1902 conditions among American workers, especially those in the anthracite industry, were woeful. Miners, laborers, and helpers saw their wages drop from $3, $2, and 80 cents per day in 1870 to $2.25, $1.40, and 75 cents in 1900. Moreover, regardless of their low wages the miners and their families paid relatively high rent, doctor's fees, and store bills to their employers. Considering the fact that overproduction made it unprofitable for most mines to work more than three days a week, mine

workers and their families constantly faced economic disaster.

To improve wages, working conditions, and everyday living, there were only two hopes—instituting immigration restriction or creating an effective union. The first hope was repeatedly dashed as more and more workers—chiefly from southern and eastern European nations—entered the fields. In 1880 only 1.7 percent of mine workers came from those regions, but by 1900, 46 percent of a vastly increased labor force came from Slavic lands and Italy. The newcomers who had escaped from dreadful European poverty, survived on incomes that older Americans deemed too low to support human existence. Pleas for immigration restriction won no major support till after World War I.

The other hope—unionization—was a dream of mine workers for many decades before 1902, but faced seemingly insurmountable opposition from employers, the state, the church, and the general public. The mine operators adamantly opposed any dealings with workers' organizations. Union men were subject to firing and blacklisting. Because the operators controlled both workers' housing and their access to food, clothing, and medical attention, none but the bravest mine workers dared to challenge their employers. Thus unions imposed secrecy on their members.

Furthermore, the Roman Catholic Church, the spiritual home of most mine workers, unconditionally condemned all secret organizations, including secret unions. Not until the 1890s did labor leaders, like Scranton's Terence Powderly of the Knights of Labor, with the help of American bishops like James Cardinal Gibbons of Baltimore and Michael Hoban of Scranton, convince Rome to allow union membership.

In case after case, the governments of the United States crippled unions. For example, the Sherman Anti-Trust Act of 1890 which declared illegal "any combination in restraint of trade," was aimed at industrial monopolies, but it had greater effect in breaking strikes than it did in shattering trusts. Strikes were, by definition, combinations of workers to restrain trade. Trusts, their owners proclaimed, existed to promote trade. No monopolies were broken under this act before 1902, but many strikes were broken by antitrust injunctions.

At the high point of the entire anthracite industry, the Kingston Coal Company maintained four breakers of this size. This is the No. 2 Breaker, which crushed hundreds of tons of coal every day. (WHGS)

In 1894 President Cleveland, a Democrat, sent troops to break a railroad strike against the Pullman Company. He felt that because national interests suffered from that strike, violence was justified to break it. His action won national approval.

In 1897 Slovak, Polish, and Lithuanian strikers in Lattimer, north of Hazleton, marched to protest abuses by the coal operators' company stores. The sheriff of Luzerne County, James Martin, ordered the marchers to disperse. When they did not break ranks quickly enough, Martin ordered his posse to shoot into the mob, killing 19 unarmed men and wounding 49. Many of these victims were shot in the back. When Martin was charged with murder, Henry W. Palmer (who was to later become Attorney General of Pennsylvania) served as his successful defense counsel. Clearly the power of government opposed unions. Workers had no chance of overpowering their employers and their government.

An anthracite mining operation required many kinds of support operations. This mill cut logs into timber props to shore up mine tunnels as the coal was extracted. The entire output of this mill was used by the Number 4 Colliery. (WHGS)

As more and more of the substrata of the Valley became honeycombed with tunnels and as the supporting timbers decayed, subsidences became more and more common. Here onlookers in 1897 observe the results of a spontaneous shift out of the perpendicular taken by the post office on West Eighth Street in Wyoming. (WHGS)

The public also viewed all unions—especially miners' associations—with suspicion. In 1877 a series of revelations by a Pinkerton detective named James McKenna shocked the nation with its "report" on union activities. After infiltrating a group of Irish-Americans whom he called "the Mollie Maguires", McKenna accused them of assault, arson, and murder. Although he never linked the Mollies with unions and despite the fact that almost none of the so-called Mollies were mine workers, antiunion propagandists led the public mind to connect unions with crime.

Another problem that impeded the organization of unions stemmed from the divisions among the workers themselves. Bituminous coal and anthracite workers saw one another as competitors and therefore resisted cooperation. Regional differences divided workers in the northern field (Scranton and Wilkes-Barre) from those in the middle fields (around Hazleton) from those in the south (around Maunk Chunk and Pottsville). Skilled miners had different needs than their unskilled comrades, and resisted joining the same union. Religious prejudices made it difficult for Protestants (chiefly of Welsh origin) to join with Catholics. Among the Catholics, ethnic difficulties separated Irish from Slovak, Pole from

Mining operations used ever-increasing amounts of electricity generated from burning anthracite. The Coalbrook Power House supplied electricity to only one of the Kingston Coal Company's collieries. The clean but somewhat old-fashioned style of the roof beams stands in incongruous contrast with the industrial power of the dynamos. (WHGS)

Italian, and so on. The disorganized workers needed a miracle man to unite them, win the support of church, state, and public opinion, and to defeat their very powerful employers.

Such a man, John L. Mitchell, emerged in 1900. He possessed a special charisma that inspired total confidence in almost everyone he met. Born in Illinois in 1870, he was only 29 years old when he became the fifth president of the United Mine Workers. Neither his Scotch-Irish background nor his Presbyterian faith (changed in a death-bed conversion to his wife's Roman Catholicism), nor his limited education, nor his profound conservatism estranged him from the Catholic workers or kept him from dealing effectively with the nation's best-trained minds. In 1900 he reluctantly called a strike of the 8,000 organized anthracite workers. To his amazement between 80,000 and 100,000 men and boys, 90 percent of the mine workers, defied their employers to heed his call. Mine operators absolutely refused to deal with Mitchell; but 33 days after the walk-out began, they yielded to political pressure. Mark Hanna, chairman of the Republican party, feared that an extended strike would throw the presidential election to William Jennings Bryan. Operators granted their workers a 10 percent increase in wages and made some

The Coalbrook Power House came to a sudden cessation of activity on the afternoon of March 14, 1921. An explosion threw the dynamos out of balance, and they destroyed not only themselves but also the building and everything else in it. The powerhouse was rebuilt and restored to active service in less than a year. (WHGS)

Left: *By all accounts, John Mitchell was a man of great strength of character. Like many other scrupulous idealists, he died broke. This pen-and-ink portrait by Edward Jazgier of Hanover Township captures something of Mitchell's quality. Courtesy, Collection of Dr. Ellis Roberts on permanent loan to the D. Leonard Corgan Library, King's College*

Below: *In the mines, mules hauled cars of coal to the bottom of the shaft, a job that was eventually taken over by electrical trolleys. The cage operator uses an air-powered device to signal the hoist room that the cage is ready to descend.*

adjustments to the most outstanding grievances.

In this settlement, the operators never negotiated with the workers or their leaders. In Mitchell's words, the concessions were "flung at them rather than granted to them." At any rate, the mines reopened and the Republican ticket of McKinley and Roosevelt won the election of 1900.

Within two years, however, a significant change had occurred in the national leadership. The conservative William McKinley was assassi-

nated in 1901 and his successor, Theodore Roosevelt, was beginning what historians would later call a progressive era in American politics. Unlike McKinley, Roosevelt believed that the government should participate actively in the management of the national economy, and he was willing to take actions that no previous president would have considered.

So, in 1902 when Mitchell sought a 20 percent increase in wages, the weighing of coal, an eight-hour day, and an industry-wide wage scale, he offered to submit these demands to arbitration. The operators, led by George F. Baer, president of the Pennsylvania and Reading Railroad Company, refused either to negotiate or to submit to arbitration. On May 12, 1902, Mitchell called on 140,000 anthracite workers to strike. Over 80 percent heard his call and began the longest strike in the anthracite industry and the most significant strike in American history.

The operators felt confident that they could break the strike. Baer identified himself as one of the "Christian men to whom God in His infinite wisdom had given the control of the property interests in this country," and identified the gentle Mitchell as a "labor agitator [who

Within the mines, other mechanization was taking place. By 1925, the air hammer (or jackhammer) had been fitted with a cruciform auger (a specially mounted drill) that made holes for the placement of dynamite charges. The dynamite loosened the surrounding rock to facilitate further excavation.

advocated] violence and crime." Baer considered the workers essentially inferior and entirely incapable of sustaining a long strike, and believed that before long they would either submit or starve. He was therefore dismayed to find the entire community supporting the workers. Men of moderate wealth like Polish brewer and banker Emil Malinowski of Nanticoke, and Slovak grocer John Kosek of Wilkes-Barre, supported the strikers. Owners of small shops, tillers of small farms, and workers in other industries gave more than excess wealth to aid the mine workers. They gave of themselves for 163 days of the walkout, sharing their possessions and the strikers' suffering. Though the workers lost $25 million in wages, no one starved. A united, committed community saw to that. Membership in the union and participation in a strike, once considered dangerous and radical activities, became sources of pride. In broken English workers of various ethnic backgrounds identified good citizenship, economic benefits, and union membership as they proudly sang "Me Johnny Mitchell Man."

In previous labor disputes the operators had counted on both the Church and the state to support the owners. But in 1902 this did not come to pass. Slavic clerics both of the Roman Catholic and of the new Polish

Cars of coal rode up to the surface in the same cages as the miners and the mules (although not at the same time). At the top of the shaft, a mechanical lever gave each car a shove that sent it rolling down into the breaker. When gravity proved inadequate, human intervention became necessary. A newswriter captioned this photo "A most modern coal mine."

Increasing mechanization of mining operations led to the introduction of the rotary mine-car dumper. Once inside the breaker, the car was gripped by this huge cylindrical device and turned upside down, dropping its contents into a waiting chute.

Their faces dirty, their bodies tired, their lunch buckets empty, and their lights extinguished, miners stream out of a tunnelhead on their way home.

National Church, including Father Hodur of Scranton, Father Malek of Plymouth, Father Szmoski of Plymouth, and Father Schlosser of Wilkes-Barre encouraged the strikers while cautioning them against violence. The Reverend John J. Curran, a former breaker boy himself and pastor of many strikers in the east end of Wilkes-Barre, offered more than encouragement. He became Mitchell's religious adviser and his agent in negotiations. Curran traveled to Philadelphia to urge Baer (unsuccessfully) to negotiate with Mitchell and to New York to seek support for arbitration from America's leading industrialist, J. Pierpont Morgan, and his partner George Perkins (a close friend of the new President Theodore Roosevelt). Finally, Curran went to the White House itself to deal with Roosevelt. Never before had an American president become involved even-handedly in a labor-management dispute; but Curran had little trouble in convincing Roosevelt to do just that.

Roosevelt forced a meeting between Mitchell whom he found most reasonable and Baer whom he found "insulting to the miners and offensive to me." Reflecting on the negotiations Roosevelt said, "If it wasn't for the high office I hold, I would have taken [Baer] by the seat of the breeches and the nape of the neck and chucked him out the window." Using all the power of his "bully pulpit," Roosevelt set up an arbitration board that included a representative of organized labor; and using J.P. Morgan as a wedge to move Baer, he forced this commission on the operators. With the creation of the board, Mitchell ended the strike on October 23, 1902, and the commission made its recommendations on March 18, 1903. The arbitration did not grant all of the workers' demands. But they did win a 10 percent raise, an eight-hour day for skilled workers and a nine-hour day for others, checks on the weighing procedures that determined their pay, and an indirect recognition of their union.

The settlement itself was not so important as the manner in which it was achieved. The strike proved beyond doubt that various ethnic and religious groups could work together, and the settlement pointed the way in which American workers could translate their numbers into power. Determined, reasonable, moderate, patient, nonviolent workers, in cooperation with a government committed to fairness to its citizens, could share the promise of American life equitably. It would take another Roosevelt to institutionalize the arbitration procedures and to recognize collective bargaining as a fundamental right. But in 1902 America's course was set in this direction by the anthracite miners, their courageous leader, their devoted priest, and a new kind of president.

As the crushed coal moved down the final chutes to the railroad cars or delivery trucks, one final check was made for remaining slag or for oversize pieces. This job was assigned to breaker boys. After the strike of 1902, their work days were limited to nine hours. Unlike their fathers, who toiled in the airless, lightless mines, breaker boys enjoyed relatively pleasant working conditions—plenty of light and adequate ventilation. (WHGS)

Many citizens started war gardens during World War I. The Kingston Coal Company turned a plot of land off Pringle Street over to the wives and children of its employees for this purpose. The gardeners in this picture—taken on August 17, 1917—seem proud of their results. The patch housing in the background shows how pleasant such buildings could be when well maintained.

For the children of laboring families, the end of the third grade often marked the end of formal education. The grimy faces of these old young men show the strain of nine-hour days as breaker boys. Courtesy, F. Charles Petrillo

Chapter Seven

THE GLORIES OF DIVERSITY

On the national level, the great Anthracite Strike of 1902 signaled a change in the way American industry, labor, and government interacted, opening the way for a sharing of the benefits of industrialism. On the local level, the strike also signaled a significant shift in the power structure. The Valley was no longer a community dominated by a single cartel centered in Philadelphia; it was no longer a region where a few could exclude the majority from decision-making. Instead, it had become a place that gloried in diversity—a place where the ongoing economic, cultural, and religious struggles would produce more lasting good than transient harm. It was, in short, a microcosm of America at the dawn of the 20th century.

The shared power structure of the Valley can be demonstrated through the second presidential visit to this area. On August 10, 1905, President Theodore Roosevelt, accompanied by the "boss" of Pennsylvania's Republican party, Senator Philander C. Knox, made a whirlwind trip to Wilkes-Barre, the Wyoming Monument, and Pittston. Roosevelt came at the invitation of the man of whom he said, "There is no friend whom I value more . . . no friend in whose friendship I take greater pride,"—Father John J. Curran, pastor of the Catholic Church of the Holy Savior in the east end of Wilkes-Barre. Sharing the platform with James Cardinal Gibbons, the progressive leader of the Roman Church in the United States, Roosevelt came to honor the Catholic Total Abstinence Society, which Father Curran led. The presidential visit recognized the growing importance of America's largest religious minority and showed the political wisdom of treating this group like first-class citizens.

Some Catholics, however, had not yet attained this status. They were moving in this direction, with considerable help from at least some of the "old Americans." No individual personified this impulse toward help more clearly than Eleanor Webster Palmer, a Valley woman whose husband, Henry, served as attorney general of Pennsylvania and as a member of Congress. Mrs. Palmer believed that America could be a "melting pot." She claimed that the horror of lower class existence resulted from an environment that led to ignorance, poverty, and crime. She made it her life's work to alter the environment of the poor by divesting them of

In the early years of the century, Pittston's primary industry—ahead of mining and textiles—was the famous Pittston Stove Works. Its factory on Broad Street manufactured great cast-iron, coalburning monsters finished in brightly colored enamel. The company's fanciest domestic models combined coal and gas for a total of two ovens, eight burners, and a broiler. (WHGS)

Father John J. Curran and President Theodore Roosevelt, who frequently mentioned their admiration and respect for one another, met at a ceremony honoring the Catholic Total Abstinence Society. Father Curran was a staunch advocate of total abstinence. Roosevelt was not, but he was an astute enough politician to recognize the importance of support from Catholics or abstainers or both. (WHGS)

their alien culture and opening them up to American ways of speech, behavior, and belief. With the county's first woman lawyer, Mary L. Trescott, as her financial assistant, she established the Boys Industrial Association (BIA). Driven by the Protestant ethic, she argued that "life is a tool to work with; not a toy to play with." She could not end child labor, but she did open a school for boys to attend after work where they could learn "proper English," good manners, personal hygiene, and trades more profitable than loading coal. The BIA exemplified perfectly the reform branch of the social Darwinist thought that gripped "progressive" America. Mrs. Palmer would improve the lot of the lower classes by giving them the culture of the dominant community.

Although Father Curran's greatest moment as a labor negotiator came during the 1902 strike, he continued to be associated with unions after the strike. In this photo, probably taken in the lobby of the Hotel Sterling in the 1920s, he met with John L. Lewis, vigorous president of the UMW for more than a quarter-century, and Thomas Kennedy of Hazleton, vice-president of the UMW and later lieutenant governor of Pennsylvania. A man of dedicated humility, Father Curran showed one manifestation of human vanity—his toupee. (WHGS)

Only in the light of the tremendous disparity between the prosperous professional class and the laboring poor does such an endeavor as the Boys Industrial Association seem understandable or indeed worthy. Here Eleanor Webster Palmer, daughter of a wealthy man and wife of an attorney and politician, appears with the breaker boys whose lot she sought to improve. (WHGS)

Although Eleanor Palmer's efforts won favorable response from many she aided, significant groups of the many Italian and Slavic migrants to the Valley had no desire to abandon their old ways of speaking and praying. Some of them, in fact, felt uncomfortable in the Roman Catholic Church, dominated as it was by the Irish bishops of Scranton and Irish pastors. To alleviate this problem, they followed the example of German Catholics who had already secured permission to establish a clearly ethnic parish (St. Nicholas, 1858) in Wilkes-Barre. Between 1883 and 1929 the bishops responded to intense ethnic pressures and established 22 Polish, 11 Slovak, 8 Lithuanian, 6 Italian, and 5 German parishes in the Valley.

Eastern Christians of several rites also established churches here. Some followed the Greek, Russian, and Syrian Orthodox practices of Christianity; others, in union with Rome, practiced the Byzantine (Ukrainian and Greek) and Maronite (Lebanese) rites. All these peoples, whether Western or Eastern Christians, sought to fulfill the economic promise of American life while retaining the languages, religious practices, and customs of the old world.

Despite the establishment of ethnic parishes, some eastern European immigrants still considered the Roman Church insufficiently responsive to their cultural and social needs. This led to two schisms in the Catholic Church in America, both beginning in the Wyoming Valley.

For young men with the money and the time, those wonderful new contraptions called bicycles were good fun and an excellent form of exercise. Here the Wilkes-Barre Bicycle Club poses before the home of William N. Conyngham (one of Isaac Perry's lost mansions) which stood on the present site of the Dorothy Dickson Darte Center for the Performing Arts. (WHGS)

Left: *German Catholics set themselves apart by establishing St. Nicholas' Church. The present church building was designed in 1886 by William Schickel. Today the church bears a large brass plaque indicating that it was founded by German immigrants, but its congregation—like those of other, similar churches—has long since adopted a much more ecumenical outlook.*

Facing page top: *Even the poorest children had at least some time for play, and the city provided playgrounds in many places. The Frances Slocum Playground was (and is) located at the corner of Scott Street and North Pennsylvania Avenue (formerly Canal Street, formerly Back Street) on the site of the old Slocum farm from which the infant Frances was abducted. The bungalow (now gone) was purportedly a replica of the Slocum house. Courtesy, F. Charles Petrillo*

Facing page bottom: *No sooner had automobiles been invented than the daring and adventurous began to race them. A prime location for a special kind of auto racing— hillclimbing—was the steep, tortuous road up Wilkes-Barre Mountain, the old Sullivan Trail, which had come to be known as Giant's Despair. This pre-1920 photo shows some of the race's participants. Courtesy, F. Charles Petrillo*

In the first case Father Francis Hodur, a Polish immigrant ordained by Bishop William O'Hara of Scranton, left his assignment as a curate in the Polish parish in Nanticoke to accept the congregation's invitation to become pastor of Holy Trinity (Polish) Catholic Church in Scranton. This action would have been normal in many Protestant communions; but in the Roman Catholic Church, it was considered a serious challenge to the bishop's authority. After Father Hodur went to Scranton, Bishop Michael Hoban, assistant to the aged Bishop O'Hara, condemned his action. Father Hodur responded by journeying to Rome to seek the appointment of Polish bishops for the United States. Failing to gain papal approval for his plan, he broke with the Church of Rome and established the Polish National Church, which combined a traditional reverence for Polish

language and culture with progressive social ideas and a democratic approach to church organization. Consecrated a bishop by an Old Catholic prelate in Utrecht, Holland, in 1907, Francis Hodur won the adherence of a small minority of Polish Americans in the Valley. Beginning with parishes in Plymouth and Wilkes-Barre from its earliest days, the Polish National Church spread to other centers of Polish culture. By 1982 a quarter of a million people, mostly in the U.S. and Canada, adhered to this communion.

Above: *Band music held a more significant spot in 19th-century America than it presently does. The Ninth Regiment of the Pennsylvania National Guard maintained Alexander's Band, which appears to have been photographed while on bivouac somewhere. (WHGS)*

The headquarters of the Ninth Regiment was the Ninth Regimental Armory, built in 1886 by Missouria B. Houpt, a prolific but undistinguished architect. After the Ninth Regiment left the structure, the building was for a time a roller skating rink and later a furniture warehouse. Now gone, the armory was a cathedral compared to the commercial structure that now occupies the site. (WHGS)

John McArthur, Jr., architect, of Philadelphia, suited his buildings to their function. His prisons were castellated Gothic affairs designed to remind the beholder of the majesty of the law and the unpleasantness of incarceration. The Luzerne County Prison was built in 1867, when Scranton and the rest of Lackawanna County were still part of Luzerne County. For that reason it is today only moderately overcrowded. Courtesy, Michael Lewis III

A comparable schism occurred among Ukrainian Catholics. Most of these peoples, who belonged to Eastern rites in union with Rome, found few priests in America who shared their rites or understood their needs. Reluctant to join Latin-rite churches, they looked to the "old country" to supply them with priests. A local Ukrainian community found such a priest in the Reverend Alexis Toth. Father Toth, a well-educated widower (eastern churches permit married priests), had come to America as a missionary but encountered a serious misunderstanding with his Latin-rite superior in Minnesota, Archbishop John Ireland. Toth agreed to come to Wilkes-Barre if the congregation would follow him into the Russian Orthodox Church. The congregation agreed, and Father Toth made Wilkes-Barre a center of Russian Orthodoxy in America, even though most of his followers were not Russians and had not been Orthodox in the "old country." Eventually, Rome responded to the special needs of Uniate Catholics by granting them what Bishop Hodur had once asked for the Poles—their own bishoprics. The majority of Uniate Christians in the Valley were then able to maintain the religion of their fathers in the land of their future.

In the mid-1870s, a young architect named Bruce Price—fresh from study in Europe (he brought several tons of Italian tile back with him)— had the good professional sense to marry a Wilkes-Barre Bennett. Had he been less ambitious and talented, he could still have earned a decent living designing mansions solely for his in-laws. This is the entrance hall of the George Bennett house of 1876, which was demolished in 1931 to make way for the YMCA. Courtesy, Michael Lewis III

Like the Episcopalians and the Presbyterians, the Methodists wanted to replace their 1840s brick church with something bigger and grander. Since the Bennetts were Methodists, Bruce Price was commissioned for the job. In 1876, he offered this extravagantly Gothic design. Courtesy, Michael Lewis III

By 1886, when the Methodists were ready to build, Price was among those architects rapidly retreating from Gothic excess—and from Victorian excesses of all kinds. As it was finally erected, the church is clearly a development of his ideas from a decade earlier, but much ornamentation has been removed, and the masses are handled with considerably more mastery. (WHGS)

The lives of Bishop Hodur, Father Curran and Father Toth illustrate the importance of the clergy in the Valley's Catholic community. But of all the local priests to influence the community and the nation, none has more claim to greatness than the Reverend Joseph Murgas, the founding pastor of Sacred Heart (Slovak) Church, Wilkes-Barre. Born, educated, and ordained in Europe, Father Murgas came to the Valley as an accomplished painter, a brilliant naturalist, a talented linguist and writer, and a devoted Slovak patriot. Despite the variety of his talents, he made his major contribution in the field of radio communication.

When Gugliemo Marconi developed the process of transmitting sounds without wires, he could send only a single sound, send it only over water, and send it only for short distances. His system of communication had little practical application until Father Murgas—tinkering in his rectory basement—developed a way to send two or more sounds (thus accommodating the Morse code) for distances of 70 miles over land and 700 over water.

Father Murgas' wireless telegraphy system was tested and proved practical on November 23, 1905, when Mayor Fred C. Kirkendall of Wilkes-Barre transmitted a message to Mayor Alexander R. Connell of Scranton. Murgas' tower rose near his church at the top of Bowman Hill. Courtesy, F. Charles Petrillo

Joined by businessmen, Murgas founded a company to test and develop his discovery and patented his inventions in 1903. Despite his many talents, Murgas was no businessman. His company failed after the death of a partner and after a storm destroyed his equipment. Marconi simply appropriated Murgas's techniques without giving him credit or compensation. In 1916, however, the priest had the satisfaction of having the United States District Court recognize him as the inventor of practical wireless communication.

Father Murgas's involvement in the life of the Slovak community, both in Wilkes-Barre and in Europe, consumed most of his talents in his later years. He founded both the Slovak Catholic Federation of America (to promote Slovak interests in America) and the Slovak League (to promote Slovak causes abroad). He took an active part in lobbying and fund raising for the Czecho-Slovak Republic established in 1919. Disappointed in this cause (many Slovaks felt that Czech oppressors replaced Hungarian oppressors), Father Murgas entered into a quiet seclusion, ministering to the needs of his parishioners until his death in 1929. He had lived to see his people so accepted in the Valley that one of his parishioners, John V. Kosek, Jr., was elected first as judge of the Court of

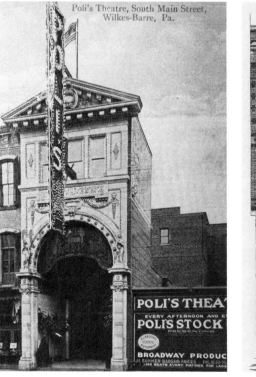

Far left: In the heyday of vaudeville and road shows, Wilkes-Barre had four legitimate theaters as well as silent movie houses. One of the best known, Poli's later became the Penn. It continued to play vaudeville into the 1950s. Local audiences were notoriously tough; show business people were fond of saying that if you could play something in Wilkes-Barre, you could play it anywhere. Courtesy, F. Charles Petrillo

Left: Bruce Price also designed Tuck's Drug Store. He then moved his practice to New York, where he prospered, but he continued to return to Wilkes-Barre to build houses for his relatives. His best known and largest building is the Chateau Frontenac, a hotel in Quebec City. (WHGS)

Common Pleas of Luzerne County and then, in 1911, as mayor of Wilkes-Barre, the first Slovak-American to hold this office.

In the early decades of the 20th century 10,000 Italians came to the Valley to escape the poverty of southern Italy and Sicily. They too established their ethnic churches, especially in the Pittston area and the heights section of Wilkes-Barre. Italian Americans sought release from the drudgery of the mines through self-employment. Almost every Italian family had its own truck farm, forcing the earth to produce good food, first for the family tables, then for sale to their neighbors. Italian men often pushed carts through the towns of the Valley, hawking foods or specialty items not readily available. When one such peddler, Amadeo Obici, discovered the local taste for his specially roasted peanuts, he became the "Peanut Man." Obici gradually expanded his business, eventually buying farmland in the South and bringing the raw peanuts to Wilkes-Barre. Using organizational skills comparable to those of Andrew Carnegie and employing friends and relatives in his store on East Market Street near the Square and in his corporate headquarters on lower South Main Street, he saw his one-man operation, called Planters' Peanuts, become a corporate giant.

Other Italian-Americans sought to establish themselves in a variety of enterprises. Andrew Sordoni built a financial empire in the Valley, based originally on the construction business. Over the years, he and his family developed a conglomerate that included interests in hotels, telephone companies, and banks. Sordoni also became a leading figure in the Republican party.

The diversity of the economic, cultural, and religious life of Wyoming Valley in the first two decades of the 20th century alarmed some who lamented the dilution of old American values and mourned the passing of American customs; and others who felt that commercial competition and religious duplication wasted money and produced confusion. Still others argued that cultural clashes could yield only harm. Clearly, this era of diversity saw much waste and bitterness; but, the perspective of several generations shows that much that was good has remained from this period and that most of its antagonisms have passed. The heirs of the disturbed old Americans and the confused new Americans can glory in the diversity of their region.

The Wyoming Seminary, established by Methodists in 1844 (despite its name and religious affiliation) is a private preparatory school that serves not only the Valley but also students of all faiths from around the country and the world. Into the 1930s, the seminary also offered a two-year business program. This photograph from the 1920s shows the campus on Sprague Avenue in Kingston. (WHGS)

Chapter Eight

WORTH AND GENIUS IN THE VALLEY

World War I, which made the United States the strongest economic unit in the world, touched Wyoming Valley in several important ways. By creating a large market for the products of local mines, mills, and factories, it reintroduced the Valley into world economy. Calling many local men to armed service and interfering with established patterns of immigration, it created a labor shortage that caused wages to rise sharply. By heightening the sense of American nationalism, moreover, it helped diminish ethnic consciousness and thus lessened the rivalries between and among different ethnic groups.

Shortly after the war (1921), the United States passed its first comprehensive law restricting immigration, thus ending the flow of Euro-

Above: *The last of the great mansions built in downtown Wilkes-Barre belonged to Fred J. Weckesser who was an executive of the Woolworth-Kirby five and dime stores. Architect C.H.P. Gilbert's 1916 design imitated French chateau style. After 1916, the area's rich and prosperous tended to live on the West Side, either in nearby Kingston or further into suburbia in the Back Mountain area. (WHGS)*

Left: *Wilkes-Barre's first art deco building is the Anthracite Institute on Old River Road. Designed by L. Verne Lacy in 1928, the building rose only a few years after the Chrysler Building started the art deco craze. Made of dark red brick, the building is heavily ornamented with starkly contrasting forms of glazed ivory terra-cotta. (WHGS)*

The Washington Street School, at the southwest corner of North Washington and Bennett streets, was typical of the small wooden school buildings maintained by the Wilkes-Barre School Board in the mid-19th century. (WHGS)

pean workers who had been coming to the region steadily for 90 years. Had normal economic conditions prevailed, this development would have led to a general improvement in the local economy; but such conditions did not prevail. Reduced markets for coal and changing techniques in manufacturing caused a long, slow decline in the anthracite and textile industries. The Valley entered a recession as early as 1919; and by the mid-1920s, the recession had become a depression suspended briefly during World War II and finally in the 1960s.

This depression affected almost every phase of local life. The county's population, which had risen in every census but one since 1790, virtually leveled off during the 1920s, and then began declining. Unemployment and underemployment became so common that the streets were often filled with idle men, wiling away the time and hoping that prosperity was indeed "just around the corner." Declining profits made the local business community, once a center of innovative practices, quite conservative and unwilling to reinvest reduced profits in new ventures. Local governments generally preferred to cut services rather than raise taxes.

Though the economy was depressed, several phases of local life demonstrated a remarkable vitality, none more important than education. The Valley's people never lost their hope for improvement or the willingness to support those institutions that could provide it. Such support came from two basic sources—the wealth of a few rich men and women who were willing to respond to philanthropic impulses and the tiny contributions of many poor people who strove to escape from their poverty through group efforts. Together these impulses led to significant achievements in popular education.

By the last quarter of the 19th century, Wilkes-Barre began erecting brick schoolhouses. The Conyngham Grades [sic] School (shown here) was probably the best architecturally. The school was designed by Willis Gaylord Hale, who practiced briefly in Wilkes-Barre before moving on to Philadelphia where he built mansions for the newly rich. In the densely populated city of the day, there was a school within walking distance of every child's home. (WHGS)

Education has played a vital part in American history since the co-lonial period. In the Wyoming Valley most people considered education the first fruit of economic democracy and the instrument of expanding that democracy. As noted earlier, the Valley's first high school, the Wilkes-Barre Academy, had been established in the first decade of the 19th century; and a system of free public elementary schools developed by the second decade. The Methodists established Wyoming Seminary in 1844 and Catholics began their separate system in the 1850s.

Unfortunately, the extensive use of child labor in the era of mining interfered with elementary education until the 20th century, when child labor laws and more sophisticated means of separating slate from coal released children from work. When that happened, most families tried to send their children to grammar school; and after World War I an increas-ing number made the sacrifices necessary to allow young people to attend high school, at least for a few years. The public grammar schools located in almost every neighborhood served most of the population without direct costs. Wilkes-Barre's impressive Central High School, built in 1881, became so overcrowded in the early 20th century that the construction of three separate schools became necessary—the James M. Coughlin Memorial (1911), the Grand Army of the Republic Memorial in the

The city was proud of its new Central High School when the building went up in 1881. Standing on the southeast corner of North Washington and East Union streets, the school became so overcrowded within 30 years that the city was obliged to build three new high schools, each several times the size of this. Even so, some Coughlin classes were held in the old building into the 1950s. (WHGS)

Facing page top: *The earliest
public schools in Wilkes-Barre were
one-room wooden structures. This
school, on Cinder Alley, was not
typical. Cinder Alley ran along the
railroad yards in the poorest part of
town. With the American genius for
euphemism, the alley was renamed
Cinderella Street, a change that did
nothing to improve the welfare of its
residents. The school, the rail yards,
and the street itself have
disappeared. (WHGS)*

Left: *As late as the 1940s, one-room
schools could still be found in rural
areas of the Valley. This one was
located in Harveyville. The
wrought-iron and hardwood desks —
often scarred by years of schoolboy
whittling — were also used in the
larger brick schools. (WHGS)*

JAMES M. COUGHLIN HIGH SCHOOL. WILKES-BARRE.

heights section (1925), and the Elmer L. Meyers Memorial in south Wilkes-Barre (1928). Almost all the towns of the Valley had high schools, offering secondary education to most young people and a college preparation to the ever-increasing number who might pursue it.

The first indication that the Wyoming Valley might become a center of post-secondary education occurred in 1916 when Pennsylvania State College agreed to sponsor courses in mining engineering in the region. This Penn State extension began on a small scale with practicing engineers teaching their art to interested students at night, first in the old YMCA, then at the new Coughlin High School, and after 1950, in the Guthrie School on North Washington Street. For many of these years students received certificates of accomplishment rather than college credits. The curriculum was gradually expanded to include courses in aeronautical, civil, electrical, mechanical, and textile engineering, reflecting the diversity of the local economy and the importance of education as a key to economic progress.

By World War II, the Penn State system played a vital role in the nation's war effort and the local extension became one of the most important centers of war-related training schools. In 1946 Penn State at Wilkes-Barre opened a day school to augment the night program and moved toward becoming a junior college, specializing in various engineering arts and sciences.

The public schools depended upon effective teachers to serve the needs of the young. The Valley produced so many teachers that the

Like the other two high schools built in Wilkes-Barre over the next two decades, the James M. Coughlin High School of 1911 shows the predilection for neoclassical public buildings then in vogue. The building's cafeteria and athletic facilities were replaced when a large annex was added to the building in the 1950s. Shortly after that, the old Central High was razed. Courtesy, F. Charles Petrillo

St. Leo's School, with the church and rectory nearby, was typical of the alternative grade schools established by the Roman Catholic community to provide religious instruction concurrently with secular teaching. Courtesy, F. Charles Petrillo

surplus allowed members of the school boards to extend the patronage system to the hiring of teachers and, it was claimed, to force those hired to contribute to the treasury of the party in power. A Wilkes-Barre Township teacher, Miss Barbara McGlynn, president of the State Teachers League, joined with the classroom teachers of the Pennsylvania State Education Association and with members of the American Federation of Teachers (chiefly from Philadelphia) to fight these abuses. They lobbied in vain for a strong tenure act until 1935, when a new state senator from Wilkes-Barre, Dr. Leo Mundy, introduced—and the legislature passed— the nation's strictest tenure act. Largely as the result of Miss McGlynn's work, Pennsylvanians could, in the future, be assured that their schools were free from inappropriate political influence.

Though the Catholic community did not have many communicants wealthy enough to make large donations for a private school system, many Catholics considered it so important to maintain parochial schools that they willingly shared their limited resources to support such a system. These schools operated at amazingly low costs, through the use of simple facilities and through the sacrifices of remarkably generous women who proclaimed and practiced poverty as a virtue. Small groups of nuns of several orders ran parish grammar schools to preserve religion and culture while preparing young Catholics to succeed in the secular society. Eventually they established eight high schools (St. Ann's, St. Mary's, St. Nicholas, and Marymount (all in Wilkes-Barre), St. Leo's (Ashley), St. John's (Pittston), Sacred Heart (Plains), and St. Vincent's

When the Sisters of Mercy opened College Misericordia in 1924, the new institution consisted of only the central part of the building shown here. By 1932 the two wings had already been added. Courtesy, College Misericordia

(Plymouth). Graduates of these schools came to appreciate the value of their education which allowed them to break the circle of poverty and to enter the white-collar world.

A small group of courageous Sisters of Mercy, encouraged by Bishop Michael J. Hoban, began to pursue what in 1924 seemed a difficult mission. They decided to build College Misericordia, a four-year institution of higher learning, "to help educate young women of high academic standing whose financial resources are limited." The work began in Dallas; and by 1927 Misericordia was able to grant the first four bachelor's degrees in Luzerne County history. On the occasion of the graduation, held in Irem Temple, the whole community had reason to join in the celebration.

The early Misericordia faculty included women with national reputations as scholars and teachers, artists and scientists. They established a variety of departments and personally assured that a College Misericordia education would provide a firm basis for a professional career. In addition to their work in Dallas, they taught evening and Saturday classes in Wilkes-Barre so that working women could achieve the degree that would allow them to advance in their professions as teachers, nurses, home economists, and office managers. College Misericordia, now vastly expanded and serving both men and women, remains a tribute to the heroic women who founded it.

Less than 10 years after Misericordia's beginning, the principals of several local high schools sought to provide their male graduates with a chance of continuing their education locally. The group convinced Bucknell University of Lewisburg, Pennsylvania, to establish a two-year extension, conducted in rented facilities in Wilkes-Barre. Begun in 1933, in the worst days of the depression, Bucknell Junior College endured four trying years. Unable to attract many students or collect sufficient tuitions to meet the costs of operation, this institution almost collapsed. A community drive in 1937 and the generosity of Mrs. John N. Conyngham and Mrs. Harold Stark saved it. The women donated two large and beautiful buildings on South River Street (Kirby and Conyngham Halls) where the college held all its classes. At the same time Bucknell hired a professional administrator, Dr. Eugene S. Farley, to take over as the director of the enterprize. Almost single-handedly, Farley kept Bucknell Junior College alive through the next 10 years.

Facing page bottom: *Frederick Clark Withers, a New York architect best known for the Jefferson Market Courthouse he codesigned with Calvert Vaux, built this sumptuous residence for S.L. Thurlow in 1872. Later it became for many years the home of Fred Kirby, whose son gave it to Bucknell Junior College in 1941. Today, without its porch roofs and missing most of its ornamental ironwork (but otherwise in superbly restored condition), the house is Kirby Hall of Wilkes College. (WHGS)*

In the meantime, the nation had entered and triumphed in World War II. As part of a national act of gratitude to those who served in that conflict, the government of the United States offered to pay the costs of higher education for all veterans. The educational provisions of the GI Bill revolutionized education in the Valley, as it did in the rest of America. Heretofore, a collegiate experience was a normal expectation only for a member of the academic, economic, or athletic elite. The GI Bill brought the possibility of college to talented members of the working class. Young adults in this region responded with enthusiasm.

Their enthusiasm was shared by the fourth bishop of Scranton, William J. Hafey, who began a charity drive shortly after World War II. Through it, he secured sufficient funds to purchase the building of the Wilkes-Barre Business College on Northampton Street. At the same time, a group of seven members of the Holy Cross Fathers, who operate Notre Dame University, agreed to come here to establish the county's second four-year college. They opened the College of Christ the King to 306 men, the vast majority veterans, in September 1946.

From that beginning a remarkable institution has developed which in many ways demonstrates the Valley's ability to transcend its social and economic problems. As a Catholic college, King's reflected the religious commitment of the vast majority of the local people—yet, it was never restricted to members of that faith. From the beginning the faculty and staff included lay people from many religious backgrounds who have shared equally in the direction of the college. Ethnic and religious prejudices, so long a barrier to genuine cooperation in the community, found no home at King's. The college became coeducational in 1970, thus removing its only obstacle to the admission of all qualified applicants. Though 90 percent of the first 10 years' graduates had to leave Wyoming Valley to find employment appropriate to their education, more recent alumni have been able to remain within the community and now serve in every profession and occupation.

Left and bottom left: *The Little Theatre of Wilkes-Barre is one of the oldest amateur theatre groups in the country. For years, performances were held in the Irem Temple; with the decline of neighborhood movie houses, the group acquired the Sterling Theatre on North Main Street from the Comerford chain. The group mounts four productions every season. These photographs show a production of* Fashion *from the late 1940s or early 1950s. (WHGS)*

Facing page top: *In 1863, Frederick Clark Withers built a mansion for Andrew Todd McClintock, one of Wilkes-Barre's leading attorneys. For a century, generations of McClintocks—all members of the bar—resided there, the last being Gilbert S. McClintock, first president of the board of trustees of Wilkes College. Ralph Dewitt photographed Gilbert McClintock's study in 1943. A bachelor, the last McClintock left no heirs; he bequeathed his house to the college he had helped to found. (WHGS)*

Facing page bottom: *The residence of Judge Stanley Woodward was another of the great Wilkes-Barre houses to become part of Wilkes College. The house was designed in 1867 by Isaac G. Perry, who abandoned his favorite French Empire style in favor of Italianate Lombardic. The house stood on South River Street next to the John N. Conyngham mansion with a great copper beech between. The tree was damaged by the fire that destroyed the Conyngham house, but it survives. (WHGS)*

While King's was getting started, Dr. Eugene S. Farley of Bucknell Junior College, encouraged by a number of public-spirited citizens and especially by attorney Gilbert McClintock and Admiral Harold Stark, investigated the feasibility of establishing a third four-year college. By 1947 Wilkes College (named more for the city than for the 18th-century politician) received its charter and began to welcome both men and women to its campus on South River Street. For almost 25 more years Farley carefully guided the institution, watching it acquire more and more of the most beautiful homes of "old Wilkes-Barre." In the area south of Market Street, Wilkes expanded almost annually so that it could accommodate the academic and housing needs of an increased student body. Originally an undergraduate school offering liberal arts and science majors as well as preprofessional programs, Wilkes added a graduate division in 1959, thus allowing local students to attain a master's degree near home. Wilkes conferred the first advanced degrees in 1965.

King's and Wilkes, located within a mile of one another, and founded within a year of one another, established a rivalry that has been,

Early Wilkes-King's games—with the rival colleges on adjacent blocks—tended to encourage the release of more youthful high spirits than the town could handle. Some of those spirits came out of a keg of Mr. Stegmaier's excellent product. Athletic contests between the two colleges were suspended for some years; when they resumed, violence no longer posed a problem. Courtesy, King's College Archives, D. Leonard Corgan Library

for the most part, a friendly one. For a time in the early 1950s, however, the rivalry became so intense that some city and college officials became worried and suspended athletic contests between the schools. After the depression decades the antagonisms waned and athletic contests began anew in 1978, after a 16-year pause. Both schools have served the same kind of student, and both schools have produced a host of graduates in which the community as a whole can take pride. The energy, talent, and money that went into Misericordia, King's, and Wilkes Colleges have brought rich rewards.

Thomas Jefferson once observed that "worth and genius would have to be sought out from every condition in life, and completely prepared by education . . . for the public trust." Nowhere in the nation is Jefferson's observation more clearly demonstrated than in the Wyoming Valley. Through their educational systems, the people of the Valley allowed the worth and genius of more than 20 nations to flourish. That the entire community benefited from this would be seen in the political as well as the economic, social, and cultural life of the Valley.

King's College students routinely took over West Northampton Street for a parade against their traditional rival, Wilkes College. If these Kingsmen look a bit tougher and more seasoned than the average undergraduate, it must be remembered that many of them entered college as veterans of World War II. Courtesy, King's College Archives, D. Leonard Corgan Library

In 1928, the Valley forgot its financial troubles for a while and celebrated the sesquicentennial of the Battle of Wyoming. Most of the buildings in this photo have survived. A 12-story annex was added to the Hotel Sterling just east of the original building in the 1930s. The Dime Deposit Bank building, although still standing, has been substantially changed by remodeling.

Chapter Nine

POLITICS AND 40 YEARS OF DEPRESSION

Architect Charles M. Burns of Philadelphia specialized in Episcopal churches. Many of them were exact copies of English churches. (He once built a transept five degrees out of true because his model had been built that way to accommodate an old tomb.) He built St. Clement's Church on Hanover Street in 1869 and returned to Wilkes-Barre 20 years later to rebuild St. Stephen's, a project that took him the better part of a decade. Courtesy, F. Charles Petrillo

Above left: *By the end of World War I, veterans of the Grand Army of the Republic of the Civil War— once a powerful political and economic force—were diminishing in number and power. Their meeting hall — the Conyngham Post, named for an eminent local officer— eventually became a movie theater and later the site for a parking garage. The life-sized bronze soldiers flanking the entrance are now on sentry duty outside the armory of the 109th Field Artillery in Kingston. Courtesy, F. Charles Petrillo*

The political life of Wyoming Valley has received only passing mention. Until the end of World War I, the politics of the Valley were the politics of the nation.

The Republican Party—led by the conservative titans of local industry and business, and supported by the majority of English, Scotch, Welsh, Italian, and Slovak voters, as well as most German Protestants and Jews—dominated local politics from the Civil War until 1958. The Democrats, usually more conservative than the Republicans before World War I, were supported by the minority of those of British origin, by the vast majority of Irish, Polish, German, and Lithuanian Catholics, and by Russian Jews. This coalition insured the Democrat's control of some towns, and occasionally resulted in the election of a Democrat to city or county office; but for the most part, Luzerne County and the Wyoming Valley adhered strongly to the policies and the candidates of the Grand Old Party.

The economic depression that began locally in 1919, however, changed local politics. The citizenry found itself falling behind the rest of the nation economically and consequently developed different expectations of government than most Americans. At the very time that the national Republican Party, once the bastion of progressivism, was becoming increasingly conservative under the leadership of Warren Harding and Calvin Coolidge, the local party, led by those who had risen

Despite general depression in the Valley (or perhaps because of it), the grand, granite Market Street Bridge went up in the late 1920s. By January 1928, part of the new bridge was open to traffic while the skeleton of the old awaited removal. From right to left beyond the bridge can be seen the car barn of the Wilkes-Barre Traction Company, the 109th Field Artillery Armory, and Artillery Park, home of the Wilkes-Barre Barons baseball team. (WHGS)

from the working classes, was becoming more progressive. A former breaker boy from Plymouth, Arthur H. James, came through the party ranks to become lieutenant governor in 1919. He sought to make the local Republican Party an instrument of progress in the community. An ardent admirer of Theodore Roosevelt and of Gifford Pinchot, the leading progressive Republican in Pennsylvania, James consistently fought the old guard of his party. A superb organizer and an effective administrator, James was elected Governor in 1938, the high point of a long political career. After his term ended in 1943, he returned to Plymouth where he remained a voice for progress in the region, the state, and the nation for many years.

The local Republican Party found another unusual leader in John S. Fine of Nanticoke. In 1922, at the age of 30, Fine became chairman of the county Republican Party and began to build a political organization that could, most properly, be called a machine. For almost 35 years the Fine organization delivered the votes to the party on election day and "delivered the goods" to the party faithful during the year. Fine held positions on the court of common pleas and the state superior court, before being elected Pennsylvania's 100th governor in 1950. During his administration, the state extended the Pennsylvania Turnpike to the Wyoming and Lackawanna valleys, thus enhancing the region's economic resources enormously. Fine will long be remembered for his crucial role in the Republican National Convention of 1952, when he helped keep the nomination from the conservative Senator Robert A. Taft and, eventually, helped deliver it to General Dwight D. Eisenhower. It was as a political organizer, however, that Fine made his most important contributions. His organization, which could serve as a model of political efficiency for any student of practical politics, was open to men of talent, without regard to their ethnic or religious backgrounds. Through it the sons of immigrants from southern and eastern Europe, such as Judges Frank Pinola and John Aponik, were able to learn the art of politics and serve the whole community.

During the Great Depression, those who worked seemed to work all the harder. Throughout the twenties and thirties, South Main Street by night was as busy as—if not busier than—it was by day. A department store clerk working as many as 60 hours a week for a flat salary of $10 would have gotten no overtime pay, no medical insurance, and paid holidays only on Christmas, New Year's, and Independence days. Courtesy, F. Charles Petrillo

In the depression decades, the Democratic Party underwent significant changes as well. Except in a few towns, local Democrats could win elections only by promoting the candidacies of unusual men—like Dan Hart, one of the most colorful characters in the history of the Valley. Born in Wilkes-Barre in 1866, the son of Irish immigrants, Hart enjoyed a notable career as a playwright and a well-deserved reputation as a story teller and humorist. His most famous plays—"The Parish Priest" and

Women were accorded the right to vote in 1920, and with that right came the privilege of serving on juries. Luzerne County impaneled its first mixed jury in 1921. (WHGS)

"The Rocky Road to Dublin"—were produced frequently on Broadway during the first three decades of this century. They revealed the warmth and depth that made him an admirable politician.

Hart was elected treasurer of Wilkes-Barre in 1906; and for 10 years he served as a watchdog over Republican administrations. In 1919 he won the first of four terms as mayor of his native city, the only man to serve so long in that office. He was such an able administrator, so honest a politician, and so vibrant a personality that the Republican Party came to the conclusion that he was unbeatable. They joined the Democrats in nominating him for his final term in 1931. At his death in 1933, the city mourned one of its most engaging characters.

While Hart was serving as mayor of Wilkes-Barre, local voters were playing a leading part in the political movement that would transform the political majority in this country from Republican to Democratic. This movement, the Al Smith-Franklin Roosevelt revolution, began with the election of 1928.

At the time of that election, the Valley was clearly and deeply depressed economically, while most of the country falsely believed that prosperity was permanent. The Republican candidate, Secretary of Commerce Herbert Hoover, who had been the engineer of national economic policies during the two previous Republican administrations, maintained in his campaign that the extension of those policies would eliminate poverty in the United States. As the national election results showed, most Americans believed Hoover's rosy predictions.

In the Valley, however, the economy was so far from prosperous that local voters, traditionally Republican, seriously questioned the wisdom of continuing the established economic policies. The Democratic candidate, Governor Alfred E. Smith of New York, had a number of special claims on local voters. As a New Yorker, he was a neighbor; as a progressive, he offered the possibility of needed change; as an opponent of Prohibition, he attracted the county's "wet" majority. But most of all, Al Smith was the child of immigrants, educated "in the school of hard knocks," and a coreligionist of the Valley's Catholic majority. All these factors combined to help local people identify with Smith and to make the election of 1928 the most significant in local history.

In the first place, despite a stable population, the county's electorate had increased by 63 percent over the number of voters in 1924. This factor reflected the increasing interest in the political process as a solution to regional problems, as well as the tremendously increased exercise of the suffrage by local women.

The oldest bus company in Pennsylvania is the White Transit Company, now a division of Frank Martz Coach Company. White continued to provide service between Wilkes-Barre and Plymouth into the 1970s when the Luzerne County Transit Authority took over the route. Courtesy, F. Charles Petrillo

Completed in 1929, the Market Street Bridge is the work of Carrere and Hastings. Designed in a neoclassical style reminiscent of some of the bridges over the Seine in Paris, the bridge provides a grand entry into the downtown area from the west. Here limousines escort the first streetcar across the new bridge. (WHGS)

When Dan Hart died, the population of Wilkes-Barre was about 85,000, exceeding today's figure by some 35,000. Parking was nevertheless still permitted on West Market Street. All these buildings are now gone, but a tall, windowless building at the end of the lane to the right of the Times-Leader Building survives midway between Franklin and River streets. Once the stage house of the Opera House (the rest of which is gone), it still bears a barely legible sign: "Times Leader Annex."

As the population became larger, developers and architects found it necessary to build row houses and apartments. This multiple dwelling at 78 West Northampton Street (site of the original Baptist Church) was designed by Kipp and Podmore in 1887 but not built until 1899. The architects tried to disguise the fact that the building comprised a number of small units. Courtesy, Michael Lewis III

Hoover received 40 percent more votes than had Calvin Coolidge in 1924, but Smith increased the 1924 Democratic tally by almost 400 percent, carrying the county by a total of 6,000 votes—the first time Luzerne County had voted Democratic since before the Civil War. More important than their contribution to a losing national effort, local voters had broken their traditional voting patterns. Many working class people, who had followed the Republican Party for two generations, began to consider themselves Democrats, at least on the national level.

That this was not an isolated phenomenon is demonstrated by the election statistics in subsequent elections. Franklin Roosevelt, Smith's successor as governor of New York and as the leader of the new Democratic coalition, received large majorities in the county in each of his four races for the presidency. The rest of the nation would catch up with the Valley in 1932, but in the anthracite region, as Samuel Lubell pointed out in *The Future of American Politics*, the Al Smith Revolution preceded the Roosevelt Revolution.

By the time Franklin Roosevelt's presidency began in 1933, the local economic situation was truly desperate. Local political leaders of both parties looked to Washington to provide relief, recovery, and reform. In

Developer, builder, contractor, entrepreneur, and architect W.W. Neuer made a substantial fortune from the building trades. His row houses, like these at the corner of West Union and North Franklin streets, lack the elegance of Kipp and Podmore's work. (WHGS)

his New Deal, Roosevelt responded with a wide variety of programs that alleviated the Depression without ending it. The National Recovery Administration (NRA) helped local businesses, at least for a time, and inspired great public enthusiasm. The Banking Act of 1933 with the Federal Deposit Insurance Corporation (FDIC) saved some local banks but came too late for others. The Public Works Administration (PWA) completed the new Wilkes-Barre Post Office (now the federal courthouse) within six months of FDR's inauguration. Of all the New Deal agencies, however, the Works Progress Administration (WPA), and its predecessors (Civil Works Administration and Federal Emergency Relief Agency) provided the most important help. Local governments and civic associations could use federally paid laborers on approved projects, such as the Forty Fort town hall and the airport, and street lighting and paving programs throughout the area. To avoid the creation of a huge bureaucracy to administer relief, WPA allowed local political units to hire workers directly. Because most local governments were controlled by Republicans, the majority of WPA workers in this region owed their jobs directly to Republican politicians, most notably John Fine. Thus, the GOP was able to maintain much of its local strength throughout the New Deal era.

Franklin Roosevelt's personal interest in the Wyoming Valley was clearly demonstrated by his two visits in 1936. On the first occasion, he inspected the damage done by a dreadful spring flood. This visit led the Army Corps of Engineers to build an extensive earthen levee system, on both sides of the Susquehanna. It was hoped that this would completely eliminate the danger posed by annual flooding. The levee system employed hundreds of workers, altered permanently the landscape of the River Common, provided the population with some ease of mind, and protected lives and property from flood damage for a generation.

From 1865 to 1936, the Susquehanna crested at over 30 feet four times: 1865, 1902, 1904, and 1936, doing considerable damage each time, as can be seen in this photo of the 1902 flood taken from the west end of the Market Street Bridge. (For this reason, the one-mile stretch from the river to Kingston Corners, which should have been a prime candidate for commercial development, remained largely farmland.) Dikes built after the 1936 flood were expected to end this problem forever. (WHGS)

South Franklin Street, photographed by O.C. Hilliard in 1896 just after a snowfall, looks both quiet and peaceful even though it is only a few blocks from the heart of the city. Many of the buildings have survived, but the trees are gone. Chestnuts and elms succumbed to disease, and the air pollution of the 20th century killed off the rest. Recent plantings of hardy oak will some day replace the lost trees. (WHGS)

The anthracite industry was in decline when the ice-filled and swollen Susquehanna broke into the Knox mine on the morning of January 22, 1959, and billions of gallons of water poured into the honeycomb of mines below, killing 12 men. The speed and force of the water formed a gigantic whirlpool. (WHGS)

When Roosevelt returned to the Valley in the fall of 1936, he came as a political candidate seeking the votes of the increasingly important blue collar workers. He was received with adulation by 300,000 citizens who lined his long parade route and cheered him constantly as he traveled up the Valley from Nanticoke to Pittston. Like Theodore Roosevelt before him, this president demonstrated that an active, caring government could help ordinary people improve their condition.

The local economic condition was restored, temporarily, by World War II. As in every previous American military activity, local men and women responded fully to the nation's needs, serving in every branch of the armed forces, in every theater of operation, and in every rank—from Admiral Harold Stark, chief of naval operations at the time of Pearl Harbor, to officers and enlisted personnel of the Army, Navy, Marines, and Air Corps.

More than this, the mines, heavy industries, and mills of the Valley operated full-time and overtime during the war, staffed not only by men excused from military service because of their essential skills but also by a vast number of women who became vital to the war industries. During the war, wages rose so that almost everyone except the soldiers prospered. Because of the many shortages caused by the war, however, much of this wealth was stored, often in the form of war bonds. This wealth provided a buffer during the hard times to come.

Ironically, the war helped promote social peace at home. Long-standing ethnic and religious rivalries paled in the face of the monstrousness of Nazism. When the community celebrated Victory in Europe in May 1945 and Victory in Japan in August of the same year, it celebrated as a united people.

With the war's end, however, the local population, unlike the rest of the nation, had to face a dismal economic future. The use of anthracite as the major home heating fuel of urban America decreased in each of the postwar years. Oil and natural gas became more attractive to consumers as intracontinental pipelines, completed in the first years after the war, brought those fuels cheaply to the industrial Northeast. More convenient

than coal, these alternative sources of energy brought about the collapse of the anthracite industry. Outside investors withdrew their capital, and one after another the collieries shut down.

The hard coal industry employed 140,000 men in northeastern Pennsylvania in 1902, and only 5,000 in 1959. In that year, the Susquehanna River broke through the roof of a mine operated by the Knox Coal Company in Port Griffith, just south of Pittston. Collusion between company and union officials had led to unsafe operation of that mine, leading in this case to the deaths of 12 men, the flooding of the honeycombed mines throughout the Valley, and the permanent cessation of deep mining in the northern anthracite field. That disaster insured a future for the Valley that would be substantially different from its past. For better or worse, men would no longer descend into pits under Wyoming Valley.

Despite the great need for imaginative leadership, few local politicians had ideas to change the Valley; but business and labor leaders did offer new approaches to the conduct of the local economy. This is best demonstrated by the garment industries, which began to play an important part in the community in the middle 1930s when shirt and dress manufacturers began operating in the Valley. Attracted by the significant numbers of talented women who could work in the needle trades, almost 200 garment factories opened from Pittston to Nanticoke between 1937 and 1962, employing more than 10,000 workers, nearly all of them women. In the early days, these workers experienced sweatshop condi-

In an effort to clog the hole in the river's bed, officials dumped anything at hand into the breach. With the anthracite industry so depressed, there was a surplus of 60-ton gondolas. Hundreds of gondolas were rolled off a spur built over the maelstrom and disappeared. The minefields beneath the entire Valley were flooded. Enough coal remains to meet demands for several centuries, but it lies beyond the reach of existing technology. (WHGS)

Walter Humanik's woodcut "Memorial to the Twelve" commemorates the 12 miners who disappeared in the Knox disaster—the last of many hundreds to perish in the Valley's mines. In another sense, Humanik's work can be seen as a requiem for the entire industry, which from the beginning had been a fickle mistress to the Valley's prosperity. Courtesy, D. Leonard Corgan Library, King's College; Edward Welles, Jr., Collection

tions, working long hours for meager wages. The National Labor Relations (Wagner) Act of 1935 recognized collective bargaining as a right of workers and helped organizers from the International Ladies' Garment Workers Union (ILGWU) to begin their union here in 1937. The ILGWU engaged in some bitter strikes in the 1930s, but it won contracts that provided better wages for workers.

Shortly after the war, Min L. Matheson took over the leadership of the local garment unions. A tough negotiator, Min Matheson inspired a great deal of anger among her opponents with her very broad concept of the rights of workers. She would be satisfied with nothing less for them than to have the opportunity to live full, decent lives, and to share the benefits of their work with the whole community. Frequently using the strike as a weapon to gain her goals, Min Matheson brought an enlightened unionism to the region.

She achieved a seven-hour day for garment workers so that they could also tend to their responsibilities as wives and mothers. She established the ILGWU Health Center on South Washington Street, where a staff headed by Dr. Albert R. Feinberg provided excellent medical care. The health center provided all garment workers with annual physical examinations and dealt with many of their chronic medical problems, thus demonstrating a new concept in practical unionism. Workers also received paid holidays and vacations, and the ILGWU helped make these more worthwhile by sponsoring day trips, opening a vacation spot (Unity House in the Poconos), and by promoting educational and recreational activities.

Min Matheson did not rest when she won benefits for workers. She was absolutely indefatigable in her support of community projects. After she exerted pressure on workers to contribute their fair shares to the Community Chest (United Fund, United Way), labor became a vital part in fund raising for local charities.

Politically, Min Matheson's strong advocacy of the Democratic Party and her union's contribution of funds and workers to political campaigns

The textile industry needed cheap labor, and the Valley remained a textile center throughout the depressed decades. The Wilkes-Barre Lace Manufacturing Company on Courtright Avenue continued to prosper. Father Murgas' wireless telegraphy transmission tower appears in the distance to the left. Courtesy, F. Charles Petrillo

accounted, in large measure, for the eventual success of her party in achieving dominance in the cities of Wilkes-Barre, Pittston, and Nanticoke, in most of the towns, and by 1958, in the county as a whole.

The working women of the Valley, indeed, prevented a complete economic disaster in the postwar years. Many men, however, were forced to go out of the Valley for work—so many that the population began to decline sharply. Thousands took what they hoped would be temporary jobs in the Philadelphia, Binghamton, or New York areas, returning each Friday to be weekend fathers to their families. Other thousands stayed at home, serving as househusbands, tending homes and gardens throughout the region. The Valley was in need of an economic boost to relieve the increasingly depressed job market.

In 1955 William O. Sword, a major force in the chamber of commerce, headed a committee of business, education, labor, and church leaders who sought to revitalize the economy. Calling themselves the Committee of One Hundred, they received support from Pennsylvania's Industrial Development Fund (established in the administration of Governor George Leader), and collected additional funds from regional donors. With this money, the Committee bought land for an industrial park at Mountaintop, secured tax breaks for new firms, and invited national corporations to take advantage of the available labor force and

President Truman campaigned in Wilkes-Barre on behalf of Adlai Stevenson in 1952, but the Valley (like the nation) went Republican for one of the few times in recent history. Even Congressman Flood (seated to the right of the President) lost his seat in the Eisenhower landslide. For Flood, it was the last such defeat. He easily gained reelection in 1954; thereafter the GOP mustered only token opposition. Flood's wife, Catharine, is seated to the left in a fur jacket.

the many cultural and educational institutions of the community. This committee and its successors accomplished great things, bringing thousands of jobs to the area. Although they were never able to supply all the work the local population could perform, they were nevertheless able to diversify the industrial base of the area and to provide an example of effective action for the future.

As in 1902 and 1933, local efforts and resources were simply insufficient to meet local needs. The only possibility for recovery would have to come through Washington, where the Valley had an effective voice in its congressman, Daniel J. Flood of Wilkes-Barre. First elected to the House of Representatives in 1944, Flood won reelection every two years until 1978, except for narrow losses in the Republican landslides of 1946 and 1952. A flamboyant character who made a national impression with his waxed handlebar moustache and flashy clothes, Flood became a national congressman early in his career. He established a secure power base in the House appropriations committee and won his colleagues' respect for his considerable intellectual and political acumen. With each reelection, the seniority system increased his power, enabling him to secure important federal installations in the district, including the huge Veterans' Hospital outside Wilkes-Barre and the Veterans' Administration regional office in central city. During the 1950s the Congress of the United States twice passed the bill Flood co-sponsored with Senator Paul Douglas of Illinois to revitalize America's most distressed areas; and twice President Eisenhower vetoed the Flood-Douglas bill.

If the Valley had any hope of emerging from the doldrums, that hope would require a major national commitment and a change in the White House. With 14 percent unemployment in 1960, with a 40-year experience of depression, with their talented and well-educated young adults forced to leave the region, the population of the Wyoming Valley renewed their interest in the art of politics.

Above: *As a young man, the Honorable Daniel J. Flood essayed a career as an actor. He boasts to this day that he has never allowed his membership in Actors' Equity, the theatrical union, to lapse. His detractors claim this is a profession he never gave up, but no one denies that he was one of the ablest and most effective congressmen in the nation and an unflagging representative of his district. This portrait dates from the early years of his career.*

Above left: *The Honorable Dan became known for his sartorial eccentricities. His white suits were famous in the corridors of the Capitol, and on formal occasions he often sported an opera cape. At one charitable affair, he shared a table with the late Rosalind Russell, herself no amateur at flamboyance. The congressman's suit nevertheless carried the day.*

One by one, the strange, brooding breakers disappeared. Here the Woodward Colliery sits abandoned, waiting to be pulled down. Those near population centers were the first to be removed; they were fire hazards, and the land could be put to other uses. The Dorrance Colliery, last survivor in the City of Wilkes-Barre (on Water Street between the prison and a cemetery) was demolished with a bang in 1983.

The Honorable Dan Flood stood in the place of honor at John Kennedy's right hand when the President signed the Area Redevelopment Act of 1961. Courtesy, John F. Kennedy Memorial Collection, D. Leonard Corgan Library, King's College

Chapter Ten
TRANSFIGURATION

On a bright, crisp day in October 1960, Wyoming Valley hosted representatives of the national communications media who accompanied a presidential candidate to the area. Only the most perceptive among the nation's journalists grasped the underlying impact of that October visit. But the people of this depressed area sensed it. A new age of reform was at hand. They were buoyed by the expectation that the day's visitor would be the instrument through which they would transform their society and reinvigorate their economy.

The reporters, anticipating correctly that the day's speeches would not be newsworthy, looked for interesting facets of the region to use as focal points for their stories. They might have noticed the magnificence of the architecture, the vestige of the old wealth that once characterized the community; but the signs of poverty that resulted from more than 100 years of inequity attracted their attention. They might have seen businesses and colleges striving to keep abreast of modern developments, but the dreariness of the slag heaps made more interesting copy. They might have conversed with well-educated and ambitious young people filled with enthusiasm for their futures, but the dismay of older men, cut off from the only livelihood they had ever known, seemed more appropriate for the reporters to relay to the nation.

As John Kennedy of Massachusetts moved through the Valley, following essentially the same route taken by Franklin Roosevelt a generation before, he was greeted with such enthusiasm that he fell

Among the great mansions to survive virtually intact is that of Colonel Ricketts at 66 South River Street, designed in 1878 by Bruce Price. Today the portico is gone, the porch to the right has been cut back, and the iron fence is gone, but the exterior is still in superb condition. The building accommodates 10 apartments.

behind his schedule. The 35,000 citizens who waited for him on Public Square, had to be entertained for almost three hours before he arrived. During that delay, leaders of the region's past, present, and future, under the chairmanship of Wilkes-Barre Mayor Frank Slattery, kept the crowd's attention. Slattery called on one of his most remarkable predecessors, 72-year-old Con McCole, to entertain. McCole, a famous raconteur who had, in his day, delighted audiences across the nation, regaled the hometown group with a seemingly endless line of stories of the coal mining days. Through his homilies, laced with ethnic dialects, McCole proved that genuine humor could be derived from the usually painful Americanizing process. Young people on the square did not understand all the ethnic references, but they joined in the laughter of their elders.

Min Matheson, then at the height of her powers, responded to Slattery's invitation by delivering a fiery speech, urging union members to redouble their efforts in support of their candidate. Mrs. Matheson, who would return to union headquarters in New York within a few years, clearly conveyed the message that the kind of progress her workers really needed could be obtained only with federal assistance. She was speaking of the economic realities and everyone understood her message.

With time to fill, Mayor Slattery looked around the podium for still another speaker. He spotted a 20-year-old King's College senior, already recognized as one of the top debaters in the nation and, without warning, asked him to speak. Thus, Frank G. Harrison got his political baptism, pleasing the assemblage with his impromptu description of the future.

Wherever he went in the Valley on his campaign visit, vigorous young Presidential candidate John F. Kennedy was met with hopeful enthusiasm. Crowds outside the Hotel Sterling held up his motorcade until well after dark. Courtesy, John F. Kennedy Memorial Collection, D. Leonard Corgan Library, King's College

In 1960, the King's College debating team finished second to Harvard in the national tournament, and King's senior Frank G. Harrison earned one of the top awards as a speaker. In this photo, debating coach Robert E. Connelly (center) holds the award, flanked by Peter Smith (King's 1962, left), and Harrison who also headed King's students for Kennedy.

He wanted his and succeeding generations to be able to live their adult lives in the community where they had been raised and educated. For them to do that, however, the Valley would have to be formed anew. The future congressman believed, and the crowd agreed, that Kennedy offered help for that reformation.

Finally, late in the afternoon, the hero of the day arrived. The people responded with ever-increasing enthusiasm as their favorite son, Dan Flood, introduced his friend of many years, Senator Kennedy. Both spoke of their shared hopes for the region and the nation, and both won thunderous ovations. Within two weeks Kennedy was president-elect of the United States; Dan Flood was in a position to bring to fruition his own aspirations for the constituency he had served so long; and the United States was prepared to embark on the third reform period of the 20th century. No place needed reform more than Wyoming Valley, and no people responded to the opportunities it provided with more energy than the people of that Valley.

One of the first legislative accomplishments of the Kennedy era was the passage of Flood's Area Redevelopment Act of 1961. The law required that the federal government give preference to contractors in areas of high unemployment, send funds to sustain and improve public services, provide assistance to local businesses through a series of loans, and encourage national businesses to locate in such regions. In addition to this law, Flood—a leading figure on (and eventually the chairman of) the House appropriations sub-committee for health, education, and labor—arranged that his district be used as a testing ground for the innovative programs advanced by Kennedy and later by Lyndon B. Johnson. Before the Great Society became a national program, ideas like food stamps, urban renewal, and low-cost housing were piloted here.

While much of the money for regional development came through Washington, it was local civic, business, and political leaders who provided the practical application of the new ideas. Luzerne County, under very capable (if usually fractious) leadership, made wide use of the new

opportunities. It opened a county nursing home in 1961 to meet some of the medical needs of the ever-increasing population of elderly in the area. Though it is indeed a large building, Valley Crest could not accommodate all who needed nursing care; but after the passage of the Medicare Act of 1965, private facilities developed throughout the region. Public and private funds allowing the General, Mercy, and Nesbitt hospitals to expand in the 1960s enabled them to serve the acutely ill more effectively. Three smaller hospitals, Pittston, Nanticoke, and Wyoming Valley, did not grow at this time, but later Pittston and Wyoming Valley Hospitals joined the Geisinger Medical Center of Danville in erecting a consolidated hospital (NPW) in 1981. Congressman Flood insured that the Veterans' Administration Hospital also expanded and modernized to keep abreast of advances in medical technology.

The county government also tended to the needs of young adults when it opened the Luzerne County Community College (LCCC) in 1967. Originally located in Wilkes-Barre and offering vocational education not available at the three private colleges, LCCC moved to Nanticoke in 1974 and expanded its offerings as well as its campus, providing many with publicly supported education.

Above: *In 1969, with redevelopment under way and a new spirit of optimism pervading the area, citizens cheerfully celebrated the bicentennial anniversary of the Wyoming Valley's first settlement. (WHGS)*

Left: *The most recent addition to the campus of Luzerne County Community College, which opened its new facilities on top of a hill in Nanticoke in 1974, is the Conference Center, designed by Bohlin Powell Larkin Cywinski. LCCC offers many vocational courses not available through other area colleges, as well as more standard academic fare. Courtesy, Bohlin Powell Larkin Cywinski, Architects, Planners, Engineers; photo by Otto Baitz*

King's College's original location on West Northampton Street was too hemmed in by commercial buildings to permit growth. By the 1950s, the college began acquiring much of the land bounded by North Main, North River, West Union, and West North streets. There a new campus was built, in part with federal assistance. The Scandlon Gymnasium is the largest such facility in the region. Courtesy, King's College Archives, D. Leonard Corgan Library

By 1964 the need for collegiate courses in engineering had expanded so greatly that the Penn State extension in Wilkes-Barre was no longer able to accommodate all the courses and equipment needed to meet the local demand. To respond to this need, the State University gratefully accepted the gift of Hayfield Farms in Chase, the country estate of Mr. and Mrs. John N. Conyngham, as a center for an expanded school. On this large estate in the Black Mountain area, the University opened a facility that allowed an ever-increasing number of engineering students to achieve an associate degree locally and prepared many of them to follow the bachelor's course at the main campus in University Park.

The private colleges—Misericordia, King's, and Wilkes—had responded to the opportunities presented by reform legislation, especially the College Facilities Act of 1963 and the Higher Education Act of 1965. With the help of federal grants and loans, College Misericordia added a dormitory, a student union, and a small music building. The city colleges took even more advantage of Washington's largesse. Wilkes built a new

The country residence of the John Conyngham family was Hayfield Farms in Chase, a rambling fieldstone house famous for its opulence. Its gold-plated toilet seats were equipped with special plumbing to keep them warm. In 1964, the houses became the Wilkes-Barre campus of Penn State, which had opened an extension office in Wilkes-Barre as early as 1916 and eventually offered a two-year program. Courtesy, Penn State/ Wilkes-Barre

dormitory and a dining hall, a substantial library (named for Dr. Farley) and a science building (named for Admiral Stark). It also continued to acquire and renovate the big older homes adjacent to its campus. King's renewed itself by building two large dormitories, a library, the Valley's largest and most complete gymnasium, a student union, and a parkade. With their new plants, the local private colleges reached their highest enrollments in 1972.

Federal and state aid to education revolutionized public and, to a lesser extent, private schooling. In 1966 Pennsylvania required the consolidation of secondary educational facilities, leading to the abandonment of the town high schools and the creation of area high schools. Wilkes-Barre continued to used the solid older buildings as high schools, while establishing large new grammar schools, one named for Congressman Flood. The other districts erected new buildings, causing such great controversy that criticisms of these changes are heard to this day. Catholic schools which also shared federal money, and were also subject to federal regulation. This factor, as well as the decreased availability of nuns to serve on faculties, led to the consolidation of nine small Catholic High Schools into three larger ones.

Housing had been one of the most neglected of local needs, with little new construction occurring in the depression decades. President Johnson and the Congress gave the community the chance to alter this in the 1960s, and the community responded with enthusiasm. Elderly people and those with low incomes found that high-rise and garden apartments were available, often with rent subsidies.

When this photograph was taken in the late 1950s, the redevelopment of Wilkes-Barre had not yet begun. In coming years, two blocks lying along South Main Street from Ross to Dana would be almost totally removed; Hazle Avenue would be rerouted; Pennsylvania Avenue would be extended south along the route of the western railroad tracks; and Wilkes-Barre Boulevard would be created along the path of the eastern tracks.

The new Heights Elementary School had been planned before the flood. After the completion of this school and the David W. Kistler Elementary School, the local school district owned a smaller number of larger, better-equipped schools offering a more comprehensive program. (WHGS)

Because the nation's general prosperity filtered to the local economy, many people were able to find new housing in buildings created by private industries, such as the new high-rise Provincial Towers on South Main Street or the luxurious apartments and private homes in the Green Acres section of Kingston. Both Dallas to the west and Mountaintop to the south, and the areas between them and the central city, grew enormously as more and more people became wealthy enough to settle there.

Business caught the spirit of building and expansion. The Narrows and Gateway shopping centers in Edwardsville and Kingston antedated the age of reform, but served as a portent of the future. In 1972 the Wyoming Valley Mall, an enclosed shopping center with 200 stores and ample parking space, appeared on the East End Boulevard. When this became the focal point of regional commerce, it threatened the older, neglected downtown areas. Businessmen of Nanticoke had already taken the lead in restoring older commercial centers. With Model Cities funds and private capital, they transformed central Nanticoke from a dated to a vibrant commercial site.

All this activity was either completed or in progress on June 23, 1972, the day that the greatest natural disaster in American history hit the Wyoming Valley. While the flood that resulted from tropical storm Agnes was one of the most important events in the history of this region,

The flood rose as high as the sign over the main entrance of the Polish Union Building on North Main Street (built by Joseph E. Fronczak of Buffalo in 1936). The flood destroyed every plate-glass window it touched, and deposited a layer of mud many inches deep—slime when wet and ubiquitous dust when dry—everywhere it went. Undoing its damage and replacing what the flood destroyed took the better part of a decade. (WHGS)

it ultimately became the catalyst, not the cause, of the transfiguration of the Valley.

Since hurricanes do not usually occur in June, meteorologists paid considerable attention to a tropical depression that formed in the Atlantic in June 1972. When it grew to a tropical storm and then a hurricane, the weathermen named it "Agnes." It hit the west coast of Florida, causing significant damage there. As it moved northward it lost its hurricane force, but not its ample moisture, bringing heavy rains wherever it passed. Once it reached the headwaters of the Susquehanna basin, however, unusual weather forces caused it to become stationary. Agnes hovered throughout the third week of June, causing almost continuous rain. Depression was the overwhelming response of the people—not alarm. The river contained only four feet of water on Sunday, June 18th, and the levees could easily hold as much as 34 feet.

As the week passed and the rain continued, the underground water table became saturated, forcing the rainwater to run off immediately to the river. The head of the regional civil defense force, General Frank Townend, became concerned as he received reports from his assistant and the official river watcher, Nicholas Souchik. Late in the day Thursday, June 22nd, Townend quietly urged evacuation of patients from hospitals in the flood plain and the removal of vital equipment and records from government installations. On the late night news, residents of low-lying areas unprotected by the levees were urged to evacuate, and a call went out for volunteers to sandbag the levee system.

Men and women of all ages responded in amazing numbers, working throughout the chilly night; but the river rose faster than the reinforced levees. During the night, residents from West Pittston to Plymouth Flats were told to evacuate, some as quickly as possible. Most obeyed, but with a sense of disbelief, as many left without a change of clothes or other necessities. Those who were not working at the river moved to the homes of friends or relatives or to the public facilities quickly established as makeshift refugee centers.

Late Friday morning the order came to abandon the sandbagging effort as the river threatened to top the levee. Thousands of men and women fled from the danger posed by the rampaging Susquehanna. The river broke through the levees at two points: on the west side, near the original Forty Fort and on the east side, near the site of Teedyuscung's camp. Walls of water violently unearthed parts of the Forty Fort ceme-

tery, resting place of Nathan Denison and many others who had settled this region 200 years before. Across the river, the water ripped apart several mansions, symbols of the great commercial and industrial wealth that had been made in the past century. Throughout the rest of the region, the river rose to 40 feet, expanding to a width of six miles. In the recorded history of the Valley, no flood comparable to this had ever occurred; in the recorded history of the nation, no flood had ever destroyed so much property.

The physical damage done by Agnes in this community boggled the imagination. When the water receded in a matter of days, the people returned to find utter destruction. Estimates of the financial damage vary, but the true figure is both unknowable and irrelevant. Two centuries of work, of growth, and of accomplishment seemed wiped out by the rage of nature. This community, so inured to tragedy, had to face its greatest challenge.

The disbelief of the earliest days of the flood changed to determination. Somehow, some way, this people would "come back, better than ever." In 1902, in 1933, and in 1961 local people had solved their own problems with the help of their government. In 1972 they looked again to Washington to help them triumph. To them, Washington meant one man: Dan Flood. Flood was so popular in his district that both parties had nominated him for reelection in 1970—and so powerful in Washington that he could move the Congress and the executive departments of government with a phone call or a personal appeal.

Although he was 68 years old, Dan Flood seemed both inexhaustible

On the east side, the river breached the dike along Riverside Drive not far from the spot where Teedyuscung's log palace had stood two centuries earlier. Here the sheer momentum of the flood created its most spectacular havoc. These two apartment buildings along Charles Street (about 500 feet from the point of the breach) were lifted from their foundations and dropped into their own basements. Elsewhere, sturdy old houses like these survived with little structural damage. Photo by John J. Rygiel, from The Great Flood of 1972 *by Paul W. Warnagiris and John J. Rygiel.*

In the late 1960s, actor Sean Connery starred in a film about the Mollie Maguires, filmed on location in Northeastern Pennsylvania. Since his role called for a moustache, he and Congressman Flood got together to compare facial growths. The man in the middle (a Ukranian-American from the southern coal fields around Hazleton, actor Jack Palance) appears to have wanted to get in on the action.

and ubiquitous. He exercised his power with abandon, cutting red tape, calling on old friends in both parties for help. After a period of initial confusion and bureaucratic delay, the government responded. The Department of Defense sent helicopters to move people and equipment; the National Guard came to protect lives and property; the Department of Housing and Urban Development provided emergency housing (campers and trailers); the Department of Agriculture made food stamps available; and the Department of Labor authorized Emergency Unemployment Compensation benefits. Flood's most significant accomplishment was winning speedy congressional and presidential approval for his bill to provide all victims with Small Business Administration loans to replace whatever had been destroyed or damaged. With interest set at the amazingly low figure of one percent, each loan carried a $5,000 forgiveness feature, especially important to those of limited resources. Those with mortgages could refinance their homes and businesses, extending their payments and saving local lending institutions from almost certain disaster.

By the early spring of 1976 most of the superficial traces of the flood were gone, but much reconstruction remained to be done. In downtown Wilkes-Barre, the canopy and the Bicentennial Building were nearing completion, but Public Square, though green and well tended, was its drab old self.

The unusual apartment building at Ten East South Street designed by Peter Bohlin was being planned when Agnes struck. Federally assisted financing made its completion possible.

President Nixon, caught up in other problems at the time of the flood, did manage a quick visit to the area to present a check to Wilkes College officials. He was guided by his personal representative to the local community, former resident Frank Carlucci. Charged by the president to facilitate all relief programs, Carlucci won the friendship and respect of the people of Wyoming Valley.

The Commonwealth of Pennsylvania helped with grants and tax rebates and provided "mini-repairs" to make houses livable as soon as possible. County, city, and town governments coordinated and augmented the restoration efforts. Private institutions lent their resources to recovery, none more generously or effectively than College Misericordia, which was transformed into a hospital, administrative center, and refuge for the homeless. The Red Cross became the private agency best able to funnel donations from across the nation; and religious groups—Mennonites, the Salvation Army, Lutherans, in fact, every Christian and Jewish organization—practiced what they proclaimed. New community and neighborhood associations began, such as the Flood Victims' Action Committee led by Min Matheson, recently returned to the Valley for what she expected would be a quiet retirement. Families and individuals made the greatest efforts, sharing tasks in a cooperative way. By Labor Day 1972, block parties marked the completion of the clean-up stage of recovery.

What had been accomplished by that point seemed tremendous, but it was only superficial. The Valley had to be rebuilt from below the ground. Extensive, expensive reconstruction of streets, replacement of all utility lines, and installation of new systems of lighting, not only in the flood plain but in the higher ground as well, took years to complete. But when all these projects were done, there was a transfiguration of the community. After 1974, revenue sharing funds allowed local governments to extend their services, without imposing greatly increased taxes on property owners.

Downtown Wilkes-Barre and the major shopping district of Kingston were overhauled in the next decade. The perimeter of Public Square was cleared of its delightful Victorian structures, replaced by new shops and office buildings, a new hotel, and a reconstructed park. A steel and plexiglass canopy surrounded about half the square and most of the first

This town clock was installed atop a tower over the canopy during the summer of 1976. To add variety to the new Wilkes-Barre, each face of the clock frequently gives a different time—all four of them generally wrong. Far more reliable are the old Westminster chimes of St. Stephen's—which are always two minutes late. Courtesy, Bohlin Powell Larkin Cywinski, Architects, Planners, Engineers

This 700-pound bell was cast in Philadelphia not long after 1800 to hang in the steeple of Old Ship Zion Church, where it tolled the passing hours and lives for nearly half a century. When the old church was pulled down just before 1850, the bell was sold to a church in Pittston. Later it became one of the heaviest items in the collection of the Wyoming Historical and Geological Society. In 1977, it was placed on a pedestal at the spot where once it hung. Courtesy, Bohlin Powell Larkin Cywinski, Architects, Planners, Engineers; photo by Lynnwood Studios

Left: *By the summer of 1977, the new park had appeared. Within four acres, architect Peter Bohlin found room for two fountains, three sizable pieces of sculpture, a miniature amphitheater backed by a high, metal scaffold, public rest rooms, game tables, and a multitude of surprises. Courtesy, Bohlin Powell Larkin Cywinski, Architects, Planners, Engineers*

Facing page top: *The fountain at the center of the Public Square adds to the carnival atmosphere on Farmers' Market days. Since the fountain is level with the ground, children can get happily soaked without danger. In midwinter the fountain's base is a handy site for the city's Christmas tree. Courtesy, Wilkes-Barre Chamber of Commerce*

Facing page bottom: *To accommodate the annual Fine Arts Fiesta, as well as other entertainments of all kinds, the new Public Square has a miniature amphitheatre with a soaring backdrop of tubular steel and colored cloth. The granite blockhouse at the extreme left contains the controls for the fountain and electrical sources for the city's bandshell. Photo by Joseph Molitor*

block of South Main Street, protecting shoppers from the elements and supplying critics with something to complain about. While not everyone approved of the new construction, the alternative—doing nothing—was never seriously considered.

Not all these significant changes came about through government planning. Some individuals—like the dynamic, innovative merchant, Al Boscov—brought renewed life to the downtown. He came to the region in 1980, bought The Boston Store, jammed it with merchandise, advertised his wares heavily, and goaded his fellow merchants into actions that attracted increasing numbers of shoppers. At the same time and in a similar way Marvin Roth combined a hobby with creative marketing techniques, when he purchased the derelict Jersey Central Railroad Station, renovated it extensively, filled it with Victoriana, and made "The Station" a fascinating restaurant, night spot, and hotel.

The decade that followed the flood, however, has not been without serious losses. Some of the oldest commercial institutions, Kresge's and Lazurus Department stores, and Percy Brown's market and cafeteria, landmarks in the community through most of this century, went out of business, leaving gaps in the central city and in the regional economy. All of the downtown movie theaters were abandoned, and the oldest motion picture house in the Valley, the Wyoming Theater in Wyoming, burned in 1982.

Ten years after the Agnes flood, Wyoming Valley is an almost completely renewed community, with more than its share of assets and with no more liabilities than any comparable urban center. A happy future is not assured; but if history is any guide, the people of this Valley will find the leadership needed and will transcend the problems of this century to enter the 21st with confidence.

South Side Public Square,
Wilkes-Barre, Pa

In the early years of the century, Wilkes-Barre architecture was dominated by Alfred Hamilton Kipp and Thomas Podmore, whose firm built a neoclassic building for the First National Bank. They then converted Isaac Perry's older Victorian building into the Savoy Theatre, a vaudeville house. Streetcars arrived and departed around the inner perimeter of Public Square from 1888 till 1950, except for a strike that lasted from October 14, 1915, to December 15, 1916. Courtesy, F. Charles Petrillo

The removal of the third courthouse in 1909 left Wilkes-Barre with a four-acre park in the heart of the city. For about a quarter-century the center of the park was graced by flower beds and the Kankakee Fountain, designed by Orestes Formiglia of Luzerne, which depicted an Indian maiden. The fountain fell into disrepair and was removed in the mid-1930s. For 40 years thereafter, Public Square remained persistently pleasant but nondescript. Courtesy, F. Charles Petrillo.

By 1848 the Presbyterian Church of 1833—with only 32 pews—was inadequate. It was pulled down, and architects Thomas H. Parker and Ashbel Bennett began a Gothic revival replacement. When Parker died and Bennett moved to New Jersey, Daniel A. Fell finished the job. Thirty-five years later—when the Presbyterians built a great stone church to rival the new stone St. Stephen's Episcopal Church—they sold the old building to the Osterhout Library for $25,000. Courtesy, F. Charles Petrillo

Palm House, River Common, Wilkes-Barre, Pa.

The Palm House, an elaborate glass conservatory housing tropical and subtropical vegetation, stood on the River Common just to the south of the courthouse. Both the greenhouse itself and its adjacent gardens were tourist attractions and sources of civic pride, but protracted, grinding depression made their upkeep prohibitive. Courtesy, F. Charles Petrillo

At one time, two passenger stations in Wilkes-Barre and a third in Kingston served railroad travelers. The largest of these was designed by Wilson Brothers in 1883 for the Lehigh Valley Railroad, whose crack train, the Black Diamond, was named for the region's primary product. The train, the station, and the railroad are all gone now, but Alice Marea Jenkins captured their spirit in "East Bound." Courtesy, D. Leonard Corgan Library, King's College; Edward Welles, Jr., Collection

At one time, commuters who lived in the Back Mountain area—the extreme western reaches of the Valley—caught trains from the Dallas station. Graydon Mayer shows the old station during a melting midwinter rain. Courtesy, D. Leonard Corgan Library, King's College; Edward Welles, Jr., Collection

None of the four brick mansions seen here was individually of great architectural distinction, but collectively they formed a wonderfully harmonious ensemble that reflected the architectural sensibility of Wilkes-Barre in the late 19th century. From left to right, they are the homes of Cosmer P. Long, Edward Payne, Henry Ashley, the Emory family, and Asa R. Brundage. The architects of the first four buildings are not specifically known. The stucco house at the far right has its own story. The Dutch gables of Edward Payne's house suggest Alfred Kipp or Thomas Podmore (individually or collectively); while the polygonal

tower on Henry Ashley's was characteristic of Missouria B. Houpt. By the time these buildings were put up, the passion for high Victorian stucco in the French or Italianate mode had burned itself out. For the most part, the brickwork is simple, except for the paneled chimneys. The overall feeling is idiomatic American eclectic. The architects clearly respect and relate to one another because all are working within the same style. All the buildings once had porches, and all originally sported elaborate cast-iron finials, of which only one on the tower of the Emory house remains. By contrast, the Brundage house is specifically Italianate Victorian stucco (if not designed by Sam Sloan, it was surely built by someone else

influenced by Andrew Jackson Downing). The brackets tucked under the overhanging eaves are almost vestigial compared to those of the Sterling house. The absence of a belvedere probably indicates that Mr. Brundage did not feel like paying for one. The house originally had a porch supported by wrought-iron pillars quite similar to those of the Sterling house.

On January 22, 1959—and for three horrible days thereafter—the ice-filled Susquehanna poured billions of gallons of freezing water into the mines below. The incident cost 12 lives and ended deep mining in the Valley for the foreseeable future. "Knox Mine Disaster," by Alice Welsh Jenkins, shows that chilling event. Courtesy, D. Leonard Corgan Library, King's College; Edward Welles, Jr., Collection

One of Fred Kirby's great gifts to the city, the 132-acre park on the west bank of the Susquehanna across from downtown Wilkes-Barre, was also completely renovated in the wake of Agnes. Along with athletic facilities of all kinds, playgrounds, picnic tables, shelters, a vita course, an arbor, and sundry whimsical wooden sculptures, Peter Bohlin and his associates supplied a pond for summer paddleboating and winter skating.

For many years, the Valley (especially West Pittston and Wilkes-Barre) has cherished and encouraged its Japanese cherry trees; Wilkes-Barre will give a tree to anyone who will plant and cultivate it. The oldest and most luxuriant trees stand along the River Common from North to South streets. An annual Cherry Blossom Festival—featuring all sorts of activities from art shows to a raft race—is scheduled for two April weekends. The festival usually occurs either just before or just after the trees have blossomed.

On November 2, 1778, at about noon, three Indians appeared at the home of Jonathan Slocum in Wilkes-Barre and carried off his five-year-old daughter, Frances. Fifty-seven years later, visitors to an Indian town near Peru, Indiana, met the widow of a Miami chief, who was clearly a white woman. Ma-con-a-quah, as she was then called, had forgotten how to speak English; as an honored member of her tribe, she had no interest in returning to the Wyoming Valley. She did remember that her home had been on the Susquehanna, and advertisements in various area papers told the story of the discovery of "lost sister of Wyoming." In 1839 Joseph Slocum was reunited at last with the sister he had not seen in nearly six decades. Other members of her white family also made the journey to Indiana to visit her, and George Winter painted her portrait. She lived until 1847. Perhaps because it seems more like legend than fact, the story of Frances Slocum has been retold up and down the Valley for generations. The site of the Slocum cabin (at the corner of North Street and Pennsylvania Avenue in modern Wilkes-Barre) is now a small park. The little town of Mocanaqua is about five miles downriver from the Wyoming Valley. Because the story of Frances Slocum seems to be the stuff of opera, perhaps it was inevitable that an opera would be made about her. Scranton-born composer Richard Wargo's concert opera, The River Flows, *received its world premiere from the Northeastern Pennsylvania Philharmonic (which commissioned the work) in Wilkes-Barre in 1982. Courtesy, Pennsylvania State Museum*

Harvard graduate Timothy Pickering, quartermaster general of the Continental army, came to the Valley to arbitrate land claims. He was able to acquire much acreage for himself, and lived in Wilkes-Barre between 1786 and 1792. Pickering left the Valley to serve in the cabinets of George Washington and John Adams. (WHGS)

Kipp and Podmore's most extravagant commercial structure was the Bennett Building, erected at the turn of the century. The brick building was richly ornamented with glazed tile, including heads in the tympanums of the fourth-story arches flanked by standing figures on the capitals. Many Valley people feel that the removal of buildings like this in the name of modernization entails a misguided destruction of the city's past. Courtesy, F. Charles Petrillo

The Mallinckrodt Convent housed the Sisters of Christian Charity, a Roman Catholic order with its origins in Germany. It also was the home of St. Ann's Academy. The original (central) building was designed by E.F. Durang (architect of St. Mary's Church), but within a few years expansion was necessary, and Willis G. Hale added the flanking wings. Courtesy, F. Charles Petrillo

Opened in 1925, G.A.R. Memorial High School was the second of Wilkes-Barre's three secondary schools. Athletic rivals in other institutions, who do not remember the Grand Army of the Republic, insist that the initials stand for garbage, ashes, and rubbish. After 50 years of hard use, the building was thoroughly renovated and enlarged in the late 1970s. Courtesy, F. Charles Petrillo

At the turn of the century George Stegmaier's brewery was the largest local beer manufacturer. The main brewery with its fantastic roofline (built in 1894 by A.C. Wagner) stands in the center flanked on the left by the stables and on the right by the bottling house. The railroad gatehouse in the left foreground was manned continuously by a guard who lowered and raised the gates manually through a system of levers, pulleys, and cables. Courtesy, F. Charles Petrillo

The five courtrooms of the Luzerne County Courthouse are different in their specific decor but alike in their opulence. Different combinations of rare wood and stone are used in each. The Orphans' Court features wainscoting of English veined white Italian marble panels with columns of Brache violetti and mahogany woodwork. The mural behind the bench, painted by Charles L. Hinton, is titled "The Symbols of Life." Courtesy, F. Charles Petrillo

One of Fred M. Kirby's two great gifts to his native city is the Kirby Health Center, a memorial to his mother, Angeline Elizabeth Kirby. This neoclassic building with a distinctly Mediterranean character was built in 1931 by Thomas Henry Atherton. Courtesy, F. Charles Petrillo

On Thursday, June 22, 1972, the intersection of South Franklin and West Northampton streets—one block from the river—was flooded as high as street level. The Valley had not endured a major flood for more than 30 years; residents uneasily and a bit giddily reasoned (or hoped) that if this was as bad as it was going to be, it wasn't going to be that bad. The stone structure right of center is the base of the First Presbyterian Church tower. Photo by Tom Beck

Two days later, all of central Wilkes-Barre—and all other low-lying parts of the Valley—was under water as high as the first-story ceilings of most buildings. On Northampton Street, the water surged as far east as the steep rise to the heights. The tower rising in the distance to the right of center is First Presbyterian Church. Photo by Tom Beck

During the Agnes Flood, helicopters were put to many uses—none more important than finding and rescuing those stranded by the rising waters.

The bucolic beauty of the Wyoming Valley can be seen in this view of Ricketts Glen State Park. Colonel Ricketts, a longtime area resident, donated the land to the state. The colonel's summer estate once stood nearby.

A great problem with culm banks—
aside from their considerable
unsightliness—was their tendency
to burst spontaneously into flame.
Burning mountains of slag defied all
attempts to extinguish their fires. By
night, they were enchanting—like
terrestrial aurora borealis—but by
day they were terrifying. J. Philip
Richards chose to show them by
night in "Burning Mountains."
Courtesy, D. Leonard Corgan
Library, King's College; Edward
Welles, Jr., Collection

Above: *The Wyoming Valley Battle Monument, erected during the 1840s and dedicated in 1878, stands now in a peaceful grove.*

Left: *Turn-of-the-century neoclassical architecture is best exemplified in the Valley by the fourth Luzerne County Courthouse. The exterior was designed by Pittsburgh architect Frederick Osterling. During construction (1906-1909), the already generous budget was exceeded over and over again; the final price tag was well over two million dollars—an enormous sum for the day. Osterling was ultimately fired, and the interior is the work of McCormick and French, a local firm. Photo by Ralph Vivian*

This apartment building, Ten East South, is the tallest and most widely praised of the downtown buildings put up in the decade since Agnes. It is in fact a 10-story optical illusion; the broad east and west elevations consist of a series of setbacks punctuated by the end walls of the terraces with their porthole openings and the solid walls with their bands of polychrome brick. As the viewer walks past, the entire building seems to shift—another of Peter Bohlin's architectural tricks.

In winter, Public Square becomes a festival of light. Added to the park's own lollipop-like lighting are strings of lights on the bare trees and cheerful light-sculptures depicting popular cartoon characters. Originally intended for pre-Christmas decoration, their brightness is continued through the midwinter months. Courtesy, Bohlin Powell Larkin Cywinski, Architects, Planners, Engineers

The steel and plexiglass canopy along the first block of South Main Street includes a covered crosswalk in the middle of the block and a clock tower with four faces—each of which usually gives a different time and all of which are consistently wrong. Nevertheless, the canopy and the planters full of seasonal flowers (with evergreens in the winter) make the shopping district a happy place—vigorously competing with the suburban plazas and malls. Photo by Mark Cohen

Above: *When the floodwaters of Agnes receded, the devastation both above and below ground was total and reconstruction took years. Beneath downtown streets, telephone lines, power lines, steam conduits, sewers, water pipes, and storm drains had to be replaced entirely;* many thoroughfares seemed more like open ditches or obstacle courses than city streets. Here the first two blocks of a renewed South Franklin Street are seen from the top of the Miners National Bank Building.

Facing page: *The newest of the Valley's colleges, Luzerne County Community College, sits on a hilltop in Nanticoke. Among the newest of its new buildings is the Conference Center (or LCCCCC). Regional architecture buffs would immediately (and correctly) associate its cheerful, colorful interior with Peter Bohlin. Courtesy, Bohlin Powell Larkin Cywinski, Architects, Planners, Engineers; photo by Otto Baitz*

The Wilkes-Barre and Wyoming Valley Traction Company inaugurated electrified streetcar service in 1888. In its heyday the system would cover the whole Valley. On the right is Ben Dilley's Tavern, the most famous watering place in turn-of-the-century Wilkes-Barre. (WHGS)

Chapter Eleven

PARTNERS IN PROGRESS

INTRODUCTION

Once the chosen hunting ground of the Iroquois Confederacy, which granted various minor Indian tribes the privilege of temporary residence, Wyoming Valley is now the heart of Luzerne County.

Born in strife of battle between the Connecticut settlers and the Pennamites from Pennsylvania, the Valley emerged as a place peopled by strong men and women sharing an undaunted spirit.

Although surrounding counties were soon established, the Valley in Luzerne County was the leader first in agriculture—which continued as the cornerstone of the area's economy until the latter half of the 19th century—and then in coal mining, following the discovery of huge beds of anthracite. The popularity of the mineral, used as a fuel for the iron forges as early as the 1760s, flourished after Judge Jesse Fell of Wilkes-Barre demonstrated in 1808 that it could be used for domestic heating.

Farming and coal mining existed side by side through the mid-1800s, until the demand for coal in the industrial Northeast made the mining industry omnipotent. As a result, the need for coal miners touched off a wave of immigration to the area, creating a diversified social background that ultimately evolved into a cosmopolitan social structure reflected in the availability of ethnic foods, festivals, and the diversity of language in the region.

The climb to prosperity in the mining era reached its peak in 1918, when 37.7 million tons of coal were mined, while peak employment numbered 67,207 workers in 1926. Then adversity struck, caused by a plummeting economy during the Great Depression. The catastrophic effects of the Depression lingered in the coal-mining towns, even as conditions eased in the rest of the nation. Consequently, the young populace of the Valley began a migration to the industrial cities of the East which, by the end of World War II, had become an exodus.

Employment in the mines by 1940 had dropped to 39,300 workers; a decade later it decreased to 34,500 miners, with production down to 17.1 million tons. Subsequently, a disaster in the late 1950s spelled the end for coal mining in the Valley.

Nonetheless, the enterprising citizenry would not succumb to a dying economy. As a foundation on which to build a new economy, civic leaders persevered in establishing a garment industry. The success of this project encouraged successive drives, led by the Greater Wilkes-Barre Chamber of Commerce, which raised millions of dollars to have nationally known corporations locate in the Crestwood Industrial Park at Mountaintop and other industrial complexes throughout the Valley. Among the various companies thus attracted were Eberhard Faber, Foster Wheeler, and Cornell Iron Works.

"Homegrown industries," such as Diamond Manufacturing and Eastern Pennsylvania Supply Company, were established as supportive coal-mining operations. As they sought new markets and introduced new product lines to successfully compete, most of these firms have grown—and a few now have satellite plants or sales offices in other parts of the nation.

The educational system of the Valley—where several townships in 1773 levied a general taxation to provide for schools, making it the forerunner of the free-school system in Pennsylvania—has in itself become an industry, with five institutions of higher learning that provide employment for hundreds of teachers, admininstrators, and staff.

Due to the foresight and determination of its early citizens and their successors, the community today rests on a diversified economy, shipping goods worldwide that were produced by skilled and proud craftsmen in the Wyoming Valley.

GREATER WILKES-BARRE CHAMBER OF COMMERCE
1884-1984

The Greater Wilkes-Barre Chamber of Commerce was founded by a group of Wilkes-Barre businessmen in the spring of 1884 and was originally known as the Wilkes-Barre Board of Trade.

The Chamber is proud to celebrate 100 years of commitment to the "encouragement and protection of trade and commerce," as is stated in its original charter. Since its founding, the Chamber has had many names and undergone many changes. It has, however, never faltered in its determination to improve the economic conditions of the greater Wilkes-Barre/Wyoming Valley area. Today the object of the organization continues to be "to advance the commercial, industrial, retail, civic, cultural, health, recreational, and general interests of those adjacent communities in Luzerne County, Pennsylvania, which are collectively known as the Wyoming Valley and its generally recognized suburbs." Throughout the past 100 years the Chamber has acted as a catalyst for community projects. No other single organization has consistently provided support for as many valued institutions. Concerned citizens, volunteering their time and energy, have provided the impetus that allowed the establishment of hospitals, colleges, and industrial parks.

The valley's excellent transportation network, including the Wilkes-Barre/Scranton International Airport and the interstate road system, were projects with which the Chamber of Commerce was closely associated. Flood control, quality of government, and tourism have long been concerns of the business community and the Chamber has been involved in each of those areas.

During the postwar '40s and '50s, the Greater Wilkes-Barre Chamber of Commerce began an experiment in industrialization that set the pace for the rest of the nation. The Industrial

The original minutes, dated March 24, 1884, of the first meeting of the Wilkes-Barre Board of Trade. (Special properties courtesy of The Wyoming Valley Historical and Geological Society. Photo by Ken Fox.)

Fund was created to raise monies to finance industrial expansion and relocation projects, and it received support from every segment of the community. Crestwood Industrial Park was established and corporations such as RCA, Eberhard Faber, Metropolitan Wire Corporation, Cornell Iron Works, and Certain Teed moved to the region.

The Chamber and the Industrial Fund continue to manage Crestwood Industrial Park, as well as Hanover Industrial Estates and other industrial properties. Attracting industries and creating jobs is still an important aspect of the organization's activities.

As the Chamber looks forward, the focus on economic growth remains steady. Chamber-sponsored groups, such as the Committee for Economic Growth, are currently undertaking major studies to assess the strengths of the area and to develop a marketing plan.

The Greater Wilkes-Barre Chamber of Commerce salutes its proud tradition but continues to look to the future. It will change to meet the needs of the business community and the region but it will not lose its vitality as a community catalyst.

WYOMING HISTORICAL AND GEOLOGICAL SOCIETY

It was on February 11, 1858, when 16 persons gathered at Judge Jesse Fell's tavern to mark the 50th anniversary of the burning of anthracite on an open grate, that the Wyoming Historical and Geological Society was born. Fell's tavern at Washington and Northampton streets in Wilkes-Barre was the site of the first known burning of anthracite, and the open grate still stands.

The thought of those gathered at the tavern was "that there are still preserved in our midst many memorials, papers, records, and relics of local and general historical interest which . . . if gathered up, would form a collection of increasing interest and value."

Throughout its 125 years the Society's purpose has been the collection, preservation, maintenance, and dissemination of materials relating to the history, geology, genealogy, architecture, and archaeology of Luzerne County. Today the more than 750 members of the group offer programs and activities of historical interest to the entire county.

The Society museum, located behind the Osterhout Library on South Franklin Street in Wilkes-Barre, contains three floors of exhibits that tell the history of the anthracite coal industry and the life-style of the early Indians of northeastern Pennsylvania. These two permanent displays are augmented by changing exhibits that illustrate specific events in local history. The Society also sponsors special lectures, films, and presentations of area history that are open to the public. The museum is open Tuesday through Saturday.

A short distance from the museum, at 49 South Franklin Street, is the Bishop Memorial Library, which houses more than 4,000 bound volumes of local history, in addition to newspapers, manuscript collections, photographs, and maps covering the entire chronology of Luzerne County. Its research facilities are available

The Wyoming Historical and Geological Society Museum contains three floors of permanent exhibits and changing displays of specific events in local history, such as "The Men Who Built Wilkes-Barre: Architecture of the City, 1860-1960."

Tuesday through Saturday for the serious scholar as well as for the avocational historian.

Swetland Homestead at 885 Wyoming Avenue, Wyoming, is another of the Society's facilities. A settler's cabin, the oldest portion of the house, was built in 1797 by Luke Swetland, a Connecticut man. The house, which traces the economic and social development of the family to the Victorian era, is open to the public during the summer and Christmas season.

The wealth of the bibliographic material in the Society's collection has been incorporated into numerous publications. The records of the original Connecticut settlers form the basis of *The Susquehanna Company Papers,* an 11-volume set, which has received national acclaim.

The Whole Valley Cookbook, an award-winning collection of ethnic recipes and menus, and the joint sponsorship of *The Wyoming Valley, An American Portrait,* with the Greater Wilkes-Barre Chamber of Commerce, are the most recent publishing endeavors of the Society.

DUNBAR BUILDERS HARDWARE INC.

Blending into a residential neighborhood in South Wilkes-Barre, Dunbar Builders Hardware is a quiet, family-owned business that has helped to spread the name of the city through the Northeast.

Architects, contractors, and home owners of the Wyoming Valley rely on Dunbar Builders Hardware for quality service and hardware, but their reputation has spread beyond the Northeast, and they now supply hardware, hollow metal, and wood doors throughout the country.

Owned and operated by Mr. and Mrs. Phillip A. Blaum since 1960, the company was founded by Ralph H. Dunbar, Mrs. Blaum's father, in 1941. Mr. Dunbar converted a small garage on Oak Street into a hardware store to supply "strictly builders' hardware."

Inventory at the start was approximately $1,000 and gross sales never exceeded $40,000 during the early years. The firm had its ups and downs, according to the state of the economy, but it experienced steady growth as its reputation for service grew.

Mr. Dunbar purchased the building at 485 South River Street, where the business is now located, in 1945. Mrs. Blaum began to work for her father later in 1945 as a bookkeeper and typist. In 1948 her husband, Phillip, joined the company as a salesman and later became a job estimator and coordinator. They have since been joined in the business by their son Phillip, daughter Sandra Tarulli, and son-in-law Neal Tarulli, and use modern merchandising methods to compete in what they describe as a highly competitive business. Competition has grown, Mr. Blaum explains, as the interstate highway system has opened up markets that once were the exclusive property of local hardware suppliers.

Among the many projects for which Dunbar has supplied hardware are the I.B.M. complex, Kingston, New York;

Revlon corporate headquarters, Edison, New Jersey; the Hungarian Embassy, Washington, D.C.; Lord & Taylor stores in Florida and Texas; officers' clubs at Redstone Arsenal, Alabama, and Fort Meade, Maryland; and Cornell University, Ithaca, New York. Locally the firm has furnished hardware for buildings at King's College, Wilkes College, Wyoming Seminary, and College Misericordia; as well as various schools, hospitals, churches, apartment complexes, office buildings, and private residences.

The owners see future growth from the recent development of electronic-security in both home and industry, and already have taken steps to ensure the company's entrance into that field.

Dunbar's first such project was at the newly constructed Wilkes-Barre police headquarters, where the firm assisted in the development of the specifications and then supplied the hardware for the electronic-security system.

Dunbar also aids architects, developers, and owners in budgeting costs for renovations or new construction, and assists in writing specifications for hollow metal doors and frames, wood doors, toilet partitions, and decorative hardware.

Some of the products supplied by Dunbar Builders Hardware for many of the finest buildings throughout the country.

PENNSYLVANIA GAS AND WATER COMPANY
A PENNSYLVANIA ENTERPRISES COMPANY

Since 1850 Pennsylvania Gas and Water Company (PG&W) and its forerunners have played a decisive role in the economic development of northeastern Pennsylvania. Located in the heartland of the Northeast Corridor, PG&W's nearly 250,000 customers utilize the company's gas and water services for domestic, commercial, and industrial purposes. This has been the case dating back to the origin of the company. PG&W is the product of acquisitions and mergers of 76 smaller firms. PG&W serves its 113,000 gas customers in 184 municipalities from Carbondale to Selinsgrove and Williamsport through 1,931 miles of gas mains, and its 128,000 water customers in 63 municipalities from Forest City to Glen Lyon, through 1,661 miles of water mains. Water is stored in 55 collecting and impounding reservoirs with a 20-billion-gallon capacity and the ability to serve 100 million gallons per day.

The development of water companies in the anthracite areas of Pennsylvania was closely tied to the now-defunct deep coal mines. Without water, coal could not be prepared for market through various "washing" processes which removed rocks, slate, and coal dust. Washing the coal took large quantities of water so it was logical that companies in the 1850s and 1860s acquired nearby stream facilities, constructed dams, and piped water to the mines for coal-washing operations as well as to the homes of their employees for domestic use.

During the same period the Wilkes-Barre Water Company, the oldest (chartered in 1850) and the then-largest water utility in Luzerne County, was extending its lines and gaining customers in the city of Wilkes-Barre. In the surrounding municipalities, smaller water firms were springing up so that by 1896 no fewer than 29 water companies served the Wyoming Valley, an area less than 15 miles long and 10 miles wide.

William Walker Scranton became president of the Scranton Gas and Water Company in 1879 upon the death of his father, Joseph Hand Scranton, who had cofounded the company in 1854. It was during William Walker Scranton's tenure, from 1879 to 1916, that the company witnessed its greatest expansion period of water service capability. Former governor of Pennsylvania and ambassador to the United Nations, William Warren Scranton, is the grandson of William Walker Scranton.

The Spring Brook Water Supply Company was organized in 1896 by a group of business leaders headed by Colonel Lewis A. Watres of Scranton. He became the firm's first president, serving from 1896 to 1927.

In 1895 a severe and prolonged drought hit northeastern Pennsylvania. Water had to be pumped from the nearby Susquehanna River and loaded on tank cars to supply the water to coal companies for their washing process. The drought brought the owners of the 29 existing water companies to the realization that their sources of supply and their distribution systems were inadequate to meet the needs of a growing and expanding residential population and future industrial growth and expansion. The Spring Brook Water Supply Company then emerged as a parent company through acquisition of the 29 smaller water firms serving the Valley, 15 other water firms serving other areas, and one small railroad company.

As consolidation of the water companies was occurring in Luzerne County, a similar evolution of gas and water service was taking place 20 miles to the north in the Lackawanna County area. The Scranton Gas and Water Company, which was chartered in 1854 to serve the village of Scranton, then a part of Luzerne County, emerged as the surviving company of the merger of 29 other gas and water companies.

During 1927 and 1928 the Federal Water Service Corporation, with offices in New York City, acquired stock of the Spring Brook Water Supply Company and the Scranton Gas and Water Company. On January 25, 1928, these companies were merged with the Spring Brook Water Supply Company in the Wyoming Valley to form the Scranton-Spring Brook Water Service Company.

About this time Federal also acquired other water companies in Pennsylvania, including the Chester Water Service Company; the Pittsburgh Suburban Water Company;

C.T. Chenery formed the Federal Water Service Corporation in 1926 and served as its chairman. He also served as president and then chairman of the Scranton-Spring Brook Water Service Company from 1931 to 1951. He was chairman of Southern Natural Gas Company (now SONAT, Inc.) and founded Meadow Stable and Farm in Doswell, Virginia, which has produced such thoroughbred racehorses as Hill Prince, First Landing, Riva Ridge, and Secretariat.

the Clear Springs Water Service Company, serving the borough of Northampton and environs outside of Allentown; the Clymer Water Company, serving the borough of Indiana; the Punxsutawney Water Service Company; the Jersey Shore Water Company; and the Citizens Water Service Company, serving Phillipsburg. All of the Pennsylvania companies became subsidiaries under a parent firm created by Federal, the Pennsylvania Water Service Company, and were managed by the same executives as Scranton-Spring Brook.

As a result of the Public Utility Holding Company Act, passed by Congress in 1935, holding companies such as the Federal Water Service Corporation liquidated their stock in utilities. Accordingly, all of the stock of the Pennsylvania water companies

controlled by Federal was sold or distributed through the 1940s. The last of the common stock in Scranton-Spring Brook owned by Federal was sold or distributed in 1951. That same year Carbondale Gas Company and Wyoming County Gas, Scranton-Spring Brook's two remaining subsidiaries, were merged into the parent firm. The acquisition of Pennsylvania Power and Light Company's manufactured gas properties in Wyoming Valley and an additional six-county area of north-central Pennsylvania in 1951 established Scranton-Spring Brook as a dominant, reliable energy supplier equipped to meet the demands that would be placed on both its gas and water systems by all area consumers over the ensuing years.

The year 1955 saw the beginning of the conversion of the company's gas properties in north-central Pennsylvania from manufactured gas to natural gas. In 1956 the company brought natural gas to northeastern Pennsylvania through a 42-mile, 12-inch gas line constructed at a cost of $2.3 million running from Uniondale in Susquehanna County to Wilkes-

Rulison Evans started with the Spring Brook Water Supply Company as a meter clerk in 1911. He served as president or chief executive officer from 1942 to 1972, and as chairman of the board from 1951 to 1973. His administration guided the company during the introduction and expansion of natural gas.

Barre in Luzerne County. By 1957 all of the company's gas customers were being supplied natural gas. This expensive, though necessary, change to natural gas resulted in the firm's aggressive growth pattern which continued throughout the 1950s and 1960s.

The company showed its faith in the Wyoming Valley and its future development by laying the gas and water lines at the site of the Crestwood Industrial Park in the 1950s even before the first industry was signed. Stock of the Berwick Gas Company was acquired in 1958 and by the following year revenues for gas exceeded water revenues, reaching 52 percent of the firm's gross revenues. By contrast, just nine years earlier gas sales had comprised only 26 percent of Scranton-Spring Brook's total revenues. To reflect the trend in the company's business, its name was changed on October 1, 1960, to Pennsylvania Gas and Water Company.

Sound company management developed over the years has given PG&W the capacity to meet market changes as well as natural adversity. For example, on June 23, 1972, the Wyoming Valley was hit by massive

J. Glenn Gooch joined the firm in 1948 as a staff accountant and was elected controller in 1967, vice-president of finance in 1971, and as a member of the board in 1974. He has served as president and chief executive officer since 1978.

PG&W's former corporate headquarters at 30 North Franklin Street, Wilkes-Barre, which had been the headquarters of the Spring Brook Water Supply Company.

flooding caused by Tropical Storm Agnes. The storm was described by President Nixon as the greatest natural disaster ever to hit the United States. The center of its heaviest destruction was the northeastern Pennsylvania area served by the company. The flooding of the Susquehanna River following the tropical storm caused 100,000 residents to be evacuated from their homes, and estimates of total damage were in the billions of dollars. Approximately 25,000 gas service accounts were affected in the area. Flooding also occurred in the Williamsport and Milton areas, where several thousand additional gas accounts were also affected. Restoration projects involved many thousands of man hours and equipment hours to replace, repair, dewater, and regas mains and service lines—all of which required thousands of service calls to customers' homes and businesses. As testimony to the dependability of the company's water delivery system, water service was maintained throughout the entire period of the disaster providing pure water at sufficient pressures for all

customers' requirements, including fire protection. PG&W sustained losses of $4.1 million from this natural disaster.

At the annual meeting on June 5, 1974, the firm's stockholders approved a plan to reorganize PG&W. A holding company, Pennsylvania Enterprises, Inc., was created to own all of the common stock of PG&W and other subsidiaries. This restructuring provided a vehicle to permit the company to diversify.

The first new subsidiary of Pennsylvania Enterprises, Pennsylvania Energy Resources, Inc. (PERI), was formed in 1974 to serve as a nonregulated service operation. The following year a land, property, and forestry management company, Theta Land Corporation (THETA), was created.

To meet the company's growth

demands, PG&W moved its headquarters in the summer of 1975 to the Wilkes-Barre Center Building on Public Square—the first new commercial office complex to be completed as part of the reconstruction of the city's downtown in the wake of Tropical Storm Agnes. The Wilkes-Barre Center location serves as corporate headquarters for the nearly 1,000-employee combination utility which in 1982 reported assets slightly in excess of $300 million. From this location, state-of-the-art technology employed by PG&W serves residential, commercial, and industrial gas and water customers with a great degree of reliability and efficiency.

The company's present corporate headquarters occupies the top four floors of the Wilkes-Barre Center Building on Public Square in Wilkes-Barre.

PENNSYLVANIA MILLERS MUTUAL INSURANCE COMPANY

In *The Millers' Review* of September 15, 1886, members of the Pennsylvania Millers' State Association read that a mutual insurance company was being formed for the purpose of providing "... insurance against fire of the flour mills of its members, and it is suggested to our readers that they at once place themselves in communication with some one of its members of the committee having charge of the matter."

Less than four months later, on January 10, 1887, Pennsylvania Millers Mutual Fire Insurance Company was chartered under the Pennsylvania Insurance Act of 1876. Ninety-six years later, on January 1, 1983, assets were reported at $48,820,000. The original surplus, created in 1900, has been maintained ever since and has grown to $24,909,000. In addition, a general voluntary reserve was established and continues to be maintained to take care of other unusual losses.

The A.M. Best & Co. has assigned the Pennsylvania Millers Mutual Insurance Company a policyholders' rating of "A+" (excellent) and has commended its management for sound operational concepts. The rating company also praises Pennsylvania Millers for an "excellent investment policy" and maintenance of voluntary reserves.

The firm's first office was established in Huntingdon, Pennsylvania, but was moved to Wilkes-Barre in 1904 following the election of Colonel Asher Miner as president. Through the years the Miner family has maintained a close relationship with the company and today Charles H. Miner, Jr., serves as chairman of the board.

To assure continued growth of the company, the board of directors, in 1906, authorized the entrance into additional classes or risks. Since that decision was made, Pennsylvania

Millers Mutual Insurance Company has continued to expand its product line in both "general business" and "agri business" areas.

As early as 1890 some policies were written in New Jersey, but it was not until 1900 that the firm began operations in other states bordering Pennsylvania. Later, policies were written in New England and some midwestern and southern states. Today Pennsylvania Millers Mutual Insurance Company is licensed to conduct business in 37 states and has approximately 50,000 policyholders. Almost 500 independent insurance agents represent the company in 21 states.

The board of directors authorized the construction in 1935 of an office building at 72 North Franklin Street, Wilkes-Barre, which served as its home office until 1978. At that time the firm moved to new facilities in the Bicentennial Building at 15 Public Square, Wilkes-Barre.

In 1982 Pennsylvania Millers Mutual Insurance Company developed a long range plan to ensure continued growth, consistent with sound underwriting and investment principles. To achieve its goals, the

Joseph Kologe (left) and Iowerth Jones are shown in the computer room of Pennsylvania Millers Mutual Insurance Company. The equipment enables the firm to maintain up-to-date information, which helps it to serve its customers more effectively.

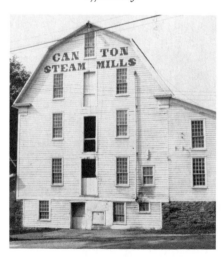

Built in 1852, this old flour mill (now owned by H. Rockwell and Son) at Canton, Pennsylvania, has been insured continually by Pennsylvania Millers Mutual Insurance Company since 1888.

firm's management team has been strengthened to provide the leadership necessary to grow in the 1980s.

WILKES-BARRE GENERAL HOSPITAL

Wilkes-Barre General, Wyoming Valley's oldest hospital, is committed to meeting the health care needs of the greater Wilkes-Barre community. That commitment, reflected in the hospital's history, likewise represents its future.

In 1870 nine area physicians put forth "an appeal in behalf of a Hospital" to be located in or near Wilkes-Barre. The appeal claimed that the position of Wilkes-Barre as a mining center especially demanded the "superior surgical and medical appliances as could be provided by a hospital." The matter was acted upon in 1872 after several fatal mine accidents occurred and miners died for the lack of medical care and facilities. The need for a hospital became tragically evident.

An organizing group first met in September in the office of ex-Governor Hoyt. On October 10, 1872, a rented factory building on Fell Street, used for the manufacture of weight scales, was transformed into a hospital. Wilkes-Barre City Hospital, as it was then named, opened with 20 beds and was conveniently located near various industrial and mining companies. Its medical staff comprised two consulting physicians, six attending physicians, and two matrons. Between the opening date and January 1873, a total of 25 patients were admitted and treated, the majority for mining-related incidents.

Until 1874 it was supported entirely by voluntary contributions from the families and industries of Wilkes-Barre. Examples of the community's support were duly noted each year in the annual report: "Three geese, Mr. Burgunder. Six sheets, made and donated by St. Stephen's Industrial School. One hundred glasses of jelly, Mr. E.P. Darling. One turkey, H. Tuck and Co."

By the end of 1874 demands on the hospital became so great that the accommodations on Fell Street were no longer suitable. Two lots were offered to the board of directors in 1875, and the four-acre plot of land donated by John Welles Hollenback was chosen as a new site for Wilkes-Barre City Hospital. The land, located on River Street in the city's north end, remains the site of the hospital.

The first hospital built at this location was occupied on April 1, 1876, and was a quadrangle, two stories high, with a large veranda and an open court in the center. It contained 60 beds in four female and five male wards, one operating room, a pharmacy, and separate dining rooms for male and female patients. Patients were charged less than one dollar per day.

By 1887 skilled nursing had taken its place among "the gainful callings of

The first facility built by Wilkes-Barre General Hospital was on River Street in 1876. This was the second building to house the hospital. The first was a rented factory building on Fell Street in South Wilkes-Barre.

Still on River Street, Wilkes-Barre General Hospital has gone through many changes to emerge as a sophisticated medical center serving the community with the latest in patient care.

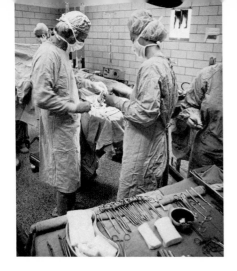

About half of Wilkes-Barre General Hospital's annual 15,000 admissions involve surgical cases. A new surgical suite, scheduled for completion in 1984, will provide a state-of-the-art setting for the surgical procedures.

life" and the Wilkes-Barre City Hospital's Nursing Training School opened. The school offered a three-year course of study in caring for the sick, and it graduated its first class of two nurses in the summer of 1890.

Ancillary growth began in 1902 with the opening of the X-ray Department. Within one year the department admitted 72 patients to undergo "Radiographs."

In 1925 the board of directors voted to change the hospital's name from City Hospital to Wilkes-Barre General Hospital to correct the mistaken belief the hospital was financed by the municipality of Wilkes-Barre.

The hospital's success in its early years was due largely to the Ladies' Auxiliary, known until 1908 as the Board of Lady Managers. Their duties in those early years entailed management of the entire hospital, from purchasing supplies to giving money to patients in need of cab fare after discharge. It was not until 1908 that a full-time administrator, Dr. D.C. Wilkins, assumed responsibility for the hospital.

It can be said that Wilkes-Barre General Hospital is synonymous with the word growth. The '30s, '40s, '50s, and '60s were years of renovation and additions. Beginning in 1959, obsolete buildings became history as they were razed to make way for an emerging "new" hospital. Wilkes-Barre General was transformed from a cluster of

individual facilities to a single structure that would also be continuously renovated and restructured.

Growth was explosive during this period, as new units and departments were born. With the renovation and expansion came the first Poison Control Center in 1959, Nuclear Medicine Department in 1963, Intensive Care Unit and Electro-encephalograph Department in 1964, Chest Clinic and Coronary Care Unit in 1966, and a 24-hour, seven-day-a-week Emergency Department in 1968. New administrative departments were created as well, and existing patient care departments were expanded and modernized.

Wilkes-Barre General celebrated its centennial, not with gala celebrations and public announcements, but by responding to the greatest challenge of its long history. June 23-24, 1972, marked the worst flood in the history of Wyoming Valley, rendering thousands of people temporarily homeless. General became the major emergency flood disaster hospital, prepared to receive scores of patients from inundated hospitals in the flood-ravaged community. People literally poured in for emergency treatment, typhoid and tetanus inoculations, and shelter. General's calm efficiency was praised by hospital president Thomas P. Saxton: "Everyone functioned normally, except at an accelerated pace—which is the highest praise of all."

While the community and

A technician prepares a patient for a CAT scan. This diagnostic equipment is used on over 5,000 patients each year.

neighboring hospitals rebuilt, General continued to upgrade and expand its services and facilities. Patient floors were added to existing buildings, and a six-level east wing was constructed. The hospital stayed abreast of the advances in medical technology with the introduction of sophisticated diagnostic equipment in patient rooms, laboratory, radiology, and other ancillary departments.

Cancer treatment became a specialty of Wilkes-Barre General in 1974 when the Evan C. and Dorothy Elizabeth Jones Cancer Treatment Center opened, providing the only radiation oncology facility in Luzerne County. That led quite naturally to a comprehensive cancer care program which now includes a cancer care unit and a host of specialized professionals, programs and facilities, all dedicated to meeting the unique needs of cancer patients.

The '80s and '90s will present new opportunities and challenges for Wilkes-Barre General. Already, construction is progressing for a new surgical suite and critical care areas that will open in 1984. Change is likewise occurring away from the North River Street site. The 1983 acquisition of Heritage House, a skilled nursing and residential care facility in downtown Wilkes-Barre, marked the beginning of a trend toward a more diversified health care organization.

As a result of over a century of services, Wilkes-Barre General has become northeastern Pennsylvania's largest community hospital. Known as a "complete health care center," it offers a wide range of general health services as well as a variety of regional medical programs. Over 1,500 people perform nearly 200 different jobs to deliver quality medical care to more than 200,000 patients each year. Wilkes-Barre General's history is a story of meeting a community's needs. That story will certainly be its future as well.

FRANKLIN FIRST FEDERAL SAVINGS AND LOAN ASSOCIATION

Franklin First Federal Savings and Loan Association, with its main office at 44 West Market Street, Wilkes-Barre, is the result of a merger on October 1, 1978, of two of the Wyoming Valley's leading financial institutions.

With assets of more than $500 million, Franklin First Federal serves customers from 18 offices in a five-county area from Stroudsburg, in the Poconos, to Tunkhannock, in the Endless Mountains, and along the Susquehanna River from Berwick to Old Forge. The savings and loan association provides complete banking services from home mortgages to student loans along with numerous savings plans, including KEOGH and IRA retirement accounts, and interest-bearing checking accounts.

To maintain community participation, four advisory boards, composed of shareholders from Berwick, Tunkhannock, Stroudsburg, and the West Side, advise and report to the 14-member board of directors led by Elmer J. Klimchak, president and chief executive officer, and Edward L. Johnson, chairman of the board.

Organized within 12 days of each other in 1934, the Franklin Federal and First Federal savings and loan associations were established to promote thrift and home ownership. That same aim today guides the board of directors and officers of Franklin First Federal Savings and Loan Association.

Friendly rivals since their inceptions, the two savings and loan associations became neighbors in 1943. At that time Franklin Federal took over the office of First Federal, which had purchased the Dime Bank Building at North Franklin and West Market streets, Wilkes-Barre.

First Federal was the first to open for business when it began operations on May 1, 1934, at 34 West Market Street. James J. O'Malley, the principal founder of the banking institution, was named its first president and

On October 1, 1978, Elmer J. Klimchak and Edward L. Johnson cut the banner, signifying the merger of two leading Wilkes-Barre savings and loan associations into the new Franklin First Federal.

continued in office until his death on March 30, 1975. Johnson was named president and served in that post until the merger with Franklin Federal. Its assets upon opening were $6,300.

First Federal opened its first branch office in Stroudsburg on November 1, 1965, and on October 1, 1976, acquired the West Side Savings and Loan Association. At the time of the acquisition, the West Side facility had offices in Kingston and Tunkhannock. Six offices of First Federal existed at the

time of the merger with Franklin.

Franklin Federal began operations on June 21, 1934, with assets of $5,300. Henry Weigand, the first president, was succeeded in office by Alexander J. Boettger, who had been elected to the board in January and was named

president on February 4, 1935.

During the institution's early years its board met in St. Clement's Parish House or at the Hanover National Bank; it was not until March 1, 1941, that the first office was opened at 644 South Main Street, Wilkes-Barre.

The first mortgage, in the amount of $1,000, was approved on August 3, 1934. On April 1, 1941, Walter Bromfield was named the first full-time manager, becoming the first employee of Franklin Federal. On January 17, 1945, he was named executive vice-president; he served until his death on November 13, 1952.

Klimchak was appointed acting manager upon Bromfield's death and on January 18, 1956, was named executive vice-president. On January 12, 1959, he was elected a director and in a reorganization of offices was named president on January 20, 1971. Boettger was elected chairman of the board; C.E. Hippensteel, vice-chairman; and Alfred P. Matthews, secretary. Klimchak also has served as president of the Greater Wilkes-Barre Chamber of Commerce and of the Pennsylvania Savings League.

In 1947 Franklin Federal merged with the Wyoming Valley Building and Loan Association, bringing the assets of the institution to more than one million dollars. The year 1959 was one of growth for the institution as it opened the first of its branch offices at the Gateway Shopping Center in Edwardsville and reported assets of more than $21 million as it entered its 25th year.

Upon the death of Boettger on November 9, 1972, Franklin Federal lost the man who had helped guide it through its early years.

A period of new growth began in 1973 as the board membership was increased, a parking lot was purchased, and two branch offices were opened. It also was the year the institution extended its influence into

The main headquarters of Franklin First Federal Savings and Loan Association is at 44 West Main Street, Wilkes-Barre.

The interior of Franklin First Federal Savings and Loan Association, Wilkes-Barre.

Columbia County with the acquisition of the Berwick Savings and Loan Association.

Less than three years after the creation of Franklin First Federal, the merged savings and loan association took over the operation of the First Federal Savings and Loan Association of Pittston, continuing the pattern of growth set by the parent institutions.

As the scope of service expands through the passage of new savings and loan association regulations, the officers and directors of Franklin First Federal face the future from the position of strength, rooted deep in the communities they serve.

This confidence in the future was exemplified by the institution's president, when he pointed out that during 1982 "... end-of-the-year assets ... showed a growth of 22.11 percent. Our savings depositors," Klimchak continued, "had an especially good year ... because we paid our depositors a record $36,452,436 in interest payments."

During the same period Franklin First Federal's mortgage portfolio increased 13.07 percent and reserves hit an all-time high of $21,036,280.

FIRST EASTERN CORP.

The merger of two downtown Wilkes-Barre banks in the 1950s produced a banking institution that has become an integral part of the Wyoming Valley, the Pocono Northeast, and Columbia County.

First Eastern Bank, N.A., a subsidiary of First Eastern Corp., marked its 120th anniversary in 1983, with assets of nearly one billion dollars, 1,000 employees, and 33 offices throughout Luzerne, Columbia, Lackawanna, and Monroe counties. The bank's continued growth in the 1980s follows a tradition established during the Civil War, when First Eastern's predecessors were founded.

One of the earliest national banks, First National Bank of Wilkes-Barre received Charter Number 30 on June 1, 1863, just four months after President Lincoln established the National Banking System. The original capital investment was $51,000, and the bank was located in the Chahoon

James McLean, first president of First National Bank of Wilkes-Barre, served from 1863 to 1864.

Thomas F. Atherton, first president of Second National Bank of Wilkes-Barre, served from 1863 to 1870.

Hall Building at 7-9 West Market Street. The bank's first president was James McLean.

First National experienced a slow but steady growth and on May 17, 1905, purchased property on the south side of Public Square for $146,000. The following year, on April 18, the construction of the bank building began, at a cost of $113,646. The building, opened on January 2, 1908, is still standing.

On October 14, 1929, William H.

Conyngham was elected president of the bank. He was to serve during the Depression and World War II periods, until his death on April 25, 1943. Conyngham guided the bank through this difficult time, which witnessed the stock market crash of 1929, the sharp decline of anthracite production, and widespread unemployment in the Wyoming Valley.

As the banking paralysis of the early Depression years spread throughout the country and as state after state established bank moratoria, a special meeting was held on March 8, 1933, concerning the Wilkes-Barre Clearing House Plan to issue Clearing House certificates covering authorized officers, pledges for collateral, application for certificates, and pledge agreements. This scrip was intended to be circulated as a medium of exchange during the bank crisis. However, on March 13, 1933, the Clearing House cancelled the plan, and scrip was never put into use in Luzerne County.

As banks struggled to maintain their assets, interest rates fell dramatically. By January 1, 1949, interest on savings accounts was down to one percent; on open accounts, it was three-quarters of one percent. However, First National

The Matheson Silent Six, manufactured in the Wyoming Valley. The advertisement appeared in the Board of Trade Journal *in 1911. The Matheson Motor Company, along with the F.M. Kirby Company, rented the entire top floor of the First Eastern Bank Building.*

The First National Bank Building, on the south side of Public Square, was occupied by the bank from 1876 to 1908.

Bank of Wilkes-Barre emerged from the Depression and World War II on a solid financial footing.

The development of Second National Bank of Wilkes-Barre nearly paralleled that of First National. It was chartered on September 19, 1863, five months after First National. Its original capital investment was $100,000 and it received Charter Number 104.

The first president was Thomas F. Atherton, who owned a store in Wyoming and was one of the first stockholders of the DL&W Railroad. One of the first directors of the bank was George Coray, the first student to register at Wyoming Seminary. Coray was later to serve a term in the state legislature from 1869 to 1870.

On October 27, 1864, the assets of the Susquehanna Bank were acquired by Second National Bank, in the first merger into what was to become First Eastern Corp.

Second National was a neighbor of First National in the Chahoon Building on West Market Street. The building was later occupied by N.P. Jordan, a men's clothing store, which was carried on by Harry E. Jordan and partners until 1958, when the building was acquired by the merged banks.

In the first years of its existence, Second National experienced a rapid growth as deposits rose from $11,783 on December 3, 1863, to more than $2 million by 1889. The growth of the bank forced expansion of the facilities and on December 22, 1904, land was purchased on the northeast corner of West Market and North Franklin

streets and an 11-story structure, costing $241,950, was erected. The completed building, including vault doors and a synchronized clock, cost $306,990. The entire top floor was leased to the F.M. Kirby Company and the Matheson Motor Car Company, a manufacturer of cars in the Wyoming Valley and a customer of the bank.

Second National experienced the same difficulties as other Wilkes-Barre banks during the stock market crash, and the minutes of the September 24, 1932, board of directors' meeting noted that the bank expressed its thanks to tellers, bookkeepers, and clerks for "the exceptional manner in which they performed their several duties under trying circumstances of recent days."

After World War II the first of several bank mergers took place, as Second National purchased the assets of First National Bank of Kingston on March 6, 1951.

Less than seven years later, on September 12, 1957, First National and Second National banks were formally consolidated to become the First-Second National Bank and Trust Company of Wilkes-Barre. Total assets of the newly merged banks were more than $57 million.

Thomas H. Kiley was elected president and was to serve in that capacity until being named chairman of the board and chief executive officer in December 1971. Maurice G. Shennan, who had been president of First National, was named chairman of the board.

During the early 1960s the bank made great strides in the computerization of bank operations, as well as in the opening of branch offices throughout the Wyoming Valley. In 1961 a Burroughs Visible Records Computer, the most advanced electronic equipment available at the time for the processing of bank transactions and the maintenance of records, was installed. At this time, First National was able to provide a

1908

1870

1864

1863

main office and at five branches. One of the bank's major problems was the restoration of data-processing operations on which Pennsylvania, New Jersey, and New York financial institutions were dependent.

The data-processing equipment was located on the third floor of the main office at 11 West Market Street and had not been affected by the flood. The problem, however, was a lack of electrical power, which was finally overcome through the leasing of one generator and the purchase of another. Employees from various correspondent banks came to Wilkes-Barre in those early clean-up days to process accounts when on-line operations failed. Limited telephone service was restored after the flood and operations began to return to normal.

The dedication plaque showing First National Bank of Wilkes-Barre as the 30th national bank organized in the United States.

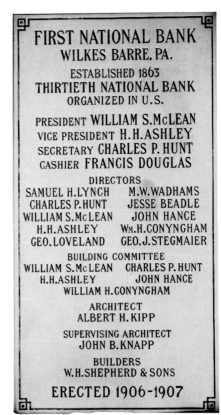

FIRST NATIONAL BANK
WILKES BARRE, PA.
ESTABLISHED 1863
THIRTIETH NATIONAL BANK
ORGANIZED IN U.S.

PRESIDENT WILLIAM S. McLEAN
VICE PRESIDENT H. H. ASHLEY
SECRETARY CHARLES P. HUNT
CASHIER FRANCIS DOUGLAS

DIRECTORS
SAMUEL H. LYNCH   M. W. WADHAMS
CHARLES P. HUNT   JESSE BEADLE
WILLIAM S. McLEAN   JOHN HANCE
H. H. ASHLEY   Wm. H. CONYNGHAM
GEO. LOVELAND   GEO. J. STEGMAIER

BUILDING COMMITTEE
WILLIAM S. McLEAN   CHARLES P. HUNT
H. H. ASHLEY   JOHN HANCE
WILLIAM H. CONYNGHAM

ARCHITECT
ALBERT H. KIPP

SUPERVISING ARCHITECT
JOHN B. KNAPP

BUILDERS
W. H. SHEPHERD & SONS

ERECTED 1906-1907

wide variety of services to correspondent banks in the area; by 1963, 39 area banks had established account relationships with First National.

During the 1960s and 1970s, the bank continued to grow with the acquisition of the White Haven Savings Bank in 1964, Conyngham National in 1966, First National of Bloomsburg in 1967, First-Stroudsburg National in 1971, and Berwick National in 1974. To more accurately describe the scope of the bank's operations, the name was changed on April 1, 1971, to The First National Bank of Eastern Pennsylvania.

The four buildings that housed the Second National Bank of Wilkes-Barre before its merger with First National Bank of Wilkes-Barre to become First Eastern Bank, N.A. The building at upper left was constructed in 1908 and is the main office of the bank today. It is located at 11 West Market Street, Wilkes-Barre.

With the promotion of Thomas H. Kiley to chairman of the board and chief executive officer late in 1971, Horace E. Kramer became the new president.

The flood resulting from Tropical Storm Agnes in June 1972 presented special challenges for First Eastern, which experienced flooding at the

Throughout this period, First National did not lose sight of the needs of its customers. Its attitude during the early days of the flood is best illustrated by an excerpt from a meeting held at the Dallas office. There was a huge demand for cash as merchants in areas not affected by the flood began running short of currency because of the disruption of normal banking procedures. It was at the meeting in Dallas that bank officials decided to cash checks in any reasonable amount. Bank chairman Thomas Kiley noted that in the emergency situation, "We are in no position to measure the needs of people . . . decisions by our people had to be made on the spot."

The year 1973 brought several major changes to First National. Effective June 1, Richard M. Ross, Jr., was to serve as president, while Horace E. Kramer was named vice-chairman of the board and chairman of the executive committee. Upon the retirement of Messrs. Kiley and Kramer the following year, Ross assumed the additional title of chief executive officer. In September the bank's Operations Center on South Washington Street, Wilkes-Barre, was opened.

Following the merger with Berwick National Bank in July 1974, the bank's name was changed to First Eastern Bank, N.A. First Eastern continued to grow throughout the 1970s and on September 19, 1980, acquired the South Side National Bank of Catawissa and North Scranton Bank and Trust Company.

A new decade saw other new and exciting directions at First Eastern. In 1980 it became the first financial institution in northeastern Pennsylvania to establish a Bond Dealer Department as part of its Investment Division. In 1981 the bank's common stock was included in the National Association of Securities Dealers Automated Quotation

(NASDAQ) System, which makes up-to-the-second quotations available to any brokerage firm in the nation. As a result of the affiliation with NASDAQ, First Eastern stock is listed in the *Wall Street Journal*, the *New York Times*, and other newspapers. Also in 1981, Keystone Equipment Leasing became a wholly owned subsidiary of First Eastern. Keystone leases a wide variety of equipment to businesses and industries and has offices in Scranton and Allentown. At the bank's annual meeting in April 1982, shareholders voted overwhelmingly to create a one-bank holding company, and the following August First Eastern Corp. became a reality. A discount brokerage service was established in 1983 and proved to be extremely popular with many self-directed investors. Discount brokerage offers customers fast, efficient service and saves them up to 70 percent in commissions.

By 1983 First Eastern served an area of 2,435 square miles and a population of more than 700,000 persons. It is the only bank in northeastern Pennsylvania to be ranked in *American Banker's* listing of the nation's top 300 correspondent banks of 1983, and provides a variety of services to more than 50 financial institutions.

From its beginning during the Civil War, through depression and flood, First Eastern has continued to grow and is facing the 21st century with optimism.

Bank notes were issued by First and Second National banks from 1929 to 1935.

The interior of First Eastern Bank's main office at 11 West Market Street, Wilkes-Barre, showing the lavish use of marble in the interior.

CORNELL IRON WORKS, INC.

A brass gate of the 1800s.

The name Cornell first became associated with iron and steel on July 19, 1828, when B. Birdsall announced in the *New York American* the sale of his iron works in Lower Manhattan to George Cornell and B. Althause, "... young men of tried integrity, industry, and capability."

One hundred and fifty-five years later Cornell Iron Works continues to prosper as a family-owned firm known for its excellence in the manufacture of rolling steel doors and grilles. Operating out of two plants, with a combined space of 125,000 square feet, the business reports annual sales of $10 million. Its average annual payroll for 110 employees exceeds $2 million.

Four generations of the Cornell family have continued to own and operate the firm, whose history has coincided with many of the historic events in our nation's history. While George Cornell is credited with the founding of the venture, his brother,

John Black Cornell, together with his son, John Milton, led the firm to prominence in the 1800s.

John Black Cornell was born in 1821 and entered the company at the age of 15. A noted businessman and inventor, he is credited with the invention of an improved method of street lighting in 1854 and was given the first U.S. patent for joining metal slats to produce revolving shutter windows and doors.

The firm made its mark in New York City as a manufacturer of iron safes in 1847. By 1859 J.B. & J.M.

Cornell had outgrown its small foundry on Centre Street and had built a larger and more modern foundry at West 26th Street, which enabled it to mold the big cast-iron building fronts for which it became famous.

During the Civil War, Cornell cast the turrets for the Ericsson Monitors that were to usher in the Age of the Iron Clads and change naval warfare.

Under J.B. and J.M. the firm continued to prosper and on July 1, 1897, Cornell acquired the West Point Foundry at Cold Spring, New York. The expansion to Cold Spring gave the Cornell firm an advantage over competition and it obtained contracts for structural work on the Astoria Hotel and the Park Row Building, which in 1898 was billed as "the tallest mercantile building ever erected." More than 8,000 tons of structural steel went into the facility.

As the manufacturing of steel and iron turned westward, Cornell experienced a loss in business. But it was J.B.'s patented rolling steel doors that were to save the company, and they continue today to be a popular product.

In 1965 Cornell relocated to the Crestwood Industrial Park at Mountaintop and has continued to grow and prosper, furnishing architectural and industrial closures to the construction industry. As it looks to the future, Cornell Iron Works remains committed to serving its customers and employees profitably.

Located in a shopping center, this modern security grille was manufactured by Cornell Iron Works in Mountaintop.

OFFSET PAPERBACK MFRS., INC.

Offset Paperback Mfrs., Inc., of Dallas, Pennsylvania, noted its 10th anniversary in 1982 as a successful business that in a few short years had grown to become the third largest paperback manufacturer in North America.

The phenomenal growth of the company is rooted in the dream of a Canadian, Saul Simkin of Winnipeg, Manitoba, who for reasons of health had moved to Phoenix, Arizona, in June 1965 and opened his own firm— Valley Paperback Manufacturers, Inc.—in the spring of 1966.

Simkin had been associated with Universal Printers Ltd. in Winnipeg, a company founded by his father in 1907 and known as one of the most successful firms in the Canadian paperback industry. He began his new venture with 30 employees. Within four years 120 workers were producing 50 million books each year.

Simkin sold his business to V.T.R., a New York-based conglomerate with diversified interests, in 1969. That same year the new owners moved the plant to Dallas to better serve their major eastern markets and, particularly, the New York publishers. This gave the firm the market advantage of an excellent highway

The 169,000-square-foot production plant and 100,000-square-foot on-track warehouse of Offset Paperback Mfrs., Inc., in Dallas, Pennsylvania, where 220 million paperbacks are printed each year.

The Offset plant in Dallas, Pennsylvania, is capable of meeting the demands of any customer from color cover printing to binding a 1,024-page book in paperback or digest format.

system that would reduce distribution costs.

Under the ownership of V.T.R., the company grew stagnant and the Simkin family, who had remained as consultants, became frustrated with the performance of the printing firm. In May 1972 Saul Simkin and a cousin, Abraham, repurchased the business and reorganized it under the name Offset Paperback Mfrs., Inc.

Simkin realized that future growth depended upon the introduction of offset printing if the company was to become a leader in paperback manufacturing. The transformation

was made and the new name, Offset Paperback Mfrs., Inc., was introduced.

Saul Simkin died in December 1975, but his dream lived on, as Offset continued to expand. Today it employs more than 400 persons printing some 220 million books with a payroll in excess of $4 million. Offsite facilities have been expanded to include a warehouse in Laflin and a distribution center at the Eastern Distribution Centre in Pittston Township.

In June 1982 Bertelsmann A.G. of Guetersloh, West Germany, the world's second-largest media company (outranked only by CBS in the United States), acquired a minority interest in Offset. This marriage of two family-owned operations ensures the continued growth of Offset as it moves into the 1980s guided by the experience and expertise of the 150-year-old international corporation.

SMITH, MILLER AND ASSOCIATES, INC.

Smith, Miller and Associates, Inc., with principal offices at 189 Market Street, Kingston, provides distinctive projects through design excellence.

From its beginning 30 years ago as a mechanical and electrical engineering firm, Smith, Miller and Associates, Inc. (SMA), has grown into a multi-discipline practice of architecture, landscape architecture, surveying, planning, project development, construction management, and structural, mechanical, electrical, civil, and sanitary engineering. Its more than 55 employees are responsible each year for between $15 million and $20 million worth of construction.

When the Agnes Flood ravaged the Wyoming Valley in 1972, SMA was one of the thousands of property owners who returned to find their buildings destroyed and possessions lost. Before the mud from the Susquehanna River was washed from the roads and streets, SMA raised a two-story office building and focused its efforts on flood recovery.

Beginning in 1972, SMA became involved in the area's redevelopment and urban renewal projects in the cities of Wilkes-Barre and Nanticoke and the boroughs of Forty Fort and Kingston. Some of the projects took a decade to complete.

The firm was established in 1953 by

Donald D. Smith, founder of Smith, Miller and Associates, Inc., of Kingston, Pennsylvania, stands behind a model of a Ecumenical Enterprises project in West Pittston.

Donald D. Smith, a professional engineer who worked for local design firms and served on the engineering faculty at the Wilkes-Barre Campus of the Pennsylvania State University.

The West Side Area Vocational Technical School in Pringle, Pennsylvania, was designed by Smith, Miller and Associates, Inc. During the Agnes Flood it served as one of the principal evacuee centers. The building is capable of supplying its own needs for heating, air conditioning, and electricity from natural gas.

Theodore S. Miller, a native of West Pittston and a distinguished architect, was a principal in the firm for 10 years before his death in 1978.

SMA is widely known for its expertise in the construction of school buildings, and one of its designs, the West Side Area Vocational Technical School, is supported by its own gas and electrical systems. Other schools designed by SMA include the Dallas Area Junior High School and the elementary and high school in the Lake Lehman School District.

SMA also has designed the geriatric campuses of Wesley Village in Jenkins Township and Ecumenical Enterprises' Meadows Campus in Dallas. The Meadows project is uniquely designed, consisting of 120 independent apartments and 120 intermediate/skilled nursing beds.

One of SMA's accomplishments was the rehabilitation of the Good Shepherd Lutheran Church on South Main Street, Wilkes-Barre. The structure, built in the mid-1800s, was damaged in the Agnes Flood and was totally restructured to today's access and space requirements.

The firm's work during the Agnes Flood recovery period attracted the attention of the Federal Emergency Management Agency. When Johnstown, Pennsylvania, and adjacent communities were

extensively damaged in the flood of 1977, SMA was recommended by the federal agency to assist in the recovery efforts. And, when Hurricane David hit Baltimore in 1979, SMA again was called upon to assist in the rebuilding efforts.

SMA has designed the headquarters of the National Society of Professional Engineers at Washington, D.C., and other structures in the northeastern United States, Dominican Republic, and Puerto Rico. One of its most recent projects was the design and rebuilding of the Harrisburg City Island, a multi-use recreational area complete with boat docks, pools, and other recreational facilities.

Donald Smith has continued to build SMA by focusing on client satisfaction and service. Relying principally on Pennsylvania State University for his staff, he has become widely recognized as an avid fan and supporter of the university and has become known as "Mr. Penn State of Wyoming Valley." The relationship between SMA and the university has continued to grow, with the firm completing more than 80 assignments.

These include the design of 17 buildings on its many campuses and the rehabilitation of the Hayfield House and conversion of the Conyngham Estate to university use at the Wilkes-Barre Campus.

SMA also has produced the master landscape plans for Bloomsburg and Kutztown state colleges.

In recent years SMA has met the demand for energy conservation through the development of a management team trained to assist clients in the reduction of soaring heating costs.

A special "Recovery Team" also has been created to respond immediately

Good Shepherd Lutheran Church, on South Main Street in Wilkes-Barre, was extensively damaged in the Agnes Flood. Built in the mid-1800s, it was totally restructured to today's needs by Smith, Miller and Associates, Inc.

to a disaster anywhere in the northeastern United States. The quick-response team is supported by personnel at the home office in Kingston.

The Meadows Campus, located in Dallas, Pennsylvania, is a uniquely designed project of Ecumenical Enterprises. The development provides housing and nursing care for the elderly.

DEEMER & COMPANY, INC.

Deemer & Company traces its origin to a partnership formed in 1905 between Harold D. Deemer of Wilkes-Barre and Philip Jaisohn of Philadelphia. Early in 1913 the partnership was dissolved with Deemer coming to Wilkes-Barre. He opened an office in the Second National Bank Building and in June 1913 he incorporated the business which carries his name.

A retail store was opened at 37 West Market Street in Wilkes-Barre and later moved to the Carpenter Building at 6 West Market Street in 1919. The company purchased this historic 96-year-old landmark in 1950 and the five-story structure served as Deemer's corporate headquarters until it was condemned in 1974 following the Agnes Flood. A retail walk-in store was opened in August of that year in the Wilkes-Barre Center complex. Corporate offices and warehousing facilities were moved to their present Kingston location at 251-255 Wyoming Avenue.

A second operation was opened in Scranton in 1916 on the sixth floor of the Scranton Life Building. The purchase of the stock of Shawger Brothers, a move to Linden Street in 1920 and a later move to its present location in 1928 at 209 North Washington Street, and the purchase of that structure in 1968 were symbolic of the firm's growth.

In 1924 the aggressive office products firm expanded into the city of Hazleton and located in the American Bank Building. Deemer & Company continues to operate a 4,000-square-foot office products store at 26 North Laurel Street today.

August 1965 saw the Paul Cook Supply Shop merged into the Deemer

---

During the 1930s these well-known Derby desks, distributed by Deemer & Company, were on display at the firm's Wilkes-Barre office. Today the organization is among the nation's top 15 percent of suppliers of office products and equipment.

operation. The Cook, Scovill, and Martin buildings were acquired by Deemer to house its expanding operations.

Chief executives over the years in addition to Harold Deemer were Charles W. Honeywell of Wilkes-Barre; Herman B. DeWitt, Forty Fort; George W. Miller, Conyngham; and presently, Donald L. Honeywell, Wilkes-Barre.

Today the Deemer organization employs 40 people and its sales are in the millions of dollars. Probably more offices have been installed and supplied by the Deemer firm over its 70 years than by any other in northeastern Pennsylvania. In addition to its office-furnishings expertise, tons of office supplies head out of Deemer locations every week to offices and industry. To maintain its leadership position, the firm has recently begun furnishing supplies and equipment for the rapidly emerging word-processing and computer industries.

BERGMAN'S DEPARTMENT STORE

When the flood waters of Agnes poured over the dikes surrounding the Narrows Shopping Center in Edwardsville on June 23, 1972, Bergman's Department Store was totally destroyed, sustaining losses of more than $1.3 million.

Bergman's stands as a monument to a family that refused to permit the muck and grime of the Susquehanna River to bury its business, and today continues as one of the Wyoming Valley's leading merchandisers of men's and women's ready-to-wear.

Former president Seymour A. Dimond, son-in-law of Charles Pfifferling who was one of the original founders, recalls that the months following the flood were difficult. "Without the help of our employees, vendors, and customers we would not have been able to reopen nine months later.

"One of the most amazing things in that difficult time was our customers," he says. "When we reopened in March 1973, 95 percent of our charge-customers were paid in full. Many of our customers had suffered a great loss during the flood, but not one tried to take advantage of the situation. It is a tribute to the character of the people of the Wyoming Valley."

Dimond also is proud of his employees, many of whom have been with the 67-year-old firm for 35 to 60 years.

It was on April 16, 1916, that Justin Bergman of Johnstown, Pennsylvania, opened Bergman's Department Store on South Main Street, Wilkes-Barre, naming his brother-in-law, Charles Pfifferling, as general manager.

The store was an immediate success and by 1920 occupied five floors of its building in central Wilkes-Barre. In 1948 a continued growth in business was marked by the lease of an adjacent building and the remodeling of the two structures.

Upon the death of Pfifferling in November 1955, Bergman continued

Seymour A. Dimond, former president of Bergman's Department Store, discusses merchandise with Margaret Carmody. She has worked for the firm for over 50 years, first as a clerk and then as confidential secretary.

to operate the business with the assistance of Seymour A. Dimond, Pfifferling's son-in-law, who had come into the business in 1938.

With the death of Bergman in July 1960, control of the partnership passed to Dimond, Justin Bergman, Jr., and Charles Pfifferling, Jr. These men were admitted into the partnership following World War II and A. John Dimond, the current president, was made a partner in 1968.

In 1959 the store made a daring move and crossed the river moving into its present facility. The store's growth continued and in 1968 it took over the two adjacent buildings, giving it 32,000 square feet of selling space on one floor.

In March 1973 the store reopened as a corporation with Seymour A. Dimond as president and his son, A. John Dimond, as vice-president.

Seymour Dimond retired from active management in 1975 and his son became president of the corporation. Under the guidance of John Dimond the firm continued to grow and in 1979 underwent a complete remodeling.

Today the business employs more than 100 persons and is one of the few stores in the Wilkes-Barre/Scranton/Hazleton area that is still family owned and operated.

A. John Dimond points out that through the years Bergman's "has continued to grow by providing the same customer service and quality merchandise that was the policy when the doors were opened in 1916."

Bergman's Department Store, Narrows Shopping Center, Edwardsville.

DIAMOND MANUFACTURING COMPANY

The history of Diamond Manufacturing Company is the story of two men and a woman who refused to admit failure and through their entrepreneurial spirit built an organization upon the ashes of the Exeter Machine Shops.

It is the story of John Newton Thomas, who founded the firm in 1915, Nellie Corcoran, and William Powell, son-in-law of Thomas, under whose management the business grew and prospered until today it has become the nation's technological leader in the perforation of steel.

Today Diamond purchases more than 50 million pounds of steel each year from U.S. companies and employs more than 155 workers in its computerized plants at Wyoming and Fort Worth, Texas. If you own a washer, dryer, refrigerator, personal computer, or air conditioning unit, chances are that your product has a part manufactured by Diamond.

The company also is the number one supplier of perforated metal for the chemical industry, in production of perforated ceiling and wall panels necessary for noise and acoustical controls, in sound-suppression

---

An old hand-operated perforating machine used in the early days at Diamond Manufacturing Company. Today the firm's plants are computerized.

systems for the aircraft industry, and in truck mufflers.

A large portion of Diamond's history is taken from the papers of Nellie Corcoran, who came to work for Thomas in 1916 and stayed to manage the firm for two years upon his death in 1920. She retired in 1962.

John Newton Thomas came to the Wilkes-Barre area from Minersville and, after a period as a cracker salesman, joined his uncle W.Y. Thomas in the operation of a small shop in West Pittston producing oil cups for the mine companies.

Upon the death of his uncle, Thomas acquired the business and through the years guided its growth. Over-expansion and diversification into risky new areas of manufacturing led to a debt load that eventually brought the firm to the point of financial collapse.

During the operation of the Exeter company, Thomas had opened a small perforating plant in hopes of entering the profitable field of perforated screens used in the mines to size the coal. Named Diamond Manufacturing Company, it survived the financial disaster of the Exeter Machine Shops. Diamond was first located in a building that was little more than a shed. With the collapse of the Exeter Machine Shops, Thomas was forced to move his shed, stock, and few pieces of

machinery to the present site of the firm on Eighth Street, Wyoming.

Thomas was 58 when he began building Diamond Manufacturing Company, an age when most men are looking forward to retirement. The road to success was long and hard, with many pitfalls inherent in a new business and in an infant industry. The perforation of metal was an unscientific business, cornered by a few firms with closely guarded secrets of the process. Thomas was forced to learn the process by trial and error.

The pressure to make the foundry and perforating shops a success took its toll and Thomas died at 62. Nellie Corcoran wrote, "The life of one of the most courageous businessmen of that era came to a close. His great spirit of courage and optimism and friendly personality I have never since seen contained in one person."

For the next two years, until William Powell married Thomas' daughter Janet in 1923, Nellie Corcoran kept the company alive. Her notes of those two years give an insight into an industrial period that has long been forgotten.

She writes of the Alan Wood Iron and Steel Co. of Philadelphia, to whom Diamond owed more than $9,000. According to her records the firm waited for over two weeks following the death of Thomas before it sent a Mr. Milliken to press for payment. She met with Mr. Milliken, "a very handsome Quaker gentleman," and told him she couldn't make any decisions until after the company's "tea party," which was the name given to the meetings between herself, Mrs. Thomas, and Janet.

After hearing of the financial problems of the firm, Milliken told her, "Do what you can, but don't worry." A few days later a package arrived from a Philadelphia delicatessen with four different brands of tea.

It was this type of faith and trust in a struggling company that gave Powell

A modern computer panel, which controls the perforating machinery in Diamond Manufacturing Company's plants at Wyoming, Pennsylvania, and Fort Worth, Texas.

the opportunity to build Diamond's financial position when he took over in 1923—giving up a secure future in mining to run his own business. Powell continued to manage the firm until his death in 1951. During his tenure he improved the financial base of the company and put Diamond on a solid financial footing.

The business was taken over by David Hall in 1951, husband of Marian Powell. Hall, as president and general manager, continued to move Diamond into the use of lighter metals, a move begun by his predecessor. When Hall left the business in 1959,

Diamond Manufacturing Company's modern computerized perforating plant at Fort Worth, Texas.

Frank Foster stepped in to manage the firm. Foster left Diamond in 1962 and Joan Powell's husband, Charles Flack, took over the president's position.

Flack steered Diamond through the '60s and '70s, making massive equipment changes and seeking new markets that were opening in the American economy. He led the firm into the aircraft appliance, and air and water pollution-control businesses, and into the growing field of noise and acoustical controls. Working with perforating machine manufacturers in Germany, Flack assisted in the development of new steel-feed systems and the growing computerization of the perforating industry.

It was during his tenure as president that the firm provided the steel for the domes of the Pittsburgh Civic Center and the Astrodome in Texas. It also was during this period that Diamond's leadership in the production of perforated steel for noise and acoustical control was noted and the

company produced the materials needed for the acoustical chambers housing the pumping equipment along the Alaskan Pipeline.

With Flack's death in 1979, the presidency passed to his son, Charles Jr., a 24-year-old economics graduate of Susquehanna University. Charles Jr. began working at odd jobs around the plant when he was 12. After entering college, he returned each summer to the plant and after graduation worked in the quality-control and production departments.

Under his guidance Diamond entered the '80s by building a completely computerized plant at Fort Worth and establishing itself as a leader in the industry.

The Lone Star Perforating Company is managed by Harold E. Flack II, Charles' 24-year-old brother. In 1983 the plant size was almost doubled as an 18,000-square-foot addition was constructed to meet the growing demand for perforated steel in the Southwest.

The firm continues as a closed corporation with stock owned by family members. It is guided by a board of five directors: Mrs. Thomas Robinson and Mrs. Charles Flack, Sr., daughters of William Powell; Charles Flack, Jr.; Thomas B. Robinson; and Joseph P. O'Connor, vice-president/finance.

WASSEROTT'S

In business for 59 years, Wasserott's Service has grown since the spring of 1976 to become the largest supplier of home-care medical equipment in northeastern Pennsylvania.

Located on the Luzerne-Dallas Highway, the firm serves its customers with 80 employees and a fleet of 32 vehicles. The highly trained staff numbers registered nurses and emergency medical technicians as well as college graduates. The family-owned enterprise is one of the fastest-growing businesses in the Wyoming Valley and is recognized nationally within the home-care health field.

Paul D. Wasserott, Jr., son of the founder, is a director of the Pennsylvania Association of Medical Suppliers and the Health Industries Distributors' Association.

The history of Wasserott's is the story of two firms. One began in 1924 by Paul D. Wasserott, Sr., his wife, Laura, and his brother.

They opened a surgical instrument, hospital, and physician's equipment and supply business at 55 South Washington Street, Wilkes-Barre, under the name of Wasserott Brothers and Company. The venture survives today as Wasserott's Inc.

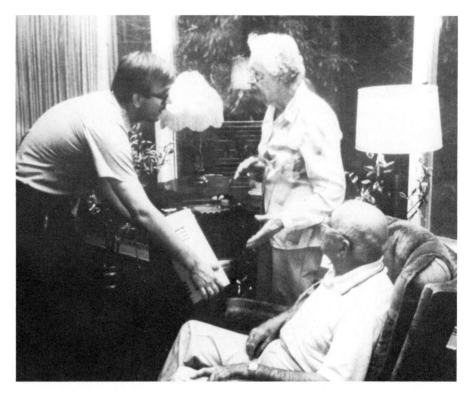

The second firm was incorporated as Wasserott's Medicare Service in the spring of 1976, when the family realized the area needed a dealer who

Wasserott's medical equipment technicians undergo extensive training to qualify for service to the firm's customers.

One of the nurses on Wasserott's Medicare Service staff instructs a mother in the use of home-care medical equipment.

could supply home-care medical equipment to the homebound patient. Within a few short years this company would be the mainstay of the Wasserott family's business.

In 1950 Wasserott's moved from Wilkes-Barre to Kingston, where the firm constructed a larger, two-story showroom. The facility sustained $250,000 damage in the Agnes Flood of 1972 and business had to be conducted from the second story while the damage was repaired.

Wasserott's Medicare Service outgrew the building in Kingston in 1978 and moved to its present headquarters on the Luzerne-Dallas Highway.

Wasserott's Medicare Service maintains a rental inventory of $3 million and a merchandise inventory of $500,000. The entire operation has been computerized as the firm prepares for the 1980s.

VALLEY AUTOMOBILE CLUB

"The purpose for which the corporation is formed is the maintenance of a Club for social enjoyment, the promotion of motoring, and to promote, aid, and support the movement for the improvement of highways."

These aims of the Valley Automobile Club were contained in its petition for incorporation to Judge George S. Ferris in the Court of Common Pleas in Luzerne County on May 8, 1908.

The original club was named the Wilkes-Barre Automobile Club and the five men who signed the incorporation papers were George F. Lee of Dorranceton, who became its president; Lyman H. Howe, vice-president; E.C. Wagner, secretary/treasurer; and W.E. Steelman and P.A. Meixell, governors.

The club's name was changed to the Wyoming Valley Motor Club in 1959 and in 1965, the Wyoming Valley Motor Club merged with the Columbia-Montour Motor Club which resulted in another name change to The Valley Automobile Club. The local club is one of more than 230 clubs nationwide with over

900 offices that are affiliated with the American Automobile Association.

Besides Lee, only five members have served as president of the club in its more than 75 years of history: E.L. Lindemuth, Peter G. Rimmer, Edward Eyerman, Sr., Senator Andrew J. Sordoni, and Aldo Franconi, who has held the post since 1963.

The club employs 33 persons at its headquarters at 100 Hazle Street, Wilkes-Barre, and its office at 128 West Main Street, Bloomsburg.

More than 44,000 persons, or more than 25 percent of passenger registrations in Luzerne, Columbia, and Montour counties, are members of the organization.

The club offers a wide variety of service to its members, including emergency road service, bail and arrest bonds, road and weather reports, notary, license, and title services. In 1983 over 17,000 members availed themselves of the emergency service. A total of 16,674 members sought the club's help in planning a trip, including personalized travel routing, reservations, and tour books.

The Valley Automobile Club and its parent organization, the AAA,

together operate the largest travel agency in the world. The club can arrange travel by plane, ship, and rail. It also can take care of details such as customs, immigration regulations, passport assistance, tours, hotel reservations, and traveler's checks.

Personal accident and travel insurance, including baggage, flight, and trip cancellation and interruption, are available from the club as well.

In its support of the community and motoring safety, the Valley Automobile Club conducts programs in schools, issues safety posters and lesson plans, and organizes safety patrols and equips them with badges and belts. In conjunction with its parent organization the club maintains and loans a safety film library; provides traffic, pedestrian, and bicycle safety programs; and offers an infant-restraint loan program.

The Valley Automobile Club, an affiliate of the American Automobile Association (AAA), has a membership of more than 25 percent of passenger registrations in Luzerne, Columbia, and Montour counties.

NPW MEDICAL CENTER

With the opening of the NPW Medical Center in Plains Township on April 20, 1981, the work of 14 years was completed and a new era in medical service was ushered in for the more than 300,000 persons in the greater Wilkes-Barre area and the Western Poconos.

The 230-bed hospital is situated on a 172-acre site, four miles from central Wilkes-Barre and within one-half hour's driving time of communities in the Back Mountain, Nanticoke, and Pittston via routes 309 and 315. Interstate 81 and the Pennsylvania Turnpike, with exchanges to Route 115, provide access to the hospital for the Western Poconos.

NPW is the only hospital in the Greater Wilkes-Barre area with a helipad within 150 feet of the emergency center. Special lighting enables night landings with complete safety for the helicopter crew and the patient.

A psychiatric unit is the only hospital-based private facility in northeastern Pennsylvania offering short-term voluntary inpatient care for adults experiencing serious emotional distress.

The outpatient physical therapy and occupational therapy unit is the most modern in the area. Unique to its design is a "daily living area" which features an actual kitchen, living room, bedroom, and bathroom where patients relearn basic skills lost through accident or sickness.

The 230-bed NPW Medical Center in Plains Township— the Wyoming Valley's newest hospital.

Specialty areas include sections designed for sports medicine, prosthetic orthotic service, and a modality-treatment area. Specialties include stroke rehabilitation programs and a chronic-pain treatment center.

Of the hospital's 230 beds, 136 are dedicated to medical surgical patients. Twenty-bed specialty units are reserved for obstetrics/gynecology,

This is the Pittston Hospital as it appeared on November 1, 1893. The building was replaced in 1927 after $300,000 was raised through public subscription. The first hospital was opened with 32 beds restricted for the care of miners.

pediatrics, and rehabilitation, with 18 beds in the psychiatric unit. A 16-bed unit in the ancillary building serves as an intensive-care unit and cardiac-care facility containing the most modern monitoring equipment necessary for the seriously ill or injured.

Diagnostic imaging and radiology services, including CAT scanning, ultrasound, and nuclear medicine, back up the four major operating suites, which include a special holding area for one-day surgery procedures, a recovery room, and a cystoscopy room.

The hospital is supported by a staff of approximately 200 physicians and more than 800 employees. Its opening created 250 additional jobs in the Wyoming Valley. The annual payroll exceeds $11 million in wages and benefits.

In keeping with its role as a community hospital, NPW has a special maternity service developed

around the entire family. Prenatal classes are held for the expectant mother and father, as well as siblings.

The hospital's commitment to community service includes fall and spring health seminars, a speakers' bureau, baby-sitting classes, preoperative teaching, and an elementary school tour program. Each year a health run is held at the center. Hundreds of runners turn out for the three-mile event and displays are developed to teach the public of the importance of physical fitness.

While the NPW facility may be new, its history is rooted in the Pittston Hospital, which opened its doors for patients on November 1, 1893, and the Wyoming Valley Homeopathic Hospital, which was opened by five physicians on June 5, 1911. The original Pittston Hospital was a two-story structure with 32 beds and admissions restricted to miners. The staff was comprised of three nurses and two graduate nurses. In those days physicians made their rounds by horse and buggy or on bicycle, and the hospital fee was one dollar a day. To feed patients and supplement the hospital's income, a farm was cultivated and by 1903 had a population of 12 cows, 12 pigs, and 2,000 chickens.

In 1903 a school of nursing was opened which still operates today under the NPW banner. The school is the lone surviving diploma awarding nursing school in the Wyoming Valley and has graduated more than 1,000 nurses, many of whom continue to practice in hospitals throughout northeastern Pennsylvania.

The Wyoming Valley Homeopathic Hospital opened in 1911 as a public charity with a free dispensary, 23 beds for charity patients, and one private and two semiprivate rooms for men and women. The original hospital, located in the Burgunder Mansion at 149 Dana Street, was purchased by the founding doctors: J.A. Bullard, Robert

The Wyoming Valley Homeopathic Hospital as it looked when dedicated on June 5, 1911, as a public charity.

Murdock, D.S. Kistler, A.D. Thomas, and E.H. Hill.

During its first year 267 patients were treated. By 1950 the hospital had grown to a modern, 100-bed health-care facility. It was the need to expand the hospital in 1967 that led to the formation of the NPW Medical Center. A long-range planning committee of the hospital reported after a feasibility study that future on-site expansion was "economically inappropriate."

The idea for a regional health-care campus was born and the Greater Wilkes-Barre Industrial Fund agreed to assist in the selection of a site.

The Agnes Flood disrupted plans for the hospital and it was not until three years later that the two hospitals, along with the Nanticoke State General Hospital, formed a planning commission to revive the plan for a

regional center. The three hospitals shared common problems: They were small, with aging facilities. In 1977 the plan received another setback when the Nanticoke hospital dropped out of the trio, leaving only Pittston and Wyoming Valley.

Approval for the construction of the new facility was received on July 26, 1977, from the state and the U.S. Department of Health, Education and Welfare. On October 9, 1978, a management agreement was signed with the Geisinger Medical Management Corporation, a subsidiary of the Geisinger Medical Center of Danville.

Geisinger Medical Center later was to guarantee the financing of NPW and construction began on March 1, 1979. Today NPW is an entity of the Geisinger System and, as a member of the multi-hospital system, can draw quickly upon the sophisticated resources of the medical center at Danville and also the Geisinger Foundation.

SUSQUEHANNA SAVINGS
A DIVISION OF ATLANTIC FINANCIAL FEDERAL

The Susquehanna Building and Loan Association was chartered in 1928 by the Commonwealth of Pennsylvania. However, it was not until 1944 that events began to take place which assured that Susquehanna would fulfill the intent of its charter. These actions, spurred by attorney Joseph Serling, were directly responsible for the beginnings of the establishment of a deposit base and the opening of a one-room, one-person public office facility. Later that same year, Susquehanna's corporate name was changed to Susquehanna Savings and Loan Association of Wilkes-Barre.

From this humble beginning, Susquehanna Savings has grown over the years to where today it employs over 100 people. Through its eight-office network, Susquehanna provides quality savings and lending programs to the people of northeastern Pennsylvania.

Susquehanna Savings introduced state-of-the-art banking to Wilkes-Barre on September 6, 1983, with the grand opening of northeastern Pennsylvania's first "Financial Service Center."

Susquehanna Savings, through the aggressive posture established by its current president, Joseph J. Olshefski, has earned a position of leadership within the local financial community. In addition, broad public acceptance has resulted because of Susquehanna's timely delivery of consumer-oriented services, such as the first financial institution locally to introduce a telephone bill-paying service; the first locally to establish a business telephone transfer account; the only local financial institution currently offering a free checking-with-interest account which does not require a specific balance or assess service charges; and the only local financial institution currently offering a $100 minimum deposit savings certificate.

To quote Joseph Olshefski, "We at Susquehanna Savings take quite seriously our responsibility to present quality products, fairly priced, which satisfy the needs of the people that we serve." Indeed, Susquehanna has established an enviable and honored record of service during its first 55 years of existence. However, it is the future that holds the highest

expectations.

Susquehanna Savings' parent firm, Atlantic Financial Federal, was formed in May 1982 through the joining together of four Pennsylvania savings and loan associations: Community Federal Savings and East Girard Savings in Philadelphia, and Greensburg Savings and First State Savings in the greater Pittsburgh area. Its purpose was to establish a management services corporation that would permit the rapidly changing and complex world of service delivery to be harnessed and directed as a positive force in tomorrow's competitive financial environment. Its unique divisional concept assured local autonomy along with local management direction and control.

In the ensuing 12 months, six other savings associations, including Susquehanna Savings, joined Atlantic Financial Federal forming Pennsylvania's first federally chartered statewide savings and loan association. Today Atlantic Financial Federal, with over 75 offices statewide and total assets exceeding $2.5 billion, ranks first in Pennsylvania among thrift institutions and 40th nationally.

Susquehanna Savings, since its alignment with Atlantic Financial Federal on August 2, 1982, has continued its already-established growth pattern. All existing savings growth and mortgage lending records have been reestablished. In 1982 Susquehanna saw its total savings deposits grow from $153 million to approximately $180 million, an increase of $27 million. This outstanding annual growth established a new all-time high. As of August 30, 1983, an increase exceeding $20 million has already been recorded, with an additional $10 million predicted by year's end.

On the lending side of the ledger, in 1982, Atlantic Financial Federal provided Susquehanna Savings with the lowest mortgage loan rates seen in the area in over two years. As a result, Susquehanna Savings was forced to expand its lending area and internal operations to meet the demands of the marketplace.

During the first eight months of 1983, Susquehanna underwrote single-family housing loans exceeding $28 million. This amount already surpasses any previous yearly totals. A monthly performance record was set

Shown here are Joseph J. Olshefski, president of Susquehanna Savings Division (left), and Raymond F. Strecker, president of Atlantic Financial Federal.

in May 1983, with 141 mortgage loans granted (totaling approximately $5.8 million). Thus far, Atlantic Financial Federal has invested some $8 million above and beyond Susquehanna's savings growth of $20 million in the local mortgage market. This financial support best exemplifies the strength and diversity of market which Atlantic Financial Federal brings to the competitive financial arena.

Susquehanna Savings is indeed proud of these mortgage loan performance records. However, greater satisfaction is derived from the knowledge that it has assisted many

area residents in making the dream of home ownership a reality.

An event of significant interest to all Wilkes-Barre residents took place on Tuesday, September 6, 1983. For it was on this memorable day that Susquehanna opened its world-class "Financial Service Center," on Public Square. This state-of-the-art banking facility represents Atlantic Financial Federal's first expansion effort. In addition, its design invites a futuristic look at the direction being taken by a financial institution that cares enough to maintain a high degree of personal banking service.

Atlantic Financial Federal, penned as a "thrift model for the future," received approval from the Federal Home Loan Bank Board in July 1983 to convert its corporate operations from a mutual savings and loan to a public stock savings and loan association. Additionally, Raymond F. Strecker, president of Atlantic Financial Federal, announced recently that the Susquehanna Savings Division has been selected to introduce ShareAmerica during the last quarter of 1983. ShareAmerica, affiliated with Atlantic Financial Federal, initially will be launched as a discount brokerage operation. However, plans have already been set to establish ShareAmerica as a full-service brokerage firm in the near future.

Susquehanna Savings, A Division of Atlantic Financial Federal, under the management of its president, Joseph Olshefski, is and will remain a positive force within the local financial community.

Atlantic Financial Federal, a financial organization which has accepted the challenges of today, looks to the future with confidence, through the leadership provided by Raymond F. Strecker, president and chief executive officer; Donald R. Caldwell, executive vice-president and chief operations officer; and Calvin D. Baker, chairman of the board.

MERCY HOSPITAL OF WILKES-BARRE

March 7, 1898, marked the official opening of the Mercy Hospital of Wilkes-Barre under the management of the Religious Sisters of Mercy, invited by seven local physicians to provide immediate care for coal miners in an area of the city where no health care facilities existed. Today, 85 years later, the Mercy Hospital of Wilkes-Barre stands on almost exactly the same spot and serves the city of Wilkes-Barre and the Wyoming Valley, providing a wide range of services for those in need.

The year 1900 saw the first graduates of the Mercy School of Nursing which for three-quarters of a century produced qualified registered nurses annually, nurses whose return of services to the local community has helped to improve the level of wellness in the entire Valley.

From the very beginning the Sisters of Mercy directed the affairs of the hospital, serving in many capacities but especially as highly qualified administrators. Early records show that concern for the health care needs of local residents was the primary reason for establishing the 55-bed hospital. Each succeeding year demonstrated the depth of that Mercy commitment as the hospital expanded its services and its facilities to the present day 300-bed structure with adjoining medical offices and parking facilities.

Free services, free nursing care, even free medical supplies characterized the beginnings of the institution from 1898 until 1911, when it became evident that voluntary contributions were an uncertain and insufficient method of business for a fast-growing hospital.

The famous Anthracite Coal Strike of 1902 caused the first serious maintenance deficit, making apparent the need for more space and more stable financing. The original building, therefore, was enlarged and remodeled in 1904, modernized in 1912, and

Sister Miriam Ruth Brennan, RSM, president of Mercy Hospital, and Joseph C. Williams, chairman of the board of directors, discuss future plans for the medical facility.

These photographs illustrate the development of Mercy Hospital from its first structure in 1898 to the modern 300-bed facility of today.

added on to in 1927, as increasing health care needs through the years demanded new or expanded services. The largest extension, however, was in 1961, when the "x"-shaped building on Church Street provided major service areas for a 200-bed facility. Two additional floors, added in 1981, helped to expand services for the 300 beds now in use.

In 1983, to provide comprehensive medical services to an expanded geographic area, Mercy began construction of a satellite medical center in Dallas, Pennsylvania. The new clinic will initially accommodate two general practitioners and a pediatrician. The center's existence will make available for Back Mountain residents quality health care including complete physical therapy, laboratory, and X-ray services.

Three times in 75 years the Susquehanna River overflowed its banks and flooded South Wilkes-Barre. In 1936 Mercy's ground floor had to be

renovated; in 1940 another flood occurred, but normal hospital routine was not interrupted. But in 1972, Hurricane Agnes damaged Mercy's ground floor and first floor, as well as the nurses' residence, to the extent of $6 million. When the hospital reopened on August 20, 1972, the slow, discouraging work of cleaning began. With the help of planners, architects, building engineers, and construction crews, Mercy made a remarkable recovery. The understanding, dedication, and service of patients, personnel, and the general

public has renewed the spirit that has characterized Mercy for almost a century.

Mercy Hospital today stands impressively large and modern; its services are sophisticated and innovative and its buildings continually expand to contain and provide those services. But most of all, Mercy personnel embody the hospital's motto, "Scientia et Compassio," Knowledge and Compassion, in the service of the sick and needy.

One hundred and fifty years ago Catherine McAuley, foundress of the Religious Sisters of Mercy, walked the streets of Dublin, looking for the sick and needy in order to help them for the sake of Christ. Today the Religious Sisters of Mercy carry on her work in modern ways: Doctors, personnel, and patients have come to Mercy to provide real healing. "Scientia et Compassio" is, therefore, more than a motto on a heraldic device: it is the deep philosophy of this entire organization; it is the Christian commitment to heal all persons with knowledge and merciful compassion.

Future services at the Mercy Hospital of Wilkes-Barre have already begun in the identification of future needs, in the present commitment to far-reaching programs of preventing illnesses and maintaining levels of wellness.

One of 120 health care facilities sponsored by the Religious Sisters of Mercy throughout America, Mercy Hospital plays a major role in future planning for future service. Mercy's current involvement in the restructuring of the larger Mercy Health Corporation places this hospital at the vital center of a network of available resources in administration, skills, services, and personnel training. "Knowledge and Compassion" together form objectives that identify a hospital dedicated to service by means of Mercy.

THE PRESSED STEEL COMPANY

The Pressed Steel Company of Wilkes-Barre was organized in 1909 with the aim not to be the "largest handlers of drawn metal. Instead, our one purpose . . . has been specialization and accuracy."

Today the third generation of the family-owned firm continues to operate in this tradition, turning out products that are known worldwide for their quality and fine workmanship.

Pressed Steel was established originally as the Dion Manufacturing Company and produced water filters. The firm was purchased in November 1909 by C.B.D. Wood, who renamed it the Wilkes-Barre Metal Drawing and Stamping Co.

On January 2, 1912, Pressed Steel was incorporated and purchased the assets of the Wilkes-Barre Metal Drawing and Stamping Co.

C.B.D. Wood continued to operate the business until his death in 1941. Its operation was passed on to his son, T.N. Wood, who was well known in the area, having served as a Luzerne County commissioner and as a Pennsylvania state senator. Upon his death in 1982 his son, T.N. (Mike) Wood, Jr., became the president of the firm.

Since its inception Pressed Steel has owned and operated a plant on North Pennsylvania Avenue consisting of press, welding, and fabricating shops.

The principal products are seamless steel cap and neck rings for compressed gas cylinders; heat-treating equipment, such as carburizing and annealing boxes, thermocouple protection tubes, radiant tubes, inner covers and base sheaths for steel mills, and welded alloy tubing for high-temperature and corrosive application; bubble caps for fractionating towers; and stainless steel specialty products for various industries.

Pressed Steel has pioneered in lightweight welded alloy units which

have produced savings for industry by lowering fuel, labor, space, and replacement costs.

In 1922 the firm made the first stainless steel container for the shipping and storage of nitric acid and

Employees of the Pressed Steel Company stand beside the huge press that bends steel for use in the firm's manufacturing process.

later it developed the first light-alloy heating equipment.

Pressed Steel's work today consists of custom-made industrial products. Mainstays for the firm are bubble cap assemblies for fractionating towers

This is a tapper built by the company to thread the cylinder caps. The machine automatically threads four caps at a time.

A worker grinds a joint in preparation for making a stainless steel tube section.

and stills, seamless drawn cylinder caps and collars for compressed gas cylinders (which it has been making since 1922), and various fabricated items for the heat treating of metals.

In recent years Pressed Steel has shipped their products to countries throughout the world, including Peru, England, India, and Germany.

The Pressed Steel Company has gross sales of $2.5 million to $3 million a year, and employs 50 skilled workers, many of whom have been with the firm for more than 30 years.

In spite of poor economic conditions and competition from Japanese firms, the company continues to maintain the quality of its products and services.

Two workmen for Pressed Steel inspect the press that draws steel into cylinder caps.

NORTHEASTERN BANK OF PENNSYLVANIA

The downtown Wilkes-Barre office of Northeastern Bank of Pennsylvania.

On December 31, 1982, the eve of its 120th year, Northeastern Bank of Pennsylvania became the first financial institution in the Pocono Northeast to exceed assets of more than one billion dollars.

Northeastern was established as a national bank in 1863 as the First National Bank of Scranton, receiving Charter No. 77. The bank's total assets on its first day of business were $200,000.

Joseph H. Scranton, president of Lackawanna Iron & Coal Co., was elected the bank's first president. Other founding directors of the new institution were Thomas Dickson, who later became president of the D&H Railroad; John Brislin, who later became president of the DL&W

Railroad; Joseph J. Albright, founder of the Dickson Manufacturing Co.; and Joseph C. Platt, superintendent of the Lackawanna Iron & Coal Co.

The bank continued to grow, and it weathered the Great Depression by taking over two banks which could not survive. In 1956 First National merged with the Scranton Lackawanna Trust Co., bringing to eight the financial institutions in Lackawanna County acquired since 1915.

The bank underwent a name change in that year. And, within two years, it became a regional bank with the acquisition of the Markle Banking & Trust Co. in Hazleton and the Wilkes-Barre Deposit and Savings Bank in Wilkes-Barre. This change to a regional banking institution prompted a name change to reflect the scope of the bank's operations.

The new name was Northeastern

Pennsylvania National Bank & Trust Co. From 1958 to 1974 the name underwent two other name changes, to finally emerge as Northeastern Bank of Pennsylvania when the board of directors voted to convert to a state bank.

Northeastern Bancorp Inc. was incorporated under Pennsylvania laws in 1981 and became the sole stockholder of the bank under the Bank Holding Company Act of 1956.

The company entered the credit life and accident and health reinsurance business in 1982 through Norbanc Life Insurance Co. It also services both existing and new customers through the Pennsylvania Trust Company of Florida, N.A., headquartered in Vero Beach, Florida. Early in 1983 Northeastern Bank entered the leasing business through Norbanc Lease Inc.

In late 1982 it was announced that the boards of directors of Northeastern Bancorp Inc. and Cement National Bank, of Northampton, Pennsylvania, had agreed to the combination of the two banking organizations. Cement National continues to operate as a subsidiary of the company, serving the counties of Northampton, Lehigh, and Carbon.

Northeastern Bank, the concern's principal subsidiary, as of December 31, 1982, was the 189th-largest bank in the United States, the 15th-largest bank in the Commonwealth of Pennsylvania, and the largest in the Pocono Northeast as measured by total deposits.

Northeastern is a full-service bank, offering deposit accounts, consumer and commercial loans, investments, discount brokerage, personal and corporate trusts, and a wide range of computer services to business. In addition, the firm offers a bank-by-phone service and 20 sites in the five-county area where customers can bank by the "electronic teller," under Northeastern's "Corner Bank" trademark.

FRANK MARTZ COACH COMPANY (MARTZ TRAILWAYS)

The history of the Frank Martz Coach Company is one of complex growth and economic upheaval in the early years, but by 1980 it had become the fourth-largest private coach operation in the United States. More than 400 employees work out of offices in Wilkes-Barre, Scranton, Philadelphia, and Washington, D.C., keeping the firm's customers happy and its 267 buses on the road.

The business was founded in 1908 by Frank Martz, Sr., as the White Transit Company. Its first route was from its office at Bull Run, Plymouth, to Nanticoke. The early customers were miners and their families as the buses ran between the Lynsey and Avondale breakers in Plymouth and the Susquehanna breaker in Nanticoke.

Martz envisioned a total transportation company, and in 1926 introduced airplane as well as bus service to the people of the Wyoming Valley. A four-passenger Bellanca airplane was pressed into service to provide flights to and from Wilkes-Barre, Newark, Buffalo, and Cleveland. Martz was also one of the original

founders of the National Trailways Bus System.

Martz continued the expansion of his company; in 1927 he moved its general offices to Wilkes-Barre and in the same year extended service to Mt. Pocono and the Poconos. Regularly scheduled runs also were inaugurated from Wilkes-Barre to New York City via Easton and in the following year to Philadelphia. Two years later Buffalo, Cleveland, Chicago, Pittsburgh, Syracuse, Rochester, and Atlantic City became regular stops for Martz buses.

When the Depression reached its height, Martz was forced to retrench and reduce its service to Wilkes-Barre, Scranton, Philadelphia, New York, and Atlantic City.

Frank Martz, Sr., died in 1936 and the operation fell to his son, Frank Martz, Jr., who slowly rebuilt the firm and placed it on a sound financial footing. Frank Jr. operated the company until his death in 1964. Frank M. Henry, a grandson of Frank Martz, Sr., assumed the presidency at that time. The '80s saw the fourth generation enter the business as Frank Henry, Jr., Scott Henry, and Marjorie

Henry began taking an active part in the daily operations in Wilkes-Barre, Philadelphia, and Washington, D.C.

Two ultramodern terminals were built in Wilkes-Barre and Scranton in 1966 and the excursion and tour departments were created to provide vacation travel. In 1975 the Gold Line in Washington, D.C., was acquired and in 1978 the Gray Line became part of Martz, adding service to the Greater Baltimore/Washington area.

The year 1982 saw continued growth as Price Bus of Scranton was purchased, providing the company with the ability to enter the school bus service area. Martz has taken an active part in the renewal of Public Square with the construction of the Martz Towers, a seven-story terminal and office complex in the heart of Wilkes-Barre.

As the Frank Martz Coach Company enters its 75th year, its officials point out that the firm's degree of success could not have been achieved without the support of its employees and of the people of the Wyoming Valley.

75TH ANNIVERSARY ★ 1908-1983

PYROS AND SANDERSON, ARCHITECTS

From their office at One South Main Street on Public Square, Nick Pyros and Don Sanderson, Architects, can take you on a one-hour tour of Wilkes-Barre's business district and show you many examples of their distinctive architectural style. The buildings they have designed are noted for their clean lines, large expanses of glass, and light, airy interiors especially designed for the modern, computerized office.

Directly across the square from their headquarters sprawls the Martz Towers while one block to the north stands the ultramodern, three-story Blue Cross Building. Anchoring the western corner of Public Square, the Bicentennial Building, its clean, white lines broken only by encircling ribbons of smoked glass, provides a unique contrast to the surrounding architectural styles. Less than a block to the south, Midtown Village, a cluster of small shops and restaurants formed in a deep broken "V," provides an eye-appealing architectural feature to the downtown shopping district.

The Pyros and Sanderson venture was formed in 1971, the result of a ten-year working relationship between the two men. The firm first established itself in three rooms over Frank Clark's Jewelry Store on South Main Street and soon found itself involved in the 1972 Agnes Flood recovery work.

The company has grown into a multidisciplined architectural and planning partnership capable of designing not only the exteriors of buildings, but also the working areas within. Projects from a few thousand dollars to $30 million have been completed throughout the Northeast.

The staff has grown steadily in numbers and expertise. New services have been developed to meet the requirements of their varied clients, ranging from commercial and industrial to public housing.

Sophisticated, computerized architectural problem-solving techniques have been applied to new

The Bicentennial Building, designed by Pyros and Sanderson, Architects. The building commands the western corner of Wilkes-Barre Public Square. (Courtesy of Bo Parker, Photographer.)

and sometimes unique situations. The need to provide additional library space at College Misericordia led to a computerized-space-utilization master plan for the campus. The process later was applied to several colleges in the state of Pennsylvania.

During the design of the Blue Cross Building, a system was developed to translate employee questionnaires into space and working-station requirements. As a result, Pyros and Sanderson has developed an expanded office-space planning and interior design service for its clients.

Pyros and Sanderson views the computer as a tool that is changing its clients' needs. The firm looks forward to these changes even as it continues to pursue its excellence in the discipline of architecture.

HANOVER BANK OF PENNSYLVANIA

To provide a service where there was none was the dream of 11 men when they founded Hanover Bank of Pennsylvania on July 17, 1911, following a meeting in a home on Hanover Street in South Wilkes-Barre.

The bank opened for business on August 19, 1911, with a capitalization of 1,000 shares and a par value of $50. William Nicholson was elected the first president; Charles H. Price, in whose home the organizational meeting was held, was named vice-president and Charles K. Gloman was secretary. William Schlingmann was hired on July 15 as cashier, two days before the state charter was issued.

On opening day 174 savings accounts and 75 checking accounts were opened and on September 11 property was leased at 639 South Main Street. Deposits during the first year totaled $48,000 with assets of $80,000.

The bank's headquarters is still located at 639 South Main Street in a two-story building which includes banking facilities, a customer service area, and offices. A portion of the property serves as a parking lot, which was created for bank customers in 1939. The bank's operation center is

Hanover Bank's branch office in Kingston opened on November 27, 1974. The bank operates three additional branches in Dallas, Glen Lyon, and Penn Plaza, Wilkes-Barre. Its main office is located in South Wilkes-Barre.

located in an adjacent building which also contains a drive-in banking service.

In August 1931 Hanover Bank purchased the assets of the Lincoln Bank and Trust Company of Wilkes-Barre. A branch bank was opened at the Penn Plaza in South Wilkes-Barre in December 1966. In December 1967 the bank acquired the Glen Lyon National Bank and in November 1974 opened its fourth office in Kingston on Wyoming Avenue. Its most recent office was opened in 1980 in Dallas along Memorial Highway.

Hanover Bank was one of the hardest hit of the area's banks during the Agnes Flood of 1972. Its main offices and Penn Plaza branch were severely damaged. Total physical damage exceeded $250,000. Bank employees, under the direction of president Russell Gardner, quickly mobilized work crews to get the bank

back into service.

On June 23, 1972, in keeping with its policy of customer service, the board of directors took an unprecedented move and granted a three month's forebearance on mortgage and loan payments on both interest and principal. Two bank teams, one on the west side of the Susquehanna River and the other on the east side, visited mortgage holders hit by the flood to advise them of the bank's policy and assist where possible. As a show of concern for its employees a special fund was established and cash assistance was provided.

During the five years ending December 31, 1982, Hanover Bank has experienced a great period of growth, increasing its deposits from $62 million to more than $90 million; its assets have grown from $67 million to more than $103 million.

Through its branch network, Hanover Bank provides a wide range of consumer banking services and in the commercial lending field it provides lines of credit, demand and term loans, and other financial accommodations.

Hanover Bank was built on service to its customers and through the years has continued that philosophy. In 1939 it became the first bank in Wilkes-Barre to offer free parking to its customers, a service that continues today.

BLUE CROSS OF NORTHEASTERN PENNSYLVANIA

Blue Cross of Northeastern Pennsylvania, serving 625,000 subscribers in a 13-county area from its headquarters in Wilkes-Barre, has long been recognized as one of the most progressive and cost-conscious of the 70 Plans operating in the United States, Puerto Rico, Canada, and Jamaica.

A nonprofit organization providing insurance against the costs of hospitalization and other related health-care expenses, Blue Cross of Northeastern Pennsylvania has conducted a vigorous program to reduce the length of hospitalization in area hospitals while ensuring the finest of medical care.

It also conducts a series of well-

prospective payment program, conducted in cooperation with two area hospitals, has become a textbook illustration as to how hospital costs can be contained within an acceptable limit.

The Blue Cross concept of health care insurance was born in 1929, when Baylor University Hospital took over a teachers' "sick benefit plan" and began to enroll other groups. This led to the creation of the first Blue Cross Plan. The American Hospital Association encouraged the program and a grant from the Julius Rosenwald Fund aided in further development of voluntary nonprofit insurance plans.

The first attempt to form a Blue Cross Plan in Northeastern

independently incorporated. However, as an affiliate of a national organization, each Plan must adhere to certain policies, standards, and contracts. It is this affiliation that gives the individual subscriber assurance of health care in any one of the 6,500 member hospitals through the country.

Under the leadership of Ralph S. Smith, president since 1965, Blue Cross of Northeastern Pennsylvania has been able to increase its services. More than 270 employees working out of the offices in Wilkes-Barre, Scranton, and Williamsport are sensitive to the needs of the subscribers and provide fast, efficient service. A 23-member board of directors, representing business, labor, industry, and education, serve without pay to ensure that the Plan is attuned to the needs of the subscribers.

In 1977 Blue Cross moved into ultramodern headquarters in central Wilkes-Barre after it had outgrown its former downtown building. The result was a modern headquarters costing $2,607,866, which greatly enhanced the area.

The unique design of the building resulted in a savings of $268,875 in construction costs, with additional savings accrued as the open-office system permitted depreciation of office furnishings in seven years instead of the usual 30 years. Important in the construction was a 10-percent increase in worker productivity and the reclamation of computer heat. The building is so constructed that an additional two floors can be erected without disturbing the existing three floors.

The new facility is only one of the examples of the cost consciousness of Blue Cross of Northeastern Pennsylvania. In 1982 the Plan paid out more than $222 million in benefits, representing a payout of $1.19 for every one dollar received in premiums. Its administrative-expense ratio is one

The headquarters of Blue Cross of Northeastern Pennsylvania, at 70 North Main Street, Wilkes-Barre. The modern building was constructed at a cost of $2,607,866. (Courtesy of Bo Parker.)

planned radio and television spots in an effort to educate the public on the value of exercise and maintenance of good-health habits. Included in the program has been the dissemination of information on the effects of smoking, drinking, and stress on the human body.

Its experiment in a per-case-rate

Pennsylvania failed in Scranton in 1936—two years before the American Medical Association gave its approval to the Plan in 1938 as a means of warding off a growing threat of socialized medicine.

That same year, in December 1938, Blue Cross of Northeastern Pennsylvania was incorporated as the Hospital Service Association of Northeastern Pennsylvania. At that time, approximately 45 voluntary hospital-service associations were operating in the nation.

Each Blue Cross Plan is

The headquarters is a model of the modern open-office system. It is designed for the efficient utilization of CRT equipment and is a critical factor in the economical processing of information.

of the best in the Blue Cross Plans nationwide, as less than three cents of every one dollar goes toward operational costs.

While the Pennsylvania Insurance Commission regulates the rates that subscribers must pay, Blue Cross of Northeastern Pennsylvania regularly reviews costs to prevent and detect excessive use of health care benefits. The aim of the administration is the elimination of duplicate services. It also has been a leader in the advocacy of ambulatory surgery, pre-admission testing, and home health care.

Its goal today, as it was in 1938, is to provide the best possible health care coverage at the lowest possible cost.

In August 1983 Ralph S. Smith retired as president and was succeeded by Gilbert D. Tough.

The reception area in the main lobby of the headquarters of Blue Cross of Northeastern Pennsylvania.

The entrance to the Blue Cross headquarters in Wilkes-Barre. Offices also are located in Williamsport and Scranton. (Courtesy of Bo Parker.)

THE TIMES LEADER

The story of *The Times Leader* can go back as far as 1810, back to a publisher named Samuel Maffet and back to a newspaper called the *Susquehanna Democrat*.

It is a story of expansion and merger and consolidation, and it is a story defined by names that appear often and honorably in the history of the Wyoming Valley, names such as Nesbitt, Stegmaier, Miner, Hourigan, and Smith.

Other names are part of the story, too, names such as *Union Leader, Plain Dealer, Morning News,* and *Sunday Herald*—names of newspapers that made their mark long ago and now are mostly forgotten.

But the story of today's *Times Leader* really begins in 1939, with the founding of the Wilkes-Barre Publishing Co., and it begins anew in 1978, with the sale of that company to the present owner of *The Times Leader,* Capital Cities Communications.

Starting with Samuel Maffet's *Susquehanna Democrat,* the evolutionary process that ultimately produced the Wilkes-Barre Publishing Co. progressed through a dozen decades and nearly a score of newspapers. Some of these papers flourished and some foundered, until merger and consolidation left only three: *The Times Leader, The Evening News,* and *The Wilkes-Barre Record.*

In 1939 these three merged and the Wilkes-Barre Publishing Co. was born. It was a merger that was noteworthy not only because it united the resources of the Wyoming Valley's leading news organizations, but because it brought together three families who had been an integral part of the local publishing scene for many years—the Smiths, the Hourigans, and the Johnsons.

At the time of the merger, *The Times Leader* was a family operation headed by Ernest G. Smith, whose two sons, A. DeWitt Smith and Harrison H. Smith, also were involved in the

The city desk of The Times Leader *—the hub of the newspaper.*

publication of the paper and later would become key figures in the operation of the publishing company. *The Evening News* was published by a partnership that included John A. Hourigan, Sr., his son, John A. Hourigan, Jr., and a daughter, Carolyn G. Hourigan.

The Wilkes-Barre Record, which numbered among its ancestors a paper called *The Record of the Times,* published in 1853 by William P. Miner, was operated in 1939 by Frederick G. Johnson. His father, Dr. Frederick C. Johnson, had purchased the paper in 1883.

Once the merger was completed, with representatives of all three families assuming active roles in the operation of the new company, the three papers were consolidated into two: *The Times Leader-Evening News,* an afternoon publication, and *The Record,* a morning paper. The two papers maintained separate printing facilities until 1952, when the entire operation was moved into *The Times Leader's* present home at 15 North Main Street, Wilkes-Barre.

But even though they coexisted under the same roof after 1952, *The Times Leader-Evening News* and *The Record* retained their individual identities for another 20 years, functioning with independent

The Wilkes-Barre Record *building after it was remodeled in 1932 before the merger of the three newspapers to form the Wilkes-Barre Publishing Company. The building today is the office of* The Times Leader.

editorial staffs and separate morning and evening distribution until havoc wrought by natural disaster promoted a major change in the publishing company's operation.

The change came in July 1972, in the wake of massive flooding generated by Tropical Storm Agnes. The flood struck in June and raged through Wyoming Valley, driving thousands of families from their homes and crippling commerce all along its path.

One of the many victims of that flood was the Wilkes-Barre Publishing Co., which was forced to use out-of-town printing facilities for weeks after the North Main Street plant was inundated. When the debris had finally been cleared away and the cost of the disaster had been tabulated, the financial losses were so staggering that publishing company executives decided to streamline their operation by eliminating the separate morning and evening papers and introducing a single, "all-day" publication. The paper was published each morning, then periodically updated with fresh news throughout the day.

At best, however, this was a short-term solution to a downturn in profitability that was magnified by the flood but certainly not caused by it. As the '70s wore on, moreover, the cost of publishing a daily newspaper increased steadily while circulation, which had reached a pre-flood peak of more than 81,000, drifted to less than

70,000 by 1977. Faced with such economic realities, and haunted by a history of labor strife that had produced no less than five newspaper strikes between 1937 and 1974, the newspaper's management decided to consider offers from potential buyers.

Several newspaper chains expressed interest in purchasing the paper, but the most attractive offer came from Capital Cities Communications, Inc., a highly profitable, New York-based firm that owns several daily newspapers, a number of television and radio stations, and Fairchild Publications, the prestigious publisher of the "bible" of the fashion industry, *Women's Wear Daily.*

The sale was finalized in May 1978 with Capital Cities paying $10.5 million for the newspaper, which by then carried the rather-unwieldy name, *Wilkes-Barre Times Leader, The Evening News, Wilkes-Barre Record.* Eventually, the name would be shortened—to *The Times Leader*—but before that change was effected, the paper would endure the most cataclysmic labor dispute in its history, a strike so bitter and divisive it would tear at the very fabric of the community the Wilkes-Barre Publishing Co. had served for so many years.

The strike began on October 6, 1978, when approximately 200 employees—nearly the entire work force—walked out in a dispute over management's refusal to accept contract provisions designed to give the newspaper's four unions extensive control over the administration of the publishing company. The walk-out erupted into violence, forcing the publishing company to suspend operations for several days, and the striking employees simultaneously began publishing a daily newspaper of their own in competition with their former employer.

The tone for *The Times Leader's* new era was established quickly as the

paper rose undaunted from the ashes of the strike and determinedly set about the arduous task of restructuring the staff and rebuilding the circulation and advertising bases that had been devastated by the work stoppage.

The driving force behind this effort was Richard L. Connor, who assumed the dual position of editor and publisher during the turbulent early days of the strike. Connor, only 31 years old in 1978 but already a newspaper veteran who had previously headed daily papers in Illinois and Michigan, initiated a program of patient but aggressive development that in the ensuing five years turned *The Times Leader* into one of the finest newspapers in Pennsylvania.

Today's *Times Leader* employs nearly 200 persons and serves the community in myriad ways, from sponsorship of community-wide recreational and cultural activities to corporate and individual contributions to local charities and civic organizations. And, of course, *The Times Leader* serves the community by providing a fresh and dependable flow of information, by reporting the news, good or bad, whenever and wherever it happens.

Samuel Maffet could not have foreseen all this in 1810 as he gathered what news he could and distributed it to his neighbors by means of the *Susquehanna Democrat.* Nor could the Smiths, the Hourigans, and the Johnsons—when they created the Wilkes-Barre Publishing Co. in 1939—have foreseen the modern and progressive institution that is today's *Times Leader.*

Likewise, no one knows now what lies ahead for *The Times Leader,* or for the Wyoming Valley. But if the past portends the future, the newspaper and the community will continue to grow together, through good times and bad, proudly adding new chapters to the noble histories of both.

EBERHARD FABER INC.

Eberhard Faber IV administers a worldwide organization with production facilities and licensees in 12 nations from Eberhard Faber Inc.'s principal production facilities and offices in the Crestwood Industrial Park at Mountaintop.

Faber is the fourth generation of a family that established America's first mass production pencil factory and freed the nation from dependency upon European supply.

Through its history Eberhard Faber Inc. has established a number of innovations in the industry, including eraser-tipped yellow pencils, tipped pencils with adjustable and removable erasers, pencils of assorted colors, nickel plating for pencil-tip protectors, the popular school box, clips on pencils, counter display assortments (which created a new era in pencil-selling methods), bayonet packing, the slide box, circular typewriter erasers, rubber erasers for cleaning, and beveled erasers. Faber also was the first to utilize the tumbling method of processing erasers.

Besides manufacturing 60 colors of lead and producing millions of pencils each year, including the world-famous MONGOL brand, other products made in the 7.5-acre plant at Mountaintop include ball pens, liquid markers, erasers, rubber bands, and a variety of art-related materials such as visual aids, artists' easels, and furnishings.

During a 24-hour period the Mountaintop plant is capable of producing one million pencils. In the rubber department the firm manufactures 5,000 pounds of rubber bands and over 1,000 gross of erasers each day.

Eberhard Faber, founder of the firm, arrived in New York City in 1849 as the agent of a business founded by his ancestor, Casper Faber, in 1761 in Germany. Faber opened his own plant in New York City in 1861 at 42nd Street and East River, the site of today's

United Nations Building. Fire destroyed the first factory in 1872 and within three months the firm was back in operation in Brooklyn's Greenpoint Section.

Eberhard Faber died in 1872 and management of the firm passed to Eberhard II and Lothar W., who together charted the course of the pencil-making business for the next 60 years.

The future course of the company was set in 1892, when in a catalog Eberhard Faber assured his customers: "All goods coming from my factories I warrant to be of the very best material, of uniform quality, most carefully finished, and always full count. It is my aim to manufacture perfect goods only."

At the turn of the century, Faber's vision and leadership in pencil manufacturing and merchandising led to the painting of pencils and the creation of the yellow MONGOL brand, now the world's best-known business pencil. Within a short time the company was finishing its pencils in every hue to match office and home decor.

Shortly before the firm celebrated its 75th anniversary, the third-generation Faber entered the business—Eberhard Faber III, Lothar's son. During the following years he worked in almost every department of the firm and eventually headed the export division, overseeing Faber's worldwide organization.

Two manufacturing subsidiaries—Fabrica Argentina De Lapices Sociedad de Responsibilidad Limitada in Buenos Aires and Eberhard Faber Industrial de Brazil in Rio de Janeiro—were established to serve the writing needs of South America.

In 1943 Lothar W. Faber died and his son, Eberhard III, was elected executive vice-president with Eberhard II as president. A tragic accident took the life of Eberhard Faber III in 1945 and the following year his uncle, Eberhard II, succumbed. Thus, for the first time in nearly a century, the company did not have a Faber at its helm.

Mrs. Julia Faber, widow of Eberhard III, joined Eberhard Faber Inc. in 1953 and served for several

Eberhard Faber, founder of the company that bears his name.

Eberhard Faber IV, chairman of the board and chief executive officer of Eberhard Faber Inc.

BROOKLYN PLANT—1950

facility in the Philippines. In 1957 Faber entered into a partnership with Jan Western and Associates in the operation of Industrial Colombiana de Lapices in Colombia, and five years later established Eberhard Faber de Venezuela in partnership with members of the Pardo family, who had served as importers of Faber products in South America since the 1890s.

In 1965 the company acquired Hampton Industries of Portland, Pennsylvania, for the manufacture of liquid markers. The factory was moved to nearby Stroudsburg in 1974.

The Eberhard Faber-Board line of visual-aid panels was established in 1967-1968 to provide a visual communication tool for education and business.

Eberhard Faber IV brought a new vigor to the organization when he became president. A graduate of Princeton University, a Fulbright scholar, and the recipient of a Fulbright teaching fellowship, he immediately initiated a series of changes to reshape the overall corporate structure.

years as vice-president and later as chairman of the board, serving until Eberhard Faber IV was elected president in 1971.

In the mid-1950s Faber outgrew its multistory buildings in Brooklyn and began a search for a new location. In 1956 the company relocated in Wilkes-Barre at its Mountaintop industrial park. The new 27-acre site, with its modern 7.5-acre one-story building, was chosen because of a favorable labor market close to major highways, permitting easy access to the nation's markets. Faber's Newark rubber

Eberhard Faber's second plant, which housed the firm's operations at Brooklyn, New York, prior to its move to Mountaintop in 1956.

factory was relocated in 1963 to Mountaintop, following expansion of the plant.

Through the years the firm has continued to expand its overseas operation by opening a manufacturing

Aerial shot of the Eberhard Faber plant at the Crestwood Industrial Park, Mountaintop.

As separate market centers were established in 1974 for overseas and domestic operations, Eberhard Faber IV became chairman of the board of directors and chief executive officer. C. Paul Mailloux, who had served as executive vice-president since 1971, was named president with responsibility for domestic operations.

The company entered into a new era of expansion and acquired an easel producer in 1976, an artists' furniture company in 1980, and a manufacturer of leather, vinyl, and cloth binders, portfolios, cases, and presentation products in 1982.

Under Faber's leadership the corporation has embarked on a worldwide program improving manufacturing, marketing, and accounting functions as it looks forward to an expanding market in the '80s.

NESBITT MEMORIAL HOSPITAL

In 1983 Nesbitt Memorial Hospital, Kingston, completed the third major expansion program in its 71-year history, bringing to the Wyoming Valley many innovations of medical care often found only in more modern medical complexes.

The latest expansion and renovation project began in 1980 with the modernization of the hospital's main facility to include additional patient rooms, new nursing stations, and a staff dining room. The second phase of the project followed with a new critical care unit, operating room, emergency room, pharmacy, physical therapy department, short stay surgical area, hospitality shop, and administration and services area.

The final stage of the expansion program resulted in one of the most modern obstetrics departments in the region as well as expanded quarters for the hospital's laboratory, radiology, cardiology, and supply processing distribution services.

On July 10, 1982, the hospital opened the doors of its new emergency room, which is constructed to provide maximum efficiency and medical services of the highest caliber. The unit is equipped with a major trauma room where emergency surgical procedures can be performed on the victims of cardiac arrest, auto accidents, and serious burns.

The facility is equipped to treat 14 patients at one time. Two of the rooms are specially designed for pelvic examinations and for ear, nose, and throat treatments.

Nesbitt Memorial is the first hospital in the area to have a complete program in nuclear medicine, diagnostic tools for the future. Now in a spacious new area, nuclear medicine makes use of computers and a "gamma camera," which is used to scan various body organs to determine disease.

In addition to its recent on-site renovations, Nesbitt Memorial Hospital has expanded services to area

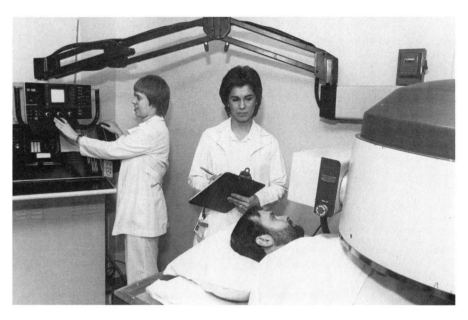

Nuclear medicine has become an important diagnostic tool, making use of computers and a "gamma camera" to scan body organs to determine disease.

residents by way of neighborhood health centers located throughout the Wyoming Valley in Dallas, Edwardsville, Exeter, Nanticoke, Pittston, and Wilkes-Barre. The health centers bring outpatient diagnostic and treatment service, including laboratory, cardiology-EKG testing, physical therapy, and radiology, to residents in these communities.

In March 1983 Nesbitt Memorial reached a milestone in medicine in the Wyoming Valley when an orthopedic surgeon on the staff performed a precedent-setting procedure in the future treatment of sufferers of acute and chronic lower back pain. The

A couple relaxes for a moment prior to delivery in one of Nesbitt Memorial Hospital's "birthing rooms." Each room provides a home-like environment and a pleasant experience for the couple.

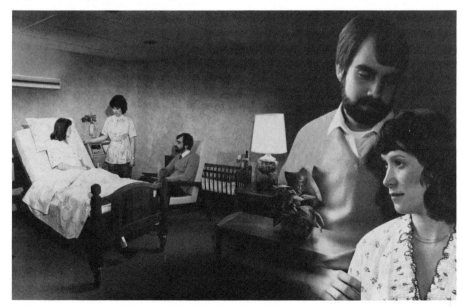

An artist's rendition of the Nesbitt West Side Hospital in 1912.

procedure, referred to as "chemonucleolysis," uses Chymopapain, a derivative of the papaya plant. Chymopapain acts as a digestive catalyst that literally dissolves a ruptured or herniated disc.

The enzyme is injected through a needle into the lumbar area. Each intradiscal therapy is accomplished in less than one hour, opposed to the traditional operating techniques involving extensive surgery. The length of hospital stay for a patient with chemonucleolysis is two or three days, compared to seven days with conventional surgery. This innovative procedure is part of Nesbitt Memorial Hospital's continued commitment to excellence in medical care established more than 71 years ago.

It was at that time that a group of doctors led by D.H. Lake, Kingston, saw a need for hospital facilities on the west side. With the assistance of

Nesbitt Memorial Hospital, 1983.

Abram Nesbitt, founder and first president, the Nesbitt West Side Hospital was chartered on May 15, 1912, at the former Jacob Sharp home.

The 30-bed hospital admitted its first patients on October 10, 1912. That same year the Nurses' Training School was established, with three students admitted to the first class. During its 61-year history the School of Nursing graduated 1,092 nurses.

A group of 30 women also organized in 1912 to form the Ladies' Auxiliary of the West Side Hospital. Since that time the group has grown to more than 500 auxilians who participate in a variety of volunteer and fund-raising activities to help support the hospital.

In 1927 the hospital was closed and completely rebuilt. Upon its reopening on December 1, 1929, the name was changed to Nesbitt Memorial Hospital. In 1941 the south wing was completed, expanding the capacity to 200 beds.

The 200,001st patient was admitted to the hospital in 1962, marking the hospital's 50th anniversary. The second renovation, in 1969, upgraded the radiology, laboratory, physical therapy, cardiology, and pharmacy departments to meet the demand of the expanded medical care in the '70s.

In June 1972 tropical storm Agnes swept through the Wyoming Valley, closing all bridges over the Susquehanna River. Nesbitt Hospital, the only hospital on the west side of the river, had to be evacuated temporarily and established its medical facilities on the campus of College Misericordia in Dallas. Before the temporary hospital closed its doors 40 days later, 300 inpatients had been admitted, 52 babies were born, and a total of 5,161 patients were treated.

As Nesbitt Memorial Hospital enters its eighth decade of service to the community, the hospital stands firm in its commitment to provide community residents with the finest in family-centered medical services.

UTILITY ENGINEERS, INC.

Innovation, within the confines of the highest standards of engineering, has been the key for the success of Utility Engineers, Inc.

Founded in 1967 by John L. Churnetski, a mechanical engineer, the firm has grown into a multidiscipline engineering company with an excellent staff of engineers and support personnel.

Whatever has wires, beams, joists, pipes, ducts, or depends on the mechanics of physics, and is built of stone, brick, wood, steel, or plastic, the staff of Utility Engineers has the expertise to design it.

The firm's staff also prides itself on its ability to solve existing problems in building systems. Utility Engineers' problem solving for industry and commercial property owners involves short- and long-range planning and extends from the cost-efficient use of existing systems to the completed installation of the most modern systems.

Its role in the developing of energy systems that use the nation's resources efficiently, while protecting the environment, is well known in industry and in the engineering field and related disciplines.

Utility Engineers was selected in 1982 by the borough of Weatherly to design a hydroelectric power plant on the Lehigh River in Luzerne County.

Utility Engineers, Inc., is a multidiscipline engineering company with an excellent staff of engineers and support personnel.

The site of the plant is the Francis E. Walter Reservoir, which controls a drainage area of approximately 288 square miles and has a storage capacity of 110,000 acre-feet. The dam is controlled by the U.S. Army Corps of Engineers as a flood-control project.

The hydroelectric plant must protect the environment and fit into the Corps' existing use of the reservoir as a prime fishing, boating, and picnicking area, and the designation of the Lehigh as a wild and scenic river.

The firm is a leader in the design of transmission and distribution of electric power.

Utility Engineers has also designed one of the early fluidized-bed boiler system applications. The new unit is designed to burn high-sulphur anthracite culm.

Culm is the waste or slack of coal mining and in the past was considered of no use. In the coal fields of the East and West the huge piles of culm dot the landscape and the release of sulphur into the water pollutes the environment.

The fluidized-bed boiler system permits the efficient burning of the culm, delivering energy at a cost below high-grade coal, gas, or oil. The process has the added advantage of ridding the landscape of eyesores and a source of pollution.

Utility Engineers has received recognition in trade publications for its use of an energy-efficient heating and cooling system involving the recapturing of heat given off by office computers. Energy expended in the cooling of the environment housing the computers is used to heat water, which is then circulated through the rest of the building.

Utility Engineers has remained active in the field of planning, storage, distribution, and protection of water supplies from hazardous wastes. It also is a leader in the design of transmission and distribution of natural gas, electric power and water, and generation of electric supplies.

TAMBLYN COMPANY

The Tamblyn Company, located at 4500 Birney Avenue, Avoca, is one of the largest word-processing and copy-duplicating distributors in northeastern Pennsylvania.

The family-owned business was founded on July 1, 1931, by C. Leonard Tamblyn and his brother, Ralph. The first offices were located on Ross Street, Wilkes-Barre, and Spruce Street, Scranton.

The brothers borrowed $6,000 to obtain a franchise from the A.B. Dick Company to sell mimeograph machines, which in the 1930s were the "state of the art" of the modern office. A.B. Dick had two models and a dozen or so supply items.

Today Tamblyn carries more than 100 different models of office equipment, from copying and offset printing equipment to computers and word-processing systems.

Today Tamblyn is marketing high technology systems such as word processors, computers, and copiers. Shown standing is Charles L. Tamblyn, Jr., with Thomas J. Tamblyn.

In 1931 the Tamblyn Company opened its doors to market the most up-to-date office product at the time: the A.B. Dick mimeograph.

Tamblyn has been associated with A.B. Dick for 52 years, making it the third-oldest distributor of the company's products in the United States covering a 10-county area of northeastern Pennsylvania.

The firm grew as A.B. Dick introduced the first offset printing equipment for the office in 1955 and became the leader in the industry. In 1957 A.B. Dick again scored a first with the photocopier.

In the early 1960s the trend was to office automation and Tamblyn began another growth period, necessitating the hiring of six additional people.

The offices in Wilkes-Barre and Scranton were closed in 1957 and a showroom, repair shop, and office were opened in Avoca. From this location Tamblyn could serve the cities of Wilkes-Barre and Scranton and have access to Route 81. The firm's headquarters was moved into a new facility located on Route 11 in 1980. The new building provided more than 14,000 square feet of space, with 5,000 square feet as a showroom.

Ralph Tamblyn died in 1954 and C. Leonard Tamblyn retired in 1974, leaving the firm in the hands of the second generation of the Tamblyn family.

Charles L. Tamblyn, Jr., was the first to join the company in 1968 after graduating from college; he is president of the firm today. Thomas Tamblyn joined the business in 1974.

With the advent of the first plain paper copier in 1972 and A.B. Dick's entry into word processing, Tamblyn had grown to 20 employees including a highly trained service staff.

In 1981 Tamblyn was chosen by Ricoh, the largest manufacturer of copiers, to become the exclusive dealer for its products in northeastern Pennsylvania. In 1983 Tamblyn added microcomputers to its list of business equipment.

Today Tamblyn employs 27 persons and is the only firm in northeastern Pennsylvania that markets and services copiers and duplicating machines as well as word processors and computers.

VALLEY VENDING COMPANY

Valley Vending Company doesn't engage in manufacturing, but fresh snacks, beverages, and candy help keep the workers in the plants and offices happy on the job.

Located on Darling Street in Wilkes-Barre, the firm since 1951 has grown into one of the foremost vending companies in northeastern Pennsylvania, serving 200 industries, offices, and colleges in three counties: Luzerne, Lackawanna, and Columbia. Valley Vending employs over 50 workers to maintain its service routes in the three-county area, and it also has a commissary at Scranton where sandwiches and baked goods are prepared each day for its customers.

The firm is a closed corporation controlled by Sam and Kathryn Bannan. Sam, after much research, found there was an opportunity in the vending business, and with a small insurance policy as collateral was able to realize enough money to buy a few soft drink vending machines.

Running into various legal technicalities, Sam contacted attorney Stephen A. Teller, who offered to become a partner. Together they contacted the Spacarb Co. and were able to purchase machines that had been repossessed. These machines were delivered to the Bannan home in Shickshinny.

Valley Vending Company supplies a wide variety of vending machines to over 200 industries, offices, and colleges in a three-county area.

The firm's first customers were the Paramount Theaters in Wilkes-Barre and Pittston and the Strand and Center theaters in Scranton. Machines were installed shortly thereafter in the Boston Store, Martz Bus Terminal, Scranton Post Office, and Consolidated Moulded Products Co.

Within its first six months of business, Valley Vending was able to add coffee vending machines to its line. At that time coffee cost five cents a cup.

Within the first year the firm expanded when it purchased the first of its competitors, Kwik Kafe Coffee. Bannan said the Kwik Kafe sold a

better cup of coffee and that the customers wouldn't object to paying 10 cents a cup.

Valley Vending soon outgrew its quarters in Shickshinny and moved to Teller's garage in Wilkes-Barre. The business continued to expand and within the year the company had to move a second time—to Darling Street.

Candy machines were added in 1954 and the first food dispenser was introduced to the public in 1956. By 1958 Valley Vending became solidly established in the food vending field when Lunch-O-Mat of Pennsylvania Inc. was acquired.

With the withdrawal from the firm of Teller, Sam and Kathryn Bannan assumed complete control of Valley Vending.

The business experienced continued growth until 1972, when the Agnes Flood hit the Wyoming Valley. The flood waters did not reach the firm's headquarters, but many of its accounts were forced to suspend business and a large portion of Valley Vending's machines were destroyed.

The company survived this disaster and entered a new growth pattern. Today annual sales exceed $2.5 million.

Sam and Kathryn Bannan are dedicated to the belief that the people of the Wyoming Valley are the area's most important asset.

BERTELS CAN COMPANY

Bertels Can Company is the United States' largest producer of tapered nesting cans in sizes ranging from one- to seven-gallon capacity.

By embossing its name and that of Wilkes-Barre on over two million cans per year, Bertels publicizes the name of its city throughout the country more than any other local industry.

The firm was founded by Raymond Bertels in 1922 when he interested local citizens in forming what was then known as Bertels Metal Ware Co. It was located on Rutter and Lathrop in Kingston, with C.F. Goeringer as its first president, W.B. Schaeffer as vice-president, and Raymond Bertels as general manager.

After Ray Bertels' death in 1946, Carrie Garner was named general manager and served until her retirement at the end of 1956. Louis F. Goeringer, the current president, was appointed general manager at that time.

Louis Goeringer poses beside a Bertels Can Company display for the 1982 International Snack Food Exposition in Las Vegas.

Bertels' modern plant in Hanover Industrial Estates.

Bertels' management team. Seated, left to right: Joan D. Kockel, vice-president; Louis F. Goeringer, president; and James C. McDonald, plant manager. Standing, left to right: Paul L. Goeringer, director of purchasing; Patrick T. Kennedy, assistant plant manager; and Theresa A. Przekop, office manager.

When C.F. Goeringer died in 1958, Marion R. Schaeffer was elected president and Louis F. Goeringer became vice-president and general manager. In 1982 Miss Schaeffer was advanced to chairman of the board and Louis F. Goeringer to president and chief executive officer.

Other officers of Bertels are Joan D. Kockel, vice-president; Allan M. Kluger, Esq., secretary; John M. Moore, treasurer; and Carolyn H. Mack, assistant treasurer.

Over the years the company has constantly updated its equipment, and in 1967 Goeringer toured can machinery manufacturing companies throughout Germany, making

purchases leading to the development of the most modern production line of its type in America.

Bertels made a major engineering breakthrough in 1970, when it created the single-side-seam tapered can; the firm is still the sole manufacturer of this type of container.

The firm changed its name in 1975 to Bertels Can Company and built a modern 27,000-square-foot plant in Hanover Industrial Estates. It was the first tenant of the park, a project of the Greater Wilkes-Barre Chamber of Commerce.

Today the major portion of Bertels business is involved with the snack food industry for the packaging of peanuts, potato chips, pretzels, and popcorn, as well as the producing of exclusively designed cans for such stores as Neiman-Marcus, Saks Fifth Avenue, Bloomingdale's, and Macy's.

Bertels' emphasis will continue to be on innovative marketing methods and an optimum standard of excellence in order to remain a viable part of the Wilkes-Barre community and an active participant in its endeavors.

PENNSYLVANIA STATE UNIVERSITY WILKES-BARRE CAMPUS

The Wyoming Valley's experiment with higher education began in 1916 with the establishment of the Wilkes-Barre Campus of the Pennsylvania State University.

The Penn State experience was more than the creation of a school. It awakened in the community an awareness of the value of higher education that was to become, in later years, the guide for other colleges in the region. The campus stands as an example of community spirit. It began when a group of citizens interested the Chamber of Commerce and the Rotary Club in the need for higher education.

The first classes were held in the YMCA and Coughlin High School, then known as the Wilkes-Barre High School Building. The school was held at night and the curriculum was mining engineering taught by practicing engineers. During those first years students received a certificate of accomplishment instead of college credits.

The curriculum has been expanded until today the first two years of more than 123 programs are offered, leading to bachelor's degrees; associate degrees in biomedical technology, telecommunications, business administration

including management information systems; and the traditional electrical, mechanical, and civil engineering technology programs are also offered.

The school grew and in 1947 day classes were instituted. In 1950 the campus was moved to the Guthrie Building on North Washington Street in Wilkes-Barre.

During the 1950-1951 academic year the engineering curricula was accredited by the Engineers' Council for Professional Development. The associate degree programs were instituted in the second academic year after the move to Guthrie.

Penn State/Wilkes-Barre Campus reached a milestone in 1968 with the donation of a permanent campus at Hayfield House in Lehman Township. The 50-room Hayfield House, with a 19-car garage, is surrounded by 43 acres.

The house was designed by Francis A. Nelson of New York City and

Michael Clupka and Jenette Faux (seated, left to right), students at Penn State, participated in an internship program in a study of local history sponsored by the Wyoming Historical and Geological Society. Standing is Burt Logan, director of the Society.

Hayfield House, the center of activities at Pennsylvania State University, Wilkes-Barre, houses the faculty and administrative offices and the student lounge and snack bar.

several European craftsmen were brought to Lehman to work on the intricate wood paneling and marble. Other special features included a 400-year-old fireplace that was removed from a castle in Holland and stained-glass windows that came from a Paris cathedral.

Hayfield House today is the center of the Wilkes-Barre Campus activities, containing faculty and administration offices, snack bar, and student lounge. Laboratories and classrooms are housed in a separate building.

The campus contains recreational facilities including a jogging and fitness path, tennis and basketball courts, and other areas for sports. In addition, the campus sponsors artistic and cultural performances. Lectures, concerts, and art and scientific exhibits are held throughout the year and are open to students and the public.

More than 800 students and an instructional staff of 40 are supported by an administrative staff of over 60 persons.

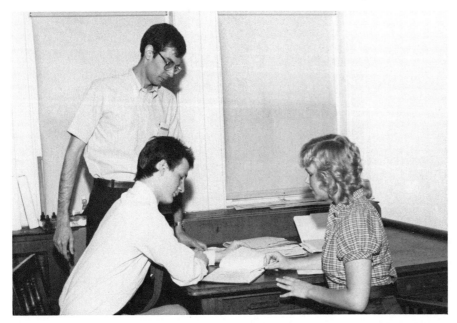

WYOMING SEMINARY

One of the first coeducational college-preparatory schools in the United States, Wyoming Seminary was founded in 1844 by leaders of the Methodist Church. Located in Kingston, Pennsylvania, the school is one of the few in the country to enroll boys and girls and boarding and day students continuously for 140 years.

Three miles north of the prep school campus in Forty Fort is the Wyoming Seminary Lower School, which has a tradition of excellence that began more than 150 years ago. The Lower School has a long history of mergers including the one in 1951 with Wyoming Seminary which made the school the only private institution in the region to offer continuous education from preschool through the 12th grade.

Through these 14 decades, the school has faced such tribulations as debt, fire, epidemic, and flood, but has rebounded on each occasion as a stronger institution. Perhaps the greatest calamity to strike this old school was the severe flooding caused by Hurricane Agnes in June 1972. All of the school buildings and properties were seriously affected and the school suffered nearly $4 million in damage, but the doors opened for the fall term only one week late.

Today 325 students at the Upper School and 320 at the Lower School, and the 68 faculty members at both divisions, make Wyoming Seminary a large enough community to provide a diversity of tastes and opinions, yet small enough to develop meaningful relationships. Boarders comprise one-third of the Upper School population. The curriculum provides a sound foundation of college-required courses and prepares students for the challenges they will meet in the world community. The primary goal is to give students every opportunity to strengthen basic academic skills and to develop study habits as well as to advance in fields of interest that usually can not be explored before college. To execute this goal effectively requires a highly personal approach and small classes.

The heritage and traditions of the school are reflected in its 19th-century ivy-covered buildings. Three new buildings constructed in the mid-1970s blend with the older structures and provide excellent facilities for the performing arts and student recreation. The Kirby Library houses a 17,000-volume collection of books as well as an extensive periodical and audio-visual section.

From its founding 140 years ago, Wyoming Seminary has recognized that each student is a distinct personality. Consequently, the school does not impose upon its students a uniform pattern of behavior and attitudes but rather attempts to help them discover the ways in which they can best serve society. It strives to furnish a curriculum and an environment that will promote personal and social usefulness, moral and spiritual concepts, and disciplined habits of thinking. The first chairman of the school's board of trustees, Dr. David Holmes, perhaps said it best in 1844 when questioned about the school's purpose: "We want an education that will produce a harmonious development of the physical, mental, and moral power . . . that will make (graduates) philanthropists, patriots, and Christians."

Looking out from the Nelson Tower to Darte, Fleck, and Swetland halls, which are on the National Register of Historic Places.

KING'S COLLEGE

The College of Christ the King began in 1945 as a dream of the Most Reverend William J. Hafey, the Bishop of Scranton, who felt there was a great need for a men's college in the Wilkes-Barre area.

He discussed his dream with his Auxiliary Bishop, Martin J. O'Connor, who shared his feelings and suggested that the Holy Cross Fathers of the University of Notre Dame would be the best choice to staff the embryonic college. The Provincial of the Congregation of Holy Cross, the Reverend Thomas A. Steiner, C.S.C., was approached and after discussions and visits with officials at Notre Dame an agreement was reached.

The King's College Administration Building, purchased in 1953 from the Lehigh Valley Coal Company.

Father Steiner appointed the Reverend James W. Connerton, C.S.C., as the first president, responsible for organizing and establishing the college. Father Steiner selected eight priests and one layman from Notre Dame's faculty to assist in the monumental task.

A group of prominent businessmen volunteered to form the Board of Organizers to get the college chartered. Spearheading the group was the Honorable Frank L. Pinola. On May 2, 1946, the college was chartered to offer B.A. and B.S. degrees by the Court of Common Pleas of Luzerne County.

In September 1946, at 29 West Northampton Street, the doors were opened to 306 freshman. At the Opening Mass Bishop Hafey stated, "The day a seed is planted is a day of rejoicing rooted in hope. The centenary celebration which recalls this planning will be glorious if the seed has become a sturdy tree, fair and fruitful."

The future of the physical plant was ensured when, in 1953, during the presidency of the Reverend Leo Flood, C.S.C., the college purchased the Lehigh Valley Coal Company building on North River Street between West Union and West Jackson streets. The designation of the area around the college as the King's College Urban Renewal Project gave the institution a solid base for planning expansion.

The expansion was carefully developed by the formulation of a master plan for the campus which, because of zoning regulations, had to be contained in a restricted area. The first building erected was the 12-story Holy Cross Hall (1966), a dormitory for students and a residence for priests. It was followed by the William S. Scandlon Center for Physical Education, opened in 1968. This impressive building, the largest facility for events in the area, houses a gymnasium which seats 4,200.

The year 1970 was an auspicious one: The college became coeducational and that September dedicated three buildings, the Sheehy Student Center, East Hall (a women's dormitory), and the D. Leonard Corgan Library.

The growth of the physical plant was necessitated by academic and student growth. Today 26 major degrees, five preprofessional programs, and several special programs are offered. Associate degrees and double majors were introduced, as well as cooperative programs with other area colleges.

The seed planted in 1946 has indeed flourished beyond all expectations, and looks to the 21st century with great hope. The development of King's College's programs to meet the needs of students during the changing times will continue.

WILKES COLLEGE

Dr. Robert S. Capin, president of Wilkes College.

It was on September 14, 1933, that Bucknell University opened a junior college in Wilkes-Barre in rented quarters on the third floor of the Wilkes-Barre Business College on Northampton Street. The first class of 193 students owed their education to the work of Dr. Frank Davis, head of the Department of Education of Bucknell University. Dr. Davis is considered "the Father of Bucknell University Junior College," but it would be the task of Dr. Eugene S. Farley, a "Quaker with an Irish name," to be "the head and heart of the college."

Bucknell named John H. Eisenhauer and eight professors as director and staff for the new junior college. Eisenhauer served until 1936. Then Dr. Farley took up the reins.

The college was reorganized and a local board of trustees was established, headed by Gilbert S. McClintock. In 1937 Admiral and Mrs. Harold Stark presented Conyngham Hall to form the nucleus of a campus which today includes six buildings on the State Historical Register.

The citizens of the Wyoming Valley contributed $150,000 as the first step in creating the endowment needed for a four-year college in 1944. Within three years Wilkes stood as an institution dedicated, in the words of Dr. Farley, to the ". . . belief that people of all backgrounds and faiths must learn to live together."

Dr. Farley retired in 1970, and Dr. Francis J. Michelini was named president at that time. Dr. Michelini drew the task of rebuilding the college following the Agnes Flood of June 22, 1972. Despite $12 million damage to its physical plant, under his leadership the college opened just 89 days later.

In 1975 Dr. Michelini left to become president of the Commission for Independent Colleges and Universities. Dr. Robert S. Capin was elected president and in 1982 announced his intention to retire in 1984. Dr. Capin provided the college with sound fiscal management and was instrumental in the development of strong academic programs. His leadership enabled the college to renovate and refurbish numerous campus buildings and allowed for the construction of a 205-unit residence hall which opened in September 1982.

Wilkes College, having established a standard for academic excellence, has never forgotten the community that gave it life. The college has been the hub of the performing arts through its support of the Fine Arts Fiesta and the Wyoming Valley Philharmonic Orchestra and its own Dorothy Dickson Darte Center for the Performing Arts; has served government through the Institute of Regional Affairs; and has supported labor-management relations through the Labor-Management-Citizens Committee. Its Sordoni Art Gallery brings important art exhibits to the Valley and is open to the public.

COLLEGE MISERICORDIA

When the Religious Sisters of Mercy purchased 99 acres in 1913 in the sleepy borough of Dallas, Pennsylvania, a seed was planted that would grow into the first four-year college in the Wyoming Valley.

The seed would lay dormant during the war years and then spring to life during the summer of 1921 when the ground was broken for the Motherhouse of the Sisters of Mercy, which would be the campus for the College Misericordia.

The college opened on the Feast of Our Lady of Mercy on September 24, 1924, with a class of 37 young women. The college would not become coeducational until 1972.

Misericordia remains a small college, with graduating classes numbering less than 300, but its academic program is what one would expect from a much larger college. In addition to the usual bachelor degrees, the program includes master of science degrees in nursing and human services administration.

The student body is composed of 1,100 undergraduates, with a faculty/student ratio of one faculty member to 13 students. About 40 percent commute from their homes in the Wyoming Valley.

In addition to serving the educational needs of the Valley, Misericordia attracts students from throughout Pennsylvania, New York, New Jersey, Maryland, and several foreign nations.

The college since its inception has played a vital role in the community. The college-community orchestra, Sinfonia de Camera, presents three annual concerts in Walsh Auditorium, while the Children's Theatre has charmed youngsters with a steady succession of performances for more than 10 years by introducing them to the fine arts.

In recent years Misericordia students have taken on an added role in the community by aiding the elderly, while the college policy provides all senior citizens free access to continuing education classes. Students are working with the elderly in the Senior Citizen Olympics, the Adopt a Grandparent program, and the Institute of Gerontology and Human Services.

College Misericordia, as it enters the '80s and looks to the future, is dedicated to the spirit of the Mercy community and to a sound liberal arts-based education which develops in the students the ability to think rationally and critically, to express themselves clearly, and to become leaders in their community.

In contrast to this 1930s typing class is this computer science class being taught at College Misericordia today.

COMFORT DESIGNS, INC.

It took a disastrous fire to make the name of Comfort Designs, Inc., as well known in the Wyoming Valley as it was in the world of furniture design and manufacturing.

The fire on February 1, 1982, which destroyed the company's main plant in Kingston, came five months before the 10th anniversary of Comfort Designs' incorporation on August 1, 1972. In that short time the firm had established a reputation in the furniture industry for unique designs and quality workmanship.

In 1975 Comfort Designs was the first manufacturer of upholstered furniture to utilize frame and panel construction for living room furniture. In 1982 the company introduced its product, Kubu, to the furniture industry. Kubu, made from a large vine that grows in the Philippines, can be applied to a flat or curvilinear surface. Comfort Designs' introduction of the product for upholstered furniture and occasional pieces set a new trend for the furniture industry.

Comfort Designs is a closed corporation, with John H. Graham as president and Adrian M. Pearsall as vice-president. The firm opened its first plant in Scranton and then moved in 1974 to West Wyoming.

In 1976 it acquired the Kingston plant that would be destroyed by fire in 1982. The plant was reopened in July 1983 and a second plant in

This upholstered sofa displays the diversity of Comfort Designs. Adrian M. Pearsall, vice-president, is the designer.

Kingston was purchased. Comfort Designs, which was started with one employee, today employs more than 100 persons and its products are distributed by representatives nationally and in various parts of the world.

All of the firm's designs are the creation of vice-president Pearsall, a registered architect. Pearsall began designing furniture in 1952 when he founded Craft Associates, an upholstering design and construction firm.

Created by Comfort Designs of Kingston, the Trade Winds collection presents wicker as a material for not just occasional furniture but as a decorative touch in any setting.

The furniture industry first took notice of Comfort Designs due to its unique designs of wicker furniture. By 1974 the company had established a reputation not only for its wicker furniture but also for its upholstered furniture designs, which have a contemporary flair using modular construction.

In 1975 Comfort Designs entered into an agreement with Mimbres de Honduras, a wicker manufacturer in San Pedro Sula, Honduras, and now most of the furniture utilizing Kubu is made at this plant.

Comfort Designs' wicker furniture has remained popular as the firm has diversified in other lines. The continuing popularity of wicker furniture has been attributed to the firm's innovative use of the age-old material. Comfort Designs has combined wicker with every possible use of furniture in the home and office. It is now available with upholstered seats and backs, suspended from a chrome steel frame to form a wicker swing chair. In Comfort Designs' line wicker is no longer used just as occasional furniture, but is considered a material to be used in the decor of even a formal dining room.

With its modern plant, and its continued experimentation in the design of furniture and of construction materials, Comfort Designs looks forward to the future and its position of leadership in the furniture industry.

NABISCO BRANDS INC.

At 10:23 on the morning of July 6, 1981, the New York Stock Exchange flashed the message to begin trading and at that instant Nabisco Brands Inc. joined the other multinational companies in the Wyoming Valley. With the merger of Nabisco Inc. and Standard Brands Incorporated, the oldest of the bakeries that in 1898 combined as the National Biscuit Company.

Standard Brands, which came into being in 1929 with the joining of the Fleischmann Company, the Royal Baking Powder Company, and Chase and Sanborn, dates back to 1863 when Royal Baking Powder Company to manufacture and market their product.

It was through Standard Brands that Nabisco Brands became a member of the Wyoming Valley industrial community. In 1961 Standard Brands acquired the Planters Nut and

The familiar Mr. Peanut was created from a schoolboy's prize-winning sketch. This early photo depicts the Planters "Peanut" Car.

fourth-largest food processor in the United States was born.

Nabisco Brands' history dates back to the first commercial bakery established in the United States in 1792 by John Pearson in the village of Newburyport. This bakery was slated to become John Pearson & Son, the

two druggists in Fort Wayne, Indiana, combined two ingredients and called it baking powder. They formed the

Chocolate Company—a business begun in Wilkes-Barre in 1906 by Amedeo Obici and Mario Peruzzi, two Italian immigrants.

Obici, who came to the United States when he was 11 years old, went to work with an uncle in Scranton. Later Obici moved to Wilkes-Barre.

Amedeo Obici (above) founded the Planters Company in 1906 with six employees and partner Mario Peruzzi (above right). Photos taken in 1915.

How the young man got his start in the peanut business depends on what story you read and whether that story was written in Wilkes-Barre or Suffolk, Virginia.

In the Wilkes-Barre version, Obici got his start when he opened a small fruit and vegetable stand. The Suffolk version has Obici owning a peanut stand and then a store and a restaurant.

Whatever story you choose to believe will lead to a remarkable man who, at 29, formed a business in 1906 in a small office with six employees and his partner Peruzzi. Success came almost instantly. Within a year a four-story building was rented to house the burgeoning operation.

The business continued to expand as new lines of merchandise were added. By 1912 the Planters Company had established a new field, one that continued to grow until it became a multimillion-dollar industry.

The success of Obici was no accident. The Italian lad who couldn't speak English when he arrived in this country was a master of modern merchandising. Within a short time the market was flooded with toys and other trinkets advertising Planters Peanuts.

Constantly looking for new ways to enhance the popularity of the peanut, the firm in 1916 offered a prize for the best sketch suitable for the adoption as the company trademark. The winning design, submitted by a schoolboy, was an animated peanut. Later a commercial artist added a top hat, cane, and monocle, and Mr. Peanut was born.

Mr. Peanut became a familiar trademark throughout the nation as it appeared on advertisements in Times Square in New York City, on toys, on Planters salesmen's cars, on mirrors, and ashtrays. Today Mr. Peanut memorabilia are sought after by antique dealers.

In Wilkes-Barre a familiar sight on Public Square was Mr. Peanut walking around with his cane, top hat, and monocle. The old gentleman was a

landmark into the early 1950s.

In 1913 Obici went to Suffolk to visit the "heart of the peanut belt" to buy a peanut-cleaning plant. He would make that city not only the peanut-growing center of the world, but also the peanut-processing capital of the world. Along the way Obici found time to improve the strain of peanuts into the big, meaty, full-flavored snacks that have made Planters Peanuts famous.

The firm opened a facility in San Francisco in 1921 and in Toronto in 1925. In 1936, 11 years before Obici's death, the firm had executive and sales offices in Wilkes-Barre and branch sales offices in New York, Philadelphia, Chicago, and Boston.

Obici left his mark not only in the processing of peanuts but on two cities—Wilkes-Barre and Suffolk. On October 4, 1946, 360 business and professional leaders of the Wyoming Valley gathered at The Hotel Sterling to pay honor to Obici at a dinner given by the Young Men's Division of the Wyoming Valley Chamber of Commerce.

Obici was presented a penned scroll with this inscription: "We are proud to offer his story as a shining example of what can be accomplished by an individual possessing vision, energy, and ambition. We are doubly proud because it all began right here in Wilkes-Barre."

Dozens of telegrams from all over the country were read at the dinner, including congratulations from the Virginia State Chamber of Commerce and the Suffolk Chamber of Commerce. Obici was honored in Virginia as a businessman who had brought an industry to the state and helped a town grow.

When Obici died his estate in trust amounted to $13.7 million. He left funds to the Suffolk Hospital under a charitable trust, to a hospital in Oderzo, Italy, and he left a trust to his friends and relatives.

AMERICAN ASPHALT PAVING COMPANY, INC.

American Asphalt Paving Company, Inc., is a leader in manufacturing and supplying crushed stone, sand, and gravel; the construction of driveways, parking lots, and tennis courts; and road construction and resurfacing. It has served, along with its predecessors, the residential, commercial, industrial, and institutional needs of the community for over three generations.

For the past 64 years the Banks family has been building the highways and streets that the commerce and industry of the Wyoming Valley needed to move their goods to market.

John and Bernard Banks manage the family corporations, comprised of American Asphalt, Banks Equipment Company, East Falls Sand and Gravel, and a number of smaller enterprises. The operations are run from the corporate headquarters on Chase Road in Jackson Township, where the firm operates an asphalt plant and a quarry.

The businesses were started by their grandfather, Joseph Banks, in the 1920s and their father, Bernard "Ben" Banks, in the 1930s and 1940s. Enterprises included Joseph Banks Construction Company, Banks Sand and Stone Company, Kelly Run Stone Quarry, Banks & Futch, West Mountain Quarry, and Nesquehoning Quarries. Ben C. Banks operated quarries in Luzerne County near the famous Hairpin Turnpike selling aggregate, sand, and gravel to contractors and coal strippings in Luzerne, Sullivan, Schuylkill, and Westmoreland counties.

These ventures were the forerunner of the present company, American Asphalt Paving Company, Inc., which was formed in 1951 as material suppliers and later as road builders and paving contractors for governmental, residential, industrial, and commercial clients.

American Asphalt was incorporated by Ben C. Banks, Frank Martz, H. Eugene Wagner, Judge Tom Lewis,

At the American Asphalt Plant in Chase, Pennsylvania, are (left to right) Richard A. Scott, controller; Gerald P. Dixon, president of Wilkes-Barre Construction Company; Bernard C. Banks, Jr., vice-president; and Richard A. Halliday, plant superintendent.

Frank A. O'Neil, Emil Rothman, and James Ruggere. This arrangement lasted for a decade, and then the Banks family bought out the other partners.

In 1954 John Banks and Bill Schiel formed Banks & Schiel Paving Company and operated it out of the headquarters of American Asphalt. That same year Ben C. Banks purchased the East Falls Sand and Gravel Corporation in Wyoming County and formed a sister company, the Banks Equipment Company. By 1961 the firms were consolidated, Banks & Schiel Paving was phased out, and the coal strip-mine operation in Pottsville closed.

The family operations are composed of American Asphalt Paving Company, crushed stone and bituminous concrete manufacturer and supplier, asphalt paving, and road and street construction; East Falls Sand and Gravel, sand and gravel and bituminous concrete manufacturer and supplier; and Banks Equipment Company: maintaining and leasing construction equipment to the affiliates. John was elected president of American Asphalt and East Falls and vice-president of Banks Equipment Company. Bernard became president of Banks Equipment Company and vice-president and treasurer of American Asphalt and East Falls.

When the Banks family gained complete control, the company accelerated its pattern of growth. In 1960 sales were listed at $136,000. In 1983 American Asphalt reported sales of $14 million and the combined group of companies reported sales of more than $16 million. There are 361 persons employed by the firm, which has an annual payroll of $3 million. The combined operations of American Asphalt and East Falls account for sales of 400,000 to 700,000 tons of stone, and the processing and sale of 150,000 to 200,000 tons of asphalt each year.

Following the Agnes Flood, the

company played a substantial role in the redevelopment of the city of Wilkes-Barre and other affected municipalities in the Wyoming Valley. Projects completed by American Asphalt include the construction of the streets and the sidewalks surrounding Public Square, the GAR redevelopment project in the Heights section of the city, Sherman Street Park, many of the streets and sewers in Kingston and Wilkes-Barre, as well as the tennis courts at Kirby Park. Some of the larger projects in the flood area are the construction of the canopy of South Main Street and Public Square, and the construction of Pennsylvania Boulevard.

John and Bernard Banks also own private companies outside the American group. In 1969 County Hauling was formed to conduct a trucking business. Wilkes-Barre

Checking out an American Asphalt Paving Company's construction job, this one on Interstate 81, are John F. Banks, president; Robert E. Schuler, retired construction superintendent; Theodor Mueller, construction supplies superintendent; Frank Wentzel, general foreman; and James E. Sterner, construction manager.

Construction Company was organized in 1974 to engage in the paving of commercial, industrial, and residential properties. Eaton Supply Company, formed in 1977, manufactures sand and gravel in a plant located off Route 309, three miles south of Tunkhannock. These three firms

Pictured from left to right are Karl F. Fries, plant superintendent; George Sloan, plant manager; Raymond Kirpa, materials manager; James P. Dermody, insurance and personnel manager; and Harold Post, quarry superintendent at American Asphalt's quarry in Chase.

merged into Wilkes-Barre Construction Company in 1980. The Meadowcrest Water Company, a public utility in Trucksville, was formed in 1974.

Bernard Banks, active in community projects, is executive board member of the Penn Mountains Boy Scout Council, president of the Newberry Country Club, treasurer of the Pennsylvania Aggregates and Concrete Association, past president of both the Dallas Kiwanis Club and the Back Mountain Council on Drug and Alcohol Abuse, and past director of the Pennsylvania Aggregates Association.

John Banks has been affiliated with the Pennsylvania Asphalt Paving Association and serves on the board of the Associated Pennsylvania Contractors' Association.

IREM TEMPLE

Irem was the 71st temple chartered by the Imperial Council of the Ancient Arabic Order of Nobles of the Mystic Shrine at its session of 1895 at Nantasket, Massachusetts.

The Shrine was organized in 1872 in New York, and some say it grew out of the "13 craze" that swept the city in the 1870s. History has recorded that the Shrine first developed in the mind of Dr. Walter Millard Fleming and his 12 companions, who met each day at 12:13 for lunch. William J. Florence, an actor, is credited as being the author of many of the Shrine's ceremonies and rituals.

From its initial charter membership of 54, Irem Temple has grown to more than 8,600 nobles in the 11,000 square miles of the temple's jurisdiction. J. Ridgway Wright was elected the first potentate of Irem, with William L. Raeder as the chief rabban, at an election held on October 15, 1895.

The mosque on North Franklin Street in Wilkes-Barre, with glazed tiles rimming the brick building and its four minarets, is considered to be one of the most beautiful in Shrinedom. The laying of the cornerstone of the mosque was a ceremony that was remembered for years as the most lavish in Wyoming Valley history.

The event was held on Thanksgiving Eve, November 27, 1907. After a "Special Ceremonial Session Extraordinary" held at Memorial Hall, the Shriners, wearing fezzes and black gowns, formed ranks and at 11:30 a.m. paraded to the site of the new temple as a large crowd lined the streets to watch. Leading the way was a platoon of city policemen and Alexander's Ninth Regiment Band. Constructed at a cost of $230,000, the mosque was formally dedicated on December 15 and 16, 1908. The two-day affair was highlighted by a banquet served to 1,200 nobles and their ladies. The exterior of the mosque was patterned after St. Sophia's Mosque in Constantinople and the

One of the most lavish ceremonies in Wyoming Valley history accompanied the laying of the cornerstone for Irem Temple on November 27, 1907. Located on North Franklin Street in Wilkes-Barre, it was patterned after St. Sophia's Mosque in Constantinople.

interior was a replica of the Court of Lions in Alhambra Palace in Granada, Spain. During the remodeling of the temple in 1931 most of the ornate decor, including the slender columns, was eliminated.

It was in 1926 that the nobles of Irem Temple first became involved actively with the Shriners' program of supporting hospitals for the treatment of crippled children. That year Irem

Seated (left to right) are Thomas E. Lehman III, past potentate and treasurer; James O. Brokenshire, high priest and prophet; Donald E. Britt, chief rabban; Edward S. Powell, illustrious potentate; Paul Schramm, assistant rabban; Peter P. Caprari, oriental guide; and Lawrence E. Pace, past potentate and recorder. Standing left to right are William Dickson, past potentate and board of governors; David M. Pierce, recorder emeritus; Sterling G. Lamoreux II, board of governors; Ray W. Hayes, board of governors; Edward L. Herbert, imperial representative; Robert E. Metzger, imperial representative; Gilbert D. Tough, board of governors; and Timothy D. Shaw, board of governors.

sent three children to the Philadelphia hospital. The following year a picnic and circus was held for the crippled children of the Wyoming Valley.

That tradition of service has grown so that each September the nobles of Irem donate their time to sponsor a three-day circus at the 109th Armory in Wilkes-Barre. Schoolchildren get a chance to see the circus at a reduced price. The youngsters, joined by their parents and friends, do their part to aid crippled children, for the money obtained from the event is given for the support of the Shriners' hospitals.

In 1928 the nobles of Irem set out to raise $650,000 for the payment of debts owed on the temple and the country club and to turn a portion of the country club into a convalescent home for the crippled children at the Shriners' hospitals. The purpose was

to free beds at the hospitals so that more children could be treated.

In the basement there were two dining rooms, one capable of seating 1,200 persons and a smaller one capable of seating 230 persons. The first floor contained an auditorium and offices, while on the second floor was a balcony. The third floor held a small dance hall that could double as a lodge hall. While the temple has lost some of its interior splendor, it is a popular auditorium for shows, meetings, and plays, and is used extensively by community groups.

Irem Temple also owns a country club in the Back Mountain complete with a golf course and a swimming pool. The club was obtained in 1920 and is a popular meeting place for civic groups in the area.

The first event to be held at the

country club was an outdoor ceremonial on August 1, 1923, to initiate a class of novices. The event was a success and has become an annual tradition.

During the Imperial Session, held in Washington, D.C., in 1921, President Warren G. Harding was made an honorary member of Irem Temple. In his response to the presentation, he told the audience that many of his ancestors had come from the Wyoming Valley.

Spearhead of the project was Frederick J. Weckesser. The nobles and many of the people of the Wyoming Valley rallied to support the drive and in a two-week period the $650,000 was pledged. Weckesser had officially

The Irem Temple Country Club, Dallas, Pennsylvania.

started the campaign with a $50,000 gift. Fred M. Kirby followed Weckesser's example and pledged $25,000, with the promise of an additional $25,000 should the $650,000 be raised.

Tragedy struck Irem Temple at this time in the form of the Great Depression. By November 1928 only $300,000 of the money that had been pledged was actually paid. By late 1929 the Depression had stolen any hope of receiving the remainder. Thus, the dream of Irem's convalescent home for crippled children remained just that— a dream.

The plight of Irem Temple in those years illustrates the depths the Depression reached in the Wyoming Valley. Membership in the four-year period of 1929 to 1932 dropped from 7,575 to 6,458 and only dues reduction slowed further dropping.

Irem's history has its lighter moments as well, one of which was the remodeling of the temple. The architectural firm of Mack and Sahm of Wilkes-Barre received the nod to draw up specifications for the remodeling.

Before the actual work began the son of the temple's original architect arrived in Wilkes-Barre. Francis W. Puckey was a prominent Chicago architect who had retained his ties with the Wyoming Valley through his membership in Irem Temple.

Puckey, after examining the plans for the renovation, discovered several flaws, the most important being the pitch of the auditorium floor. He pointed out that if the floor was pitched according to the specifications, there would be insufficient room between the main floor and the balcony for anyone to stand erect.

The building committee proceeded with the plans, nevertheless, and, as Puckey had predicted, only a small child could walk erect into the auditorium. Several rows of seats in the balcony were removed, but did not

The beautiful Irem Temple auditorium is popular with community groups for meetings and entertainments.

Overlooking the scenic 18-hole golf course at the Irem Temple Country Club.

Located among the rolling hills of northeastern Pennsylvania, the Irem Temple Country Club includes a spacious clubhouse, dining facilities, and guest rooms.

result in the needed headroom. Lowering the pitch was out of the question. The solution was the famous "dip" in the auditorium floor of the temple.

The history of Irem Temple records that many of the nobles were critical of the renovation because the beauty and grandeur of the interior was sacrificed in the name of "functionalism." But that history fails to record that with the remodeling of the temple, Irem

gave to the Valley an auditorium which even today serves as the largest playhouse in the area.

Irem weathered the years of World War II and by 1945 reversed its drop in membership and freed itself of any indebtedness. This also was the era of the Irem Horse Shows and the Mounted Patrol.

During the '60s and '70s Irem registered many firsts. George C. Smith was elected potentate in 1963, making him the first potentate to occupy an office held by his father. In 1974 Thomas J. Reese became the first potentate in Irem's history to be elected president of the Mid-Atlantic Shrine Association.

As the '70s unfolded Irem was presented with difficulties the chapter had not been forced to contend with in its early days. Irem arose to the challenge of the 1972 Agnes Flood, which destroyed the social area of the temple but left the auditorium undamaged. More than 200 nobles and their families displaced by the flood were housed at the country club, and a relief program was established to aid victims of the flood.

In 1975 Irem Temple's Legion of Honor won a national championship for precision drilling and two years later Irem won 17 trophies, the most ever won by a temple, in the Mid-Atlantic Shrine Association convention.

As the 1980s unfolded, Irem rededicated itself to aiding crippled children as the Philadelphia unit of the Shriners' hospitals established a spinal cord injury center. In 1983 the Great Hospital Crusade was held by Irem to raise funds for the Shriners' hospitals.

In the year 1983 Irem Temple's 7,600 nobles of the Mystic Shrine were led by the Illustrious Potentate Edward S. Powell.

Irem Temple remains a viable force in the Wyoming Valley, giving service through its nobles and its Shriners' affiliation.

BEDWICK & JONES

Bedwick & Jones was organized in 1961 by Robert Jones, a printer, and Raymond Bedwick, a salesman. Jones, 19, and Bedwick, 21, worked for Planters Peanuts and had a common dream—owning their own business. With a secondhand press they set up a print shop in Wilkes-Barre.

Jones worked full time at the print shop, while Bedwick held down his sales job and worked part time at the print shop and solicited customers. Within a year Bedwick & Jones was a going business and both men became full-time printers.

In 1964 the firm moved to Kingston. After the 1972 floor the print shop was located on the Sans Souci Highway until 1977 and then moved into a new facility in the Hanover Estates.

Jones continues to handle the print shop and oversees the work of the eight full-time and three part-time

Raymond Bedwick

Robert Jones

employees, while Bedwick handles sales and customer relations.

At Bedwick & Jones, design is fundamental to an effective printed piece. The firm provides art, photography, maps, and graphs to go with a client's work.

Modern cameras, combined with automatic plate-making equipment, assure good impressions. It is on the

company's modern offset press that the careful work of the darkroom and the plate-making department pays off. Bedwick & Jones' pressmen are skilled craftsmen in the tradition of the industry.

A completely equipped bindery folds, gathers, collates, punches, perforates, stitches, and trims any brochure, catalog, magazine, and book before it is checked and packed for delivery.

Bedwick oversees a salesman in the Philadelphia/Allentown area and maintains contact with an ad agency in Philadelphia and New York. Some of the firm's work has been seen in nationwide publications such as the *Ladies' Home Journal*. The firm publishes monthly magazines. For the past eight years the monthly publication *Arabesque*, a magazine of international dance, has been published by Bedwick & Jones.

The partners agree that there are no special formulas or solutions to quality printing. Each client's needs and wishes are a special job that must be handled on an individual basis. The design, typography, photography or art, and the printing must be appropriate to the client's objectives.

The Bedwick & Jones pressmen, such as Ken Lewis (shown here), are skilled craftsmen.

265

FOSTER WHEELER ENERGY CORPORATION

When Foster Wheeler Energy Corporation moved to Mountaintop in 1953, it heralded a rebirth of heavy industry in northeastern Pennsylvania.

The Wilkes-Barre area prior to the Depression had been noted for its heavy industry, train-repair shops, and coal. By the end of World War II the economy was troubled and the area was listed by the federal government as a depressed region.

Foster Wheeler demonstrated its faith in the future of the area when, in 1952, it set up a modest manufacturing operation at an existing plant on Ruddle Street in downtown Wilkes-Barre. Construction of a much larger facility was already moving forward. On March 20, 1953, a 120,000-square-foot plant was officially opened at Crestwood Industrial Park at Mountaintop. By April 9 the initial crew of 75 men had made the first shipment of heat-exchange equipment.

Since then the Mountaintop plant has grown into a complex covering almost 170,000 square feet situated on 104 acres. The main building is 100 feet by 800 feet long and stands 75 feet high. Two side bays and a plate shop cover 60,875 square feet. Adjacent service areas, including stores, outside inspection, and a detached X-ray building, total approximately 29,000 square feet.

Foster Wheeler Energy Corporation—the major United States subsidiary of Foster Wheeler Corporation—designs, fabricates, and constructs steam generating equipment as well as process plants for the petroleum and chemical industries. Formed by the 1927 merger of two companies established at the turn of the century, Foster Wheeler Corporation today is an international engineering, manufacturing, and construction organization.

Foster Wheeler furnishes electric utilities with boilers, condensers, feedwater heaters, and major auxiliary equipment. Foster Wheeler marine steam generators power thousands of the world's ships, while industrial units serve a wide range of customers.

The Mountaintop facility produces Foster Wheeler's largest pieces of steam equipment, including drums, headers, and feedwater heaters. A special area provides for the assembly of critical, high-tolerance, extremely close quality-control components. Some of the largest steam drums ever built in the United States have been shipped from the Mountaintop plant.

One of the plant's major tools is an 8,000-ton beam press weighing more than three million pounds. The largest of its type ever made, it is capable of bending steel plate up to eight inches thick and 40 feet long to form half shells. When welded together by automated equipment, these parts become steam drums or feedwater heater shells.

Holes for tube stubs are then drilled in the cylinder. The plant is equipped with five radial drills on an elevated

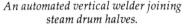

An automated vertical welder joining steam drum halves.

This 8,000-ton beam press is capable of bending eight-inch steel plate.

The main bay of Foster Wheeler's Mountaintop plant.

track. Each has an eight-foot arm and a 19-inch column. The drills can bore precisely located holes up to four inches in diameter through steam drums and headers having a shell thickness in excess of eight inches.

Strict quality control standards are maintained in the handling and insertion of long, U-shaped tubing into feedwater heater shells. Techniques include "clean and dry" materials, "clean rooms," and "white glove" treatment of tubes by workers. Welding of internal tubing in feedwater heaters and tube stubs to drums and headers is accomplished by specially designed automated equipment.

During all phases of fabrication, various nondestructive test procedures are employed to assure that the vessel satisfies all requirements of the particular specifications to which it is built. A two-million-volt X-ray machine in an adjacent building can detect faults to a maximum thickness of 12 inches. Hydrostatic tests to pressures well beyond those anticipated in use further certify the integrity of the vessel.

Conscious of the necessity to develop and apply new manufacturing methods, Mountaintop's engineers continously direct their efforts toward achieving better techniques to assure reliability. Over the years this work has resulted in advanced procedures and specialized equipment.

Railroad facilities at the Mountaintop plant enable direct delivery of its products to all areas of North America. Steam drum shipments from the plant have ranged up to those built for the largest units in the United States. Port Newark, the largest cargo facility of the Port of New York Authority, less than 200 miles away, can accept equipment for overseas shipment. Other boiler components have been forwarded to overseas customers through the port facilities at Baltimore.

A giant boiler steam drum being readied for shipment.

GEORGE L. RUCKNO, INC.

George L. Ruckno (1904-1982), founder of the firm that bears his name.

For more than 47 years, the name George L. Ruckno has been synonymous with custom home design and construction in the Wyoming Valley.

Born in 1904, George Ruckno was a "self-made man." Gaining early skills during World War I when he worked at the Hog Island Shipyards in Philadelphia, at the age of 15 he had already begun an energetic and enterprising career. Working days and attending school at night, he earned a diploma from the University of Pennsylvania Wharton School of Business in 1929. A year later he started his building career as a partner in Delong and Ruckno. By 1937 Ruckno owned his own construction company and with a friend, Ralph Garrahan, began developing the northern Westmoor section of Kingston. During World War II, with private home construction at a standstill, Ruckno built housing for the government in Berwick. It was after the war, however, that George Ruckno became widely known for building top-quality, affordable homes both for the working man and the professional.

In 1943 he married Elizabeth Caffrey, who became vice-president and partner in the expanding business. The construction company was incorporated in 1945 and one year later Forty Fort Lumber Company was started as a companion venture. Throughout the '50s and '60s the Ruckno business grew and prospered. It developed the residential complexes of Shrine Acres in the Back Mountain; Foothills Manor, White Rock Terrace, "Toy Town," and Exeter Park on the west side; and Merrywood Hills in Mountaintop. During this period George Ruckno gathered around him a competent and loyal staff of carpenters and office personnel. (In 1973 he proudly honored 27 employees with a cumulative total of 689 years of service with his firm.)

In the 1970s the housing market changed dramatically as a result of inflation. The business was expanded to include home remodeling and light commercial construction as well as home building. In 1981 the lumber company added a modern home center and hardware store to complement the traditional lumberyard.

George L. Ruckno, Inc., today continues to grow and diversify under the ownership of the seven Ruckno children who strive to maintain the ideals and spirit of its founder, George L. Ruckno.

WILKES-BARRE CLAY PRODUCTS COMPANY

"Weaver Bass Bugs" might be credited with keeping alive Wilkes-Barre Clay Products Company, Forty Fort, during the Great Depression, explains Peter S. Weaver, a member of the third generation of the family that has operated the firm since its founding in 1918 by his grandfather, Harry Richards Weaver.

Weaver explains that his grandfather was an avid sportsman and environmentalist. The construction business was slow during the Depression, and his grandfather tied bass bugs that during the summer he distributed to shops in New England under the trade name of "Weaver Bass Bugs."

Until the Depression Wilkes-Barre Clay Products was a thriving concern, with offices in Syracuse, Albany, Rochester, and Philadelphia. The firm was the broker for much of the bricks and building tiles that were used in New York and Pennsylvania. Out of the company's main office in the Brooks Building in Wilkes-Barre moved bid prices for the major construction jobs taking place in the two states. Brick was, and still is, a

Harry Richards Weaver, founder of Wilkes-Barre Clay Products Company.

relatively inexpensive building material. During the Depression days, brick sold for one cent per brick.

After the Depression Wilkes-Barre Clay Products retrenched and prospered—until World War II put a halt to all but defense construction. Harry Richards Weaver died in 1943 and the business was closed until his son, Harry Robert, was discharged from the Navy in 1945. The firm was moved to the present location in Forty Fort.

H. Robert Weaver, a graduate of Lehigh University, worked for Bethlehem Steel before entering the Navy. Wilkes-Barre Clay Products took advantage of the postwar building boom.

The company regained much of its business and moved back into New York State. It continued in its role as a distributor for the building industry. In 1968 Peter S. Weaver joined Wilkes-Barre Clay Products after spending two years with Sperry Rand after his graduation from Lehigh University. When his father died in 1980 he assumed the presidency of the firm and his brother, H. Robert Weaver, Jr., assumed the vice-presidency. Under their guidance Wilkes-Barre Clay Products has continued to grow and now employs 14 persons.

Wilkes-Barre Clay Products has supplied building materials for many of the most important construction projects in the 1970s and early 1980s in the eastern part of Pennsylvania. Among those projects were Allentown/Bethlehem Airport, Hilltown Hotel at Allentown, Blue Shield headquarters at Camp Hill, the Lycoming County Courthouse, the N.P.W. and Veterans' hospitals in Wilkes-Barre, and Wilkes and King's colleges.

The firm's main office is located at 140 Dilley Street, Forty Fort.

BALESTER OPTICAL COMPANY

The modern facilities of the Balester Optical Company.

In 1934, when Fred Balester, Sr., bought a secondhand machine and started doing surfacing of lenses for local optometrists, no one knew that 50 years later it would grow into one of the largest wholesale laboratories on the East Coast.

The Balester Optical Company existed for the first two years of its life in the basement of the Balester home on Dagobert Street, Wilkes-Barre. That first year Fred Balester, Sr., did $1,700 worth of business. Today the firm employs more than 150 persons and has an annual payroll of $2 million and sales of over $5.5 million.

During the next two years Balester hired and trained two neighborhood boys, setting in motion a company training system that exists to this day.

Balester Optical moved out of the Balester basement into the First Federal Building at Market and Franklin streets following the 1936 flood. The firm had now grown to six employees.

The venture flourished during the war years. In late 1945 Fred Balester, Jr., returned home from the service and the following year a partnership was formed by Fred Balester, Sr., and his two sons, Fred Jr. and James.

Fred Balester, Sr., died in 1975, and James retired in 1982, leaving the operation of Balester Optical to Fred Jr. and his son, Jonathan, executive vice-president. Five other family members are associated with the business today.

In 1960 Balester Optical constructed a building on South Franklin and soon added a second floor. Within two years the firm built another facility on North River Street. The old structure on

South Franklin Street is now the home of the Greater Wilkes-Barre Chamber of Commerce.

Balester Optical scored a first in the history of eyeglasses in the 1970s when the company invented "equine eyeglasses." During training at Pocono Downs, Lord Hanover, a trotter, had been jumping over shadows on the ground, which caused him to lose his

Fred Balester, Sr. (center), founder of the Balester Optical Company, and his sons, James (right), who retired from the business in 1982, and Fred Jr. (left), current president, at the grand opening of the North River Street plant in 1962.

stride. An optometrist tested the horse and found that Lord Hanover was farsighted. Balester Optical came to the rescue and produced a pair of "equine eyeglasses" ground to Lord Hanover's individual prescription and mounted in the horse's blinkers with nylon fishing line.

In 1972 the firm was sold to the Itek Corporation of Lexington, Massachusetts, but in 1979 the Balester family bought back the enterprise and formed a corporation.

Balester Optical is one of the leading wholesale distributors of custom-made eyeglasses and prescription safety glasses for industry—as well as an occasional race horse. Its 10 salesmen cover a market area extending from the mid-Atlantic states through the Virginias.

Fred and Jonathan are active in national organizations in their industry. Jonathan is on the board of directors of the Better Vision Institute of America and is the regional board chairman for the Optical Laboratories Association; Fred is chairman of the board of the Qualified Laboratories of the Optical Laboratory Association of America.

FIT-RITE HEADWEAR, INC.

Fit-Rite Headwear, Inc., is one of the area's industries that delivers a Wilkes-Barre product throughout the United States and Canada. Considered a leading producer of hard hat winter liners, Fit-Rite also manufacturers other safety accessories such as highway safety vests, disposable sweatbands, industrial painting hoods, welding caps, and mining caps and belts. The company was founded in 1922 as the Wilkes-Barre Cap Manufacturing Company by Louis Scherz, a European immigrant whose family cap-making tradition dated back to the mid-19th century. The firm was incorporated as Fit-Rite Headwear in 1957 and remains a family-owned business to this day.

Scherz originally catered to the area's and the nation's mining industry by producing some of the nation's first mining and fire-fighting helmets, patented seamless aluminum lunch kits, work gloves, battery belts,

and cloth miner caps with a patented "Double Safety" lamp holder. During this period Wilkes-Barre Cap also produced a line of children's and men's headwear, including souvenir caps for the 1939 World's Fair.

In 1946, upon his discharge from service as an Army Air Corps captain, Scherz's son-in-law, Martin Schonwetter, joined the firm. After World War II, as northeastern Pennsylvania's coal-mining industry declined, and cloth and vulcanized fiber mining headwear were being replaced by fiberglass hard hats, Wilkes-Barre Cap concerted its marketing efforts toward a more commercial line of children's dress hats and caps and men's hunting, fishing, and yachting caps while finding a new market for its mining caps and belts in the mushroom industry where light was required for the dark mushroom houses and caves. In the late 1950s, with the influx of imported headwear from the Far East, the company, now incorporated as Fit-Rite Headwear, once again rerouted its marketing path back toward the industrial market with its production of winter liners for hard hats.

Following the death of Louis Scherz in 1965, Martin Schonwetter headed the firm, and under his leadership Fit-Rite continued to increase its share of the marketplace and prosper. Upon her husband's untimely death in 1970, Sarah Schonwetter took over as president. In the early 1970s, when OSHA required the use of hard hats throughout U.S. industry, Fit-Rite found its production of winter liners to literally double overnight, and under Mrs. Schonwetter's guidance the firm continued to expand into other safety equipment areas such as traffic safety vests, cellulose sponge sweatbands, and various welding and patented fire-fighting accessories.

After the disastrous Agnes Flood of 1972, Fit-Rite moved to its present location at 92 South Empire Street. Today the family has its third generation active in the business as Mrs. Schonwetter has been joined by her son Steven, daughter Patricia, and son-in-law John Bonner in the operation of the company.

Louis Scherz, founder of Fit-Rite Headwear, Inc. (as he appeared in 1941), held a number of U.S. patents including one received in 1927 for one of the earliest automobile directional signals.

Martin Schonwetter (president from 1965 to 1970) guided the firm from a fashion line of children's headwear to its present-day line of industrial and safety products.

BARTIKOWSKY JEWELERS

Max Bartikowsky founded the original Bartikowsky Jewelers in 1905 on Main Street in Kingston.

Bernard Bartikowsky, son of the founder, is chairman of the board of the company.

Jewelers have come and gone over the decades since the settlements along the Susquehanna River grew into boroughs and cities.

But the oldest jeweler still remains, giving the same personal service Max Bartikowsky gave in 1887 as he traveled throughout the Wyoming Valley by horse and buggy as an itinerant jeweler.

Bartikowsky arrived in the Valley from his home on the border between Germany and Lithuania in 1880, when Wilkes-Barre's population was only slightly more than 23,500.

He became friends with another budding itinerant merchant, F.M. Kirby, and they talked about going into business together. They parted when they could not agree on what to sell. Bartikowsky wanted to sell gold, silver, and diamonds; Kirby wanted to peddle pots and pans. Kirby went on to become one of the founders of the biggest five-and-dime store chain in the world.

Bartikowsky traveled around the Valley selling jewelry until 1905, when he established a store on Main Street, Kingston. The store would be moved back and forth from the west side of the river to the east before settling in Wilkes-Barre. Max Bartikowsky died in 1927 and his son Bernard took the helm of the company at that time.

In 1948 Bartikowsky purchased the Ernst Building on Public Square and the store remained at that location until the Agnes Flood. The store was displaced by redevelopment and Bartikowsky moved to a temporary modular facility at 38-44 North Main Street. The firm purchased its current large building on South Main Street and moved there in October 1978.

Bernard Bartikowsky today remains as chairman of the board, but the day-to-day operation of the business is in the hands of his son-in-law, Jay Karnofsky, president, and his sons, Leonard, vice-president, and Max, treasurer. Mac Ahmad is the fourth generation of the family now actively participating in the business.

Over the years Bartikowsky Jewelers has grown to become one of the nation's leading diamond organizations. Diamonds, gold, silver, and fine jewelry are what Bartikowsky is best known for in the Valley. However, 13,000 feet of showroom space makes it possible for the company to offer a wide selection of fine crystal, china, luggage, leather goods, and gift ware.

Bartikowsky offers special services to customers including a trade-in privilege for diamonds. Customers are allowed full purchase price paid toward a larger diamond or higher priced piece of jewelry.

The firm also has watch and jewelry repair shops on the premises and provides silver cleaning and polishing, engraving, gold stamping, and all types of jewelry repairs including creative designing.

In 1957 Bartikowsky became one of the early pioneers in catalog showroom merchandising by publishing in a four-color catalog all stock items and their prices. The catalog sales produced a big spurt in growth. In the 27 years since that first catalog, sales have jumped 4,000 percent; the firm now employs more than 50 persons.

The officers of Bartikowsky are all graduates of the Gemological Institute of America's Diamond Course and as such the company's diamond and jewelry appraisals are acceptable by all insurance companies. All diamonds sold by Bartikowsky are accompanied by a "diamond guarantee certificate," which is a legal certification of the exact quality, weight, and value of the purchase.

Bartikowsky has operated a thriving business in the repurchase of diamonds, precious stones, and gold

After several moves Bartikowsky Jewelers located in this store on Public Square, Wilkes-Barre, from 1948 until the 1972 Agnes Flood destroyed the building.

and silver jewelry. The concern is well known for its service in liquidations and bankrupt stock.

The company and the individual owners are active in the community. Bartikowsky Jewelers is a member of the Wilkes-Barre and United States Chambers of Commerce and the Wilkes-Barre Business and Professional Association.

Bernard Bartikowsky is president of the University of Pennsylvania Club of Greater Wilkes-Barre, and a member of the Century Club and President's Club of King's College, the President's Club and President's Circle of the University of Scranton, the John Wilkes Club and President's Club of Wilkes College, the Crime Clinic of Wyoming Valley, Inc., and the National Crime and Delinquency Citizens' Committee.

Jay Karnofsky was president of American Merchandisers Inc. for two years, and serves on the board of trustees of the Penn State Alumni Association. He has been a member of the Wilkes-Barre Kiwanis Club for 25 years and is a member of the Kiwanis Foundation. He also writes a column on gemstones for a Wilkes-Barre newspaper.

Max Bartikowsky is a director of the Wilkes-Barre Lions Club; Leonard Bartikowsky is a member of the Commercial Association of Scranton.

The firm has created a reputation throughout northeastern Pennsylvania for integrity and service. Every customer is treated with the same respect and courtesy and is given personal service (very often by one of the principals of the business). Every customer complaint is handled by one of the owners. No doubt this is why the people of the Wyoming Valley have been coming back to Bartikowsky Jewelers for 96 years.

The new showroom of Bartikowsky Jewelers on South Main Street, Wilkes-Barre.

LIBERTY THROWING COMPANY, INC.

Liberty Throwing Company, Inc., of Kingston is the largest independent manufacturer of elastic yarns north of the Mason-Dixon Line and ranks among the 10 largest in the industry.

The firm, which was founded in 1919, also features the largest installation of high-speed, American-made elastic yarn-manufacturing machines in the world. Liberty also specializes in high-speed warping and winding equipment which permits it to exclusively supply many of the branches of the textile field. Many of the high-speed machines have been crafted in Liberty's own shops.

The founders of the company were S.J. Aronsohn of Paterson, New Jersey, and Ben Levi and Charles M. Epstein of Wilkes-Barre. The Epstein family has operated the business since its founding. With the death in 1949 of Charles Epstein, Sr., the company came under the direction of his son, Charles M. Epstein, Jr.

In the late 1920s Aronsohn sold his interest in the firm to Epstein and Levi, and shortly thereafter Levi withdrew from an active role in the management of the firm.

The original plant and offices were located in Nanticoke, and the Kingston plant was acquired in 1929. A year later the office of the company was established at the Kingston plant and the sales office was opened in New York City.

The work force in those early years was approximately 30 persons. By the 1930s, when the manufacture and sale of silk products reached its peak in the Wyoming Valley, the work force rose to 300 persons. Today it stands at 110. Throughout its existence Liberty has had to change with the times to keep pace with the taste and preference of the buying public.

Immediately following World War I, silk was the rage for hosiery and outerwear for men and women. With the advent of rayon in the 1930s and nylon in the 1940s, the change in the

Charles M. Epstein, Jr., president of Liberty Throwing Company, Inc.

industry was radical.

In the late 1940s and continuing into the early 1950s, nylon was processed almost exclusively by the industry. When Du Pont developed Lycra, Liberty moved aggressively into elastic yarns—supplying the clothing, industrial, and medical sectors of the economy.

As the textile field moved south from the Northeast, Liberty took up the challenge and opened a sales office in Hickory, North Carolina, under the direction of Gerald E. Wagner, vice-president of sales. The firm also has developed and maintains a steady export trade, especially with elastic fabric manufacturers.

Liberty management displayed the aggressiveness which has kept it at the forefront of the industry when the Agnes Flood hit the Valley in 1972.

The disaster resulted in the inundation of the office and main manufacturing plant at Kingston. The firm suffered more than $2 million in flood damage and loss of sales. It was six months before the plant was able to resume full production.

Epstein has played a number of key roles in the civic affairs of the Valley. He chaired the United Way Drive in 1969, the General Hospital Capital Funds Drive in 1976, and the Wilkes College Drive in 1973. He is currently a director of the Children's Service Center, Greater Wilkes-Barre Chamber of Commerce, First Eastern Bank, the North Mountain Club, and General Hospital.

Liberty faces the 1980s with modern machinery, an aggressive sales approach, and a young, progressive management team led by vice-president of manufacturing Leonard Mallol, Dennis Wagner, and Larry Sprankle.

GRAHAM'S OFFICE SUPPLIES & EQUIPMENT, INC.

Today we find Thomas J. Graham still active in the office supply business. He is pictured here with son Thomas J. Graham, Jr., who succeeded his father as president in 1970.

Thomas J. Graham traces the beginning of his office supply business back to the year 1888, when John C. Madden first established a stationery store in downtown Wilkes-Barre.

After Madden's death in 1922, the firm was sold to Walter J. Kressly, and later was acquired by Thomas and Helen Graham in 1940. As an employee of Kressly for 14 years, Thomas Graham first preserved his former employer's name, and continued to furnish customers with a

The Graham stationery and office supply company, 96 South Main Street, as it appeared in 1940. Note the preservation of the Kressly name.

wide variety of stationery items and school supplies.

Today Graham's Office Supplies & Equipment, Inc., still provides the same broad range of office products, but has grown to offer customers of northeastern Pennsylvania an extensive line of high-quality office

furniture, space-saving filing systems, and a complete planning and design service.

Noted as specialists in innovative, cost-saving filing solutions, Graham's is a leader in the installation of mobile shelving systems and automated document retrieval units used wherever extensive files are required.

Generations of customers continue to rely on the Graham's name for the best in office supplies, as well as the newest and finest names in office furnishings and accessories.

TJL CONSTRUCTION COMPANY

This is the lobby of the New Bridge Center in Kingston, built in 1977 by the TJL Construction Company.

Torre J. Lippi, a 1974 graduate of Clemson University in South Carolina, began his career as a builder during his high school and college years while renovating homes.

A lifelong resident of the Wyoming Valley, he now heads and directs a very successful building and contracting firm which he began in 1977. The business was incorporated under the laws of the Commonwealth of Pennsylvania in 1981.

In recent years, the construction work done by TJL Construction in the greater Wilkes-Barre area has topped one million dollars annually. The company has built or renovated churches, office buildings, apartments for the elderly, medical centers, schools, banks, fraternal headquarters, and park and recreational developments.

In 1977 the firm built the $2-million New Bridge Center and in 1983 the $2-million Park Building. The centers are located on Third Avenue in Kingston and represent modern office facilities featuring energy efficiency and tenant comfort. TJL Construction in 1983 also began work on the waste-water treatment facility for the borough of Clarks Summit.

Most of the work the firm has done was awarded via competitive bidding. However, construction management for owners and fixed-price projects are also undertaken.

TJL Construction was originally located on 234 South River Street, Wilkes-Barre, before moving to its present office building on Page Avenue, Kingston.

Lippi looks forward to the resurgence of the construction industry in the Wyoming Valley. He and his company will be an important element in the area for many years to come.

A member of the Greater Wilkes-Barre, Hazleton, Pittston, and Scranton chambers of commerce, Lippi also belongs to the Contractor's Association, the American Institute of Contractors, the American Concrete Institute, and the National Fire and Protection Agency.

In the foreground is the New Bridge Center and in the left background is the $2-million Park Building erected by TJL Construction and completed in 1983.

ENERGY CONVERTORS, INC.

Every day people throughout the United States, Canada, and overseas heat their homes as well as bake and cook with appliances using heating elements manufactured in Dallas, Pennsylvania, by Energy Convertors, Inc. Known as ENCON, this corporation is a prime producer of heating elements for the electric baseboard heating industry and for many leading small-appliance companies.

The founding of ENCON in 1973 was the result of the combined efforts of many people of the Wyoming Valley. Headed by Hanford L. Eckman, several local persons experienced in the heating-element field recognized the need for a new facility that could supply the expanding appliance and heating industry. The proposed plan called for the construction of a new plant situated to employ displaced local people skilled in the production of heating elements. With the aid of the Greater Wilkes-Barre Chamber of Commerce and its affiliated agencies, who provided site selection advice and

direction, the plan became a reality.

ENCON began production and from the beginning was accepted in its field as a producer of high-quality products. Quality control, essential to the success of the product, has continued to be excellent, thanks to workers and management who possess the qualities of good workmanship and attention to detail.

Initially ENCON specialized in the manufacture of baseboard heating elements. Soon, capitalizing on its technical expertise and production capabilities, it expanded into the manufacture of heating elements for small electric houseware appliances including heating elements for coffee makers, popcorn machines, frying pans, and griddles. Most recently, it has moved into the production of specialty elements for the automotive market, agricultural and environmental products, as well as elements for major household appliances, including refrigerators.

Well aware that energy conservation is a national priority, ENCON is actively involved in the

design and research of electric elements that can provide accurately controlled heat efficiently. This capability has contributed to the growth of the company.

Starting with a work force of 20 people, ENCON now normally employs 150 people. Located at the original site on Lower Demunds Road in Dallas, the building has been expanded to three times its original size.

ENCON, with its roots deep in the Wyoming Valley, has always been aware of its community. The founders have set an example of community participation, having served as members of the local zoning and planning boards, as college trustees and advisory board members, and as active members of the Chamber and the Industrial Fund. Community responsibility continues as a second generation enters the business and becomes committed to community service in the Wyoming Valley.

The ENCON plant, built in 1973, is located in Dallas, Pennsylvania.

THE STERLING

Once the showplace of the Wyoming Valley, frequented by Presidents and heads of industry, The Sterling is embarking on a new era in its history as a private, semi-luxury apartment building.

At present there are 193 tenants in residence. When the renovation is finished, it is expected that 245 to 280 people and 40 commercial tenants will call The Sterling home.

The hotel was built in five stages over a period of 53 years. The main hotel was finished in 1897 by Walter G. Sterling. The high-rise of 14 floors was begun in 1928 and partially completed in 1930. However, the 10th, 11th, and 12th floors were not completed until 1934, and the penthouse was not completed until 1936. The building that had been the Plaza Hotel and incorporated into The Hotel Sterling was torn down in 1949 and a four-story structure was completed the following year.

After the death of Sterling, Homer Mallow became the owner of the hotel.

During Mallow's period of ownership the high-rise was begun. The expansion was ill-fated, with the Depression halting the construction and bringing bankruptcy to Mallow.

It was in Mallow's time that the hotel became known as the "Hotel of the East," rivaling fine New York City hotels for splendor and service. The most popular restaurant in Wilkes-Barre was The Hotel Sterling's Peacock Room, which seated only 65 persons but on any single day served 500 to 600 patrons.

Senator Andrew Sordoni was the third owner of The Hotel Sterling. It was during the senator's reign that the hotel decor was enhanced by expensive art hangings in the main dining and ballrooms.

The original architectural drawings for The Hotel Sterling called for intricate towers and fancy ornamental work. However, dwindling funds resulted in the elimination of the ornate designs.

It was here that the "Big Bands" of the '40s and early '50s came to play on weekends. It was here that John L. Lewis stayed when he came to the Valley during World War II to rally the anthracite miners.

In 1968 the hotel was acquired by the prominent Engle family of Wilkes-Barre, manufacturers of the famous Roxzanne bathing suit. The Engles set about combining the smaller rooms into various-sized apartments. Several years after Engle's death the hotel complex was sold to Susquehanna Partners in 1981. Susquehanna engaged Orion Corporation of New Jersey to manage the apartment building into its new life.

Among the prominent guests over the years at the hotel were Mrs. Eleanor Roosevelt, President and Mrs. Nixon, Robert Kennedy, Jack Anderson, and a host of the famous and near-famous actors and actresses who came to Wilkes-Barre to perform at the Poali and Penn theaters when vaudeville was in its prime.

LACKAWANNA JUNIOR COLLEGE

The Wilkes-Barre Center of Lackawanna Junior College offers associate degrees in sciences and arts. A full curricula of business courses, such as this secretarial class, are offered.

For almost 100 years Lackawanna Junior College has been serving the needs of industry and business in northeastern Pennsylvania with clerical workers, bookkeepers, and accountants. With headquarters at Scranton, the college conducts classes in centers at Scranton, Wilkes-Barre, Hazleton, and Honesdale.

The development of business colleges in the eastern part of Pennsylvania closely paralleled the country's rush toward industrialization as the railroads bound the nation with ribbons of steel into one big marketplace.

In Lackawanna County the booming coal industry demanded more trained personnel than the city's school system could supply and led to the formation of the Scranton Business

College by H.D. Buck and A.R. Whitmore. The school was merged with the Lackawanna Business College in 1911 by John H. Seeley.

In 1976 Lackawanna Junior College and the Wilkes-Barre Business College merged, tying together two of the most widely known and prestigious business-oriented colleges in northeastern Pennsylvania.

The Wilkes-Barre Business College was founded in 1883 as a night school by a Professor Schneider, chief bookkeeper for the Lehigh Valley Coal Company. Daily sessions were begun

in 1887 and by 1890 the faculty and staff numbered eight persons.

The college grew and moved its site five times before ground was broken on September 15, 1924, for its own three-story building. The facility was occupied until 1935, when the college moved to the IBE Building on Public Square.

The college's building on Northampton Street in Wilkes-Barre is only a memory, having given way to redevelopment. However, it occupies a unique niche in the history of education in the Wyoming Valley.

Besides being the home of the college for 11 years, it was the home of Wilkes College when it began as Bucknell University Junior College in 1933 and was the first home of King's College in 1945.

Successors of Professor Schneider who kept the college alive and growing through the past 100 years were A.W. Moss, 1891-1896; G.L. Baldwin, 1890-1892; F.E. Wood, 1896-1897; Fred M. Allen, 1897-1910; Victor Lee Dodson, 1910-1945; William Aston, 1945-1951; and Dr. Ellis W. Roberts, 1951-1976.

In 1958 Lackawanna Junior College was granted the right by the Commonwealth of Pennsylvania to award associate degrees. During the late 1970s it took the lead in the development of the "weekend college" concept whereby persons can earn college credits by attending classes on Saturdays and Sundays. To better serve the adult working population of its market area, the college also expanded its offering in continuing education and evening college.

Today the college offers curricula leading to associate degrees in science and arts in the fields of accounting, banking and finance, business administration, business science, criminal justice, information systems, liberal arts, marketing, medical secretarial, public administration, and secretarial science.

BOHLIN POWELL LARKIN CYWINSKI

Wilkes-Barre Public Square, reconstructed by Bohlin Powell Larkin Cywinski and completed in 1979, is the historic and psychological center of the city. Photo by Joseph Molitor.

In 1965 Peter Q. Bohlin and Richard E. Powell established an architectural firm in Wilkes-Barre known as Bohlin & Powell. Almost from the time of its founding the firm has been recognized for its superior design work.

After the Agnes Flood in 1972, Bohlin & Powell became intimately involved with the reconstruction of downtown Wilkes-Barre, including Public Square and the South Main Street urban improvements. This work included the reconstruction of streets and underground utilities, the planting of more than 1,000 new trees along downtown streets, and the construction of the 1,800-foot glazed canopy that links stores along South Main Street and Public Square.

Additionally, the firm was responsible for numerous other buildings constructed in Wilkes-Barre since the 1972 flood, including the Ten East South Street Apartments, the Hampton Corners Commercial Building, and the City Heights Commercial and Elderly Housing Complex. Bohlin & Powell also undertook an extensive amount of recreation-related work, including the reconstruction of Kirby Park and the construction of Coal Street Park with its swimming center and ice skating facility.

Today the firm's involvement in Wilkes-Barre's growth continues with the renovation of the former George W. Guthrie School on North Washington Street, which will serve as the new headquarters for the InterMetro Industries Corporation.

As the firm grew, expansion took place in other cities. In 1978 an office was opened in Pittsburgh and in 1979, when John F. Larkin and Bernard J. Cywinski joined as principals, a Philadelphia office was established. Today the firm, now known as Bohlin Powell Larkin Cywinski, has a staff of more than 35, with five associates and four principals.

While the organization has the capacity to handle large and complex projects, it has maintained the ability to respond efficiently to smaller circumstances. This is reflected in the broad range of its current practice, which ranges from larger projects such as a new passenger terminal for the Harrisburg International Airport, a law library for the College of Law at Syracuse University, and a School for the Humanities and Social Sciences at Rensselaer Polytechnic Institute, to smaller projects such as private residences, small commercial buildings, and renovations of existing structures.

Bohlin Powell Larkin Cywinski is committed to design excellence in the broadest sense of the term. One measure of this is the numerous awards it has received for its completed projects. Since its founding, the firm has received more than 50 design awards from regional, state, and national awards programs.

A further mark of the company's reputation is the extensive publication its projects regularly receive. Bohlin Powell Larkin Cywinski's work has appeared in such prestigious architectural journals as *Architectural Record, Progressive Architecture,* and the *AIA Journal.*

The Conference Center at Luzerne Community College is organized along a central circulation "spine" flanked by lounges, auditoriums, meeting rooms, and dining areas. Photo by O. Baitz, Inc.

LUZERNE PRODUCTS INC.

Luzerne Products Inc. uses a precision operation known as warping to process synthetic fibers onto beams which knitters and weavers can use more economically.

James E. Bell, owner of Luzerne Products Inc.

Luzerne Products Inc. began operations in the Wyoming Valley in August 1967 by building a plant to serve the E.I. du Pont organization in the processing and repackaging of synthetic fibers in the northeastern United States market. The firm is owned by James E. Bell, Wilmington, Delaware, a former du Pont executive.

The plant was under construction in 1967, and the first warp-knit beams were produced in February 1968. The facility has been in continuous operation since that date, producing more than 300 million pounds. The plant, which began as a 20-warper operation, expanded to a 32-warper plant in 1974 and remains at that level today. The approximate annual capacity is 35 million pounds of 40-denier product. This capacity, of course, will vary significantly according to the task being met.

Luzerne Products employs a work force exceeding 200 people who have an average experience level of almost eight years. The management group has an experience level of just under 11 years. The Wyoming Valley has a readily available work force that is familiar with the textile industry. Added labor requirements have never been a problem.

During the history of Luzerne Products, its management has constantly endeavored to improve the technology and has been responsible for several improvements in the plant's operation. Some of the significant improvements are higher running speeds, development of a broken-end detector which eliminates drop wires, reduction of beam conditioning time, magnetic reversal-whorl creels, external transfer units whorl creels, and variable-speed control.

James Bell is very proud of his employees, who have excelled in product quality and in lower average product cost per pound. Hurricane Agnes in June 1972 brought four feet of water into the lower manufacturing and warehouse areas and resulted in the loss of one million pounds of yarn. Due to the extraordinary efforts of the firm's employees, the entire plant was back in full operation in less than two weeks.

EASTERN PENNSYLVANIA SUPPLY COMPANY

Eastern Pennsylvania Supply Company (EPSCo) was established in December 1889 as a partnership by Woodward Leavenworth and John N. and William H. Conyngham to supply the mines with their plumbing, heating, and building materials.

During its 94-year history the firm has been a family-owned corporation based in Wilkes-Barre. In 1911 EPSCo purchased property on South Pennsylvania Avenue and remained there until the Agnes Flood destroyed its warehouse and offices.

In 1974 the headquarters moved to an ultra-modern plant on 700 Scott Street, Wilkes-Barre. The warehouse has 1,304,000 gross cubic feet of storage space and 1,560 square feet in a self-service area. The plant contains 9,600 square feet of office space on two floors. At its headquarters EPSCo employs 66 workers.

The firm has weathered two floods, the Great Depression, a fire, and the

An aerial view of the warehouse and office of the Eastern Pennsylvania Supply Company, 700 Scott Street, Wilkes-Barre, built in 1973.

closing of the mining industry to become the main supplier of wholesale plumbing, heating, building materials, and industrial supplies in northeastern Pennsylvania, with branches in Allentown, Athens (Bradford County), Stroudsburg, and Throop.

EPSCo focused entirely on the wholesale business. The years 1936 to 1938, were to be hard times for EPSCo as the Susquehanna River overflowed

its banks. In 1938 four of the major coal companies went under, taking with them a large chunk of business.

The year 1938 also saw the area's first appeal for funds for industrial development, and EPSCo and its management played a major role in this endeavor.

By 1951 coal company business comprised only 10 percent of the total business of EPSCo. As EPSCo expanded it acquired the first of its branches in the Northeast with the Allentown property in 1953. In 1958 the firm purchased a new location in Allentown and expanded the business. Stroudsburg was added to the growing market for EPSCo three years later.

The opening of the Throop branch for industrial operations was accomplished in 1970. EPSCo began to plan for the warehouse on Scott Street in 1971 and this was hastened by the Agnes Flood. The warehouse and office was opened in 1974, the same year that the C.B. Scott Company was purchased on August 24 from the Scott family. In 1977 the two concerns were merged into one corporate entity.

Various types of nails used in the mines are illustrated in this 1920s Eastern Pennsylvania Supply Company catalog.

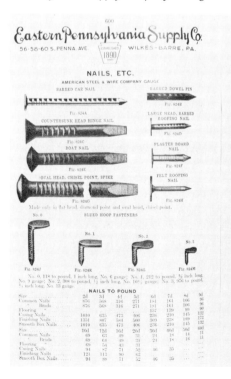

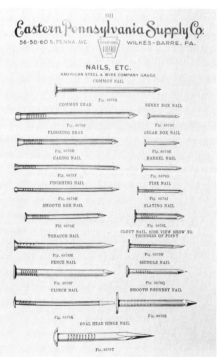

PATRONS

The following individuals, companies, and organizations have made a valuable commitment to the quality of this publication. Windsor Publications, the Greater Wilkes-Barre Chamber of Commerce, and the Wyoming Historical and Geological Society gratefully acknowledge their participation in *Wyoming Valley: An American Portrait.*

American Asphalt Paving Company, Inc.*
Balester Optical Company*
Bartikowsky Jewelers*
Bedwick & Jones*
Bergman's Department Store*
Bertels Can Company*
Blue Cross of Northeastern Pennsylvania*
Bohlin Powell Larkin Cywinski*
College Misericordia*
Comfort Designs, Inc.*
Cornell Iron Works, Inc.*
Deemer & Company, Inc.*
Diamond Manufacturing Company*
Dunbar Builders Hardware Inc.*
Eastern Pennsylvania Supply Company*

Eberhard Faber Inc.*
Energy Convertors, Inc.*
First Eastern Corp.*
Fit-Rite Headwear, Inc.*
Foster Wheeler Energy Corporation*
Franklin First Federal Savings and Loan Association*
Graham's Office Supplies & Equipment, Inc.*
Hanover Bank of Pennsylvania*
Irem Temple*
King's College*
Lackawanna Junior College*
Liberty Throwing Company, Inc.*
Dr. and Mrs. Edward A. Lottick
Luzerne Products Inc.*
Frank Martz Coach Company (Martz Trailways)*
Medical Oncology Associates—Dr. David Greenwald
Mercy Hospital of Wilkes-Barre*
Nabisco Brands Inc.*
Nesbitt Memorial Hospital*
Northeastern Bank of Pennsylvania*
NPW Medical Center*
Offset Paperback Mfrs., Inc.*
Pennsylvania Gas and Water Company*
Pennsylvania Millers Mutual

Insurance Company*
Pennsylvania State University Wilkes-Barre Campus*
The Pressed Steel Company*
Pyros and Sanderson, Architects*
George L. Ruckno, Inc.*
Smith, Miller and Associates, Inc.*
The Sterling*
Susquehanna Savings A Division of Atlantic Financial Federal*
Tamblyn Company*
The Times Leader*
TJL Construction Company*
Utility Engineers, Inc.*
Valley Automobile Club*
Valley Chevrolet
Valley Vending Company*
Wasserott's*
Wilkes-Barre Clay Products Company*
Wilkes-Barre General Hospital*
Wilkes College*
Wyoming Seminary*

*Partners in Progress of *Wyoming Valley: An American Portrait.* The histories of these companies and organizations appear in Chapter 11, beginning on page 202.

BIBLIOGRAPHY

Atherton, Sarah H. *Survey of Wage Earning Girls Below Sixteen Years of Age in Wilkes-Barre, Pennsylvania, 1915.* New York: National Consumers League, 1916.

Atkins, Herbert E., ed. *The Wyoming Valley Floods of 1936.* Wilkes-Barre: Collins Press, n. d.

Barrett, Mary I., comp. *Catalogue of the Edward Welles, Jr. Collection of Paintings by Artists in Wyoming Valley,* rev. ed. Wilkes-Barre: King's College Press, 1974.

_____ . *Luzerne County: A Bicentennial Bibliography.* Wilkes-Barre: Luzerne County Tourist Promotion Agency, 1976.

Berthoff, Rowland. "The Social Order of the Anthracite Region, 1825-1902," *Pennsylvania Magazine of History and Biography* 89 (July 1965), 261-291.

Bodnar, John E. *An Ethnic Bibliography of Pennsylvania History.* Harrisburg; Pennsylvania Historical and Museum Commission, 1972.

Brewster, William. *History of the Certified Township of Kingston, Pennsylvania, 1769-1929.* Wilkes-Barre: Smith Bennett Corporation, 1930.

Broehl, Wayne G. *The Molly Maguires.* Cambridge: Harvard University Press, 1964.

Bushman, Richard L. *From Puritan to Yankee: Character and Social Order in Connecticut, 1690-1765.* Cambridge: Harvard University Press, 1967.

Carmer, Carl L. *The Susquehanna.* New York: Rinehart, 1955.

Conway, Alan, ed. *The Welsh in America: Letters from Immigrants.* Minneapolis: Minnesota Press, 1961.

Cornell, Robert J. *Anthracite Strike of 1902.* Unpublished (WHGS)

Crook, Wilfred Harris. *Social Conflict Patterns in Wyoming Valley, Pa.* Lewisburg: Bucknell University Press, 1941.

Delaney, Leslie L. *Search for Friedenshutten, 1772-1972.* Wyoming: Cro Woods, 1973.

Drayer, Adam. M. *A History of Catholic Secondary Education in the Diocese of Scranton.* New York: Fordham University Press, 1953.

Farley, Eugene S. *Essays of an Educator.* Wilkes-Barre: Wilkes College, 1975.

Gallagher, John P. *A Century of History: The Diocese of Scranton, 1868-1968.* Scranton: Diocese of Scranton, 1968.

Gluck, Elsie. *John Mitchell, Miner: Labor's Bargain with the Gilded Age.* New York: The John Day Company, 1929.

Greene, Victor R. *For God and Country: The Rise of Polish and Lithuanian Ethnic Consciousness in America, 1860-1910.* Madison: The State Historical Society of Wisconsin, 1975.

_____ . *The Slavic Community on Strike: Immigrant Labor in Pennsylvania Anthracite.* Notre Dame: The University of Notre Dame Press, 1968.

Haberly, Loyd. *Pursuit of a Horizon: A Life of George Catlin, Painter and Recorder of the American Indian.* New York: MacMillan, 1948.

Hartmann, Edward G. *Americans from Wales.* New York: Farrar, Straus and Giroux, 1967.

Harvey, Oscar Jewell and Ernest G. Smith. *A History of Wilkes-Barre, Luzerne Country, Pennsylvania,* 6 vols. Wilkes-Barre : Reader Press, 1909-1930.

Hindle, Brook. "March of the Paxton Boys," *William and Mary Quarterly,* 3rd Series, 3 (1946), 461.

Hughes, Michael V. *The History of Plains Township.* Plains: The Plains Rotary Club, 1969.

Izbicki, Thomas M. *Newport Township, 1807-1900: A Study of the Transformation of an Agricultural Community into a Mining Community.* (Unpublished, King's College Special Collections).

Jennings, Francis. "The Indian Trade in the Susquehanna Valley," *American Philosophical Society Proceedings,* 110 (1966), 406.

Johnson, Frederick Charles. *Rev. Jacob Johnson, M.A.: Pioneer Preacher of Wyoming Valley, 1772-1797.* Wilkes-Barre: Wilkes-Barre Record, 1911.

Jones, Benjamin R. *The Settlement of the Pennsylvania Connecticut Territorial Dispute, 1753-1807.* (Unpublished, WHGS)

Joyous Struggle: A Brief Pictorial History of King's College. Wilkes-Barre: King's College Press, 1973.

Knowles, Nathaniel. "The Torture of Captives by the Indians of Eastern North America," *American Philosophical Society Proceedings,* 82 (1940), 151.

Korson, George G. *A History of the United Mine Workers of America,* 2 vols. Serialized in the *United Mine Workers Journal,* 1965-67, 1971.

_____ . *Minstrels of the Mine Patch: Songs and Stories of the Anthracite Industry.* Hatboro, Pennsylvania: Folklore Associates, 1964.

Lewis, Arthur H. *Lament for the Molly Maguires.* New York: Harcourt, Brace and World, 1964.

McCracken, Harold. *George Catlin and the Old Frontier.* New York: Bonanza Books, 1959.

McCullough, Robert and Walter Leuba. *The Pennsylvania Main Line Canal.* York: The American Canal and Transportation Center, 1973.

Merrick, R.S.M., Sr. Mary Annunciata. *A Case in Practical Democracy: Settlement of the Anthracite Coal Strike of 1902.* Notre Dame: Notre Dame University, 1942.

Miner, Charles. *History of Wyoming.* Evansville, Indiana: Unigraphic, Incorporated, 1976. (Reproduction)

Mussari, Anthony J. *Appointment with Disaster: The Swelling of the Flood.* Wilkes-Barre: Northeast Publishers, 1974.

Myers, Richmond E. *The Long Crooked River.* Boston: Christopher

Publishing House, 1949.

Myers, Wilbur A., ed. *The Book of the Susquicentennial of the Battle of Wyoming, July lst-4th, 1928.* Wilkes-Barre; Smith Bennett Corporation, 1928.

_____ and Edward F. Hanlon. *Historical Album of Wilkes-Barre and Wyoming Valley.* Wilkes-Barre : The Luzerne County Bicentennial Commission, 1976.

Nash, Gay B. "Quest for the Susquehannah Valley: New York, Pennsylvania, and the 17th Century Fur Trade," *New York History* 48 (1967), 3.

Nichols, John P. *Skyline Queen and the Merchant Prince: The Woolworth Story.* New York: Trident Press, 1973.

Novak, Michael. *The Guns of Lattimore: The True Story of a Massacre and a Trial, August, 1897-March, 1898.* New York: Basic Books, Incorporated, 1978.

Palickar, Stephen J. *A Pictorial Biography of Rev. Joseph Murgas: Pioneer in the Field of Wireless Telegraphy and Radio.* Wilkes-Barre: The Murgas Memorial Foundation, 1954.

Powderly, Terence V. *The Path I Trod: The Autobiography of Terence V. Powderly.* New York: Columbia University Press, 1940.

Price, William E. *A Frontier Community in Transition: The History of Wilkes-Barre, Pennsylvania, 1750-1800.* Kent, Ohio: Kent State University, 1979.

Raddin, George G. *Centennial Survey of the Episcopal Diocese of Bethlehem, 1871-1971.* Wilkes-Barre: King's College Press, 1972.

_____ . *The Wilderness and the City: The Story of a Parish, 1817-1967.* Wilkes-Barre: St. Stephen's Episcopal Church, 1968.

Rohrbeck, Benson W. *Wilkes-Barre Railways Company.* West Chester: B. Rohrbeck Traction Publications, 1975.

Scott, W. Roger. *Wyoming Valley: A Social History of an Immigrant Community.* (Unpublished, King's College Special Collections).

Slaff, Jonathan S. *Pennsylvania's Wyoming Valley, 1925-1938 and the Decline of the Anthracite Industry During the Roosevelt Years.* (Unpublished, WHGS).

Smith, Harrison H., comp. *History of the First Presbyterian Church of Wilkes-Barre, 1772-1972.* Wilkes-Barre: Mebane Offset Printing and Publishing Company, 1972.

Smith, Samuel R. *The Wyoming Valley in the Nineteenth Century.* Wilkes-Barre: The Wilkes-Barre Leader, 1894.

Stevens, Sylvester K. *Pennsylvania: Keystone State,* 2 vols. New York: American Historical Company, 1956.

The Susquehannah Company Papers, 11 vols, Julian P. Boyd, ed. vol. I-IV, and Robert N. Taylor, ed. vol. V-XI. Ithaca, New York: Cornell University Press for the Wyoming Historical and Geological Society, 1930-1971.

Tarasar, Constance J., ed. *Orthodox America, 1794-1976: Development of the Orthodox Church in America.* Syosset, New York: The Orthodox Church in America, 1975.

Tierney, Judith, comp. *A Description of the George Korson Folklore Archive.* Wilkes-Barre: King's College Press, 1973.

Trash, Roger R. "Pennsylvania and the Albany Congress, 1754," *Pennsylvania History* 27 (1960), 273.

Ukrainians in Pennsylvania: A Contribution to the Growth of the Commonwealth. Philadelphia: Ukrainian Bicentennial Committee, 1976.

Valletta, Clement, ed. *Ethnic Heritage Studies.* Wilkes-Barre: King's College Press, 1975.

_____ . *Ritual and Folklore in Pennsylvania's Wyoming Region.* (Unpublished).

Walensky, Robert Paul. *The Aftermath of the Great Agnes Disaster: An Analysis of Emergent Groups and Local Government Officials in the Wyoming Valley of Pennsylvania.* Ann Arbor, Michigan: Xerox University Microfilms, 1977.

Wallace, Anthony F.C. *King of the Delawares: Teedyuscung, 1700-1763.* Philadelphia: University of Pennsylvania Press, 1949.

Wallace, Paul A.W. *Conrad Weiser, 1696-1760: Friend of Colonist and Mohawk.* Philadelphia: University of Pennsylvania Press, 1945.

_____ . *Indians of Pennsylvania.* Harrisburg: Pennsylvania Historical and Museum Commission, 1961.

_____ . *Pennsylvania: Seed of a Nation.* New York: Harper and Row, 1962.

Weyburn, Samuel F. *Following the Connecticut Trail to the Susquehanna Valley.* Scranton: The Anthracite Press, 1932.

Whittemore, Charles P. *A General of the Revolution: John Sullivan of New Hampshire.* New York: Columbia University Press, 1961.

Wilkes-Barre Record Almanac: A Handbook of Local and General Information. Wilkes-Barre: The Wilkes-Barre Publishing Company, 1885-1961.

Wlodarski, Stephen. *The Origin and Growth of the Polish National Catholic Church.* Scranton: The Polish National Catholic Church, 1974.

Wright, Hendrick B. *Historical Sketches of Plymouth.* Philadelphia: T. B. Peterson and Brothers, 1873.

Wyoming Historical and Geological Society. *Proceedings and Collections of the Wyoming Historical and Geological Society, 1884-present.*

INDEX

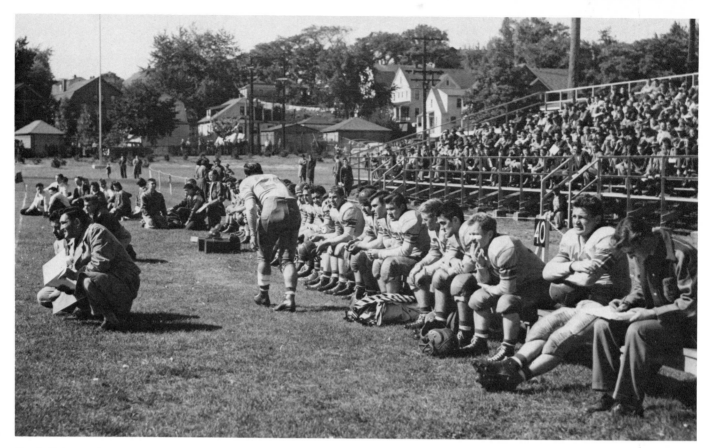

Football fostered a strong rivalry between King's College and Wilkes College. King's played at Scandlon Field, on the northern fringe of Kingston, seen here in a photo from the 1950s. Courtesy, King's College Archives, D. Leonard Corgan Library

Advisory Committee for <u>The Wyoming Valley: An American Portrait</u>

Ben Badman
NPW Medical Center

James O. Brokenshire
Crestwood School District

Robert Capin
Wilkes College

Jack Conyngham
Eastern Penn Supply Company

M. Keen Cornell
Cornell Iron Works, Inc.

Charles Davis
Nanticoke Area School District

John Dimond
Bergman's Department Store

Joseph Fink
College Misericordia

Louis Georinger
Bertels Can Company

Dominic Graziano
Hanover Area School District

Elwood Jacoby
Wyoming Valley West School District

Donald Jennings
Hanover Bank of Pennsylvania

Elmer Klimchak
Franklin First Federal Savings & Loan Association

Rev. James Lackenmier
King's College

Roy E. Morgan
WILK

Gerard Musto
Pittston Area School District

Joseph Olesky
Wyoming Area School District

Edmund H. Poggi
Howell and Jones, Inc.

George Pyle
West Side Area Vocational Technical School

Paul Radick
Pennsylvania Miller's Mutual Insurance

Richard Ross
First Eastern Bank, N.A.

James Ryan
Penn State Wilkes-Barre Campus

David Preston
Lake-Lehman School District

Richard A. Shipe
Dallas Area School District

Ralph Smith
Blue Cross of Northeast Pennsylvania

Leo E. Solomon
Wilkes-Barre Area School District

Wallace Stettler
Wyoming Seminary

David Tressler
Northeastern Bank of Pennsylvania

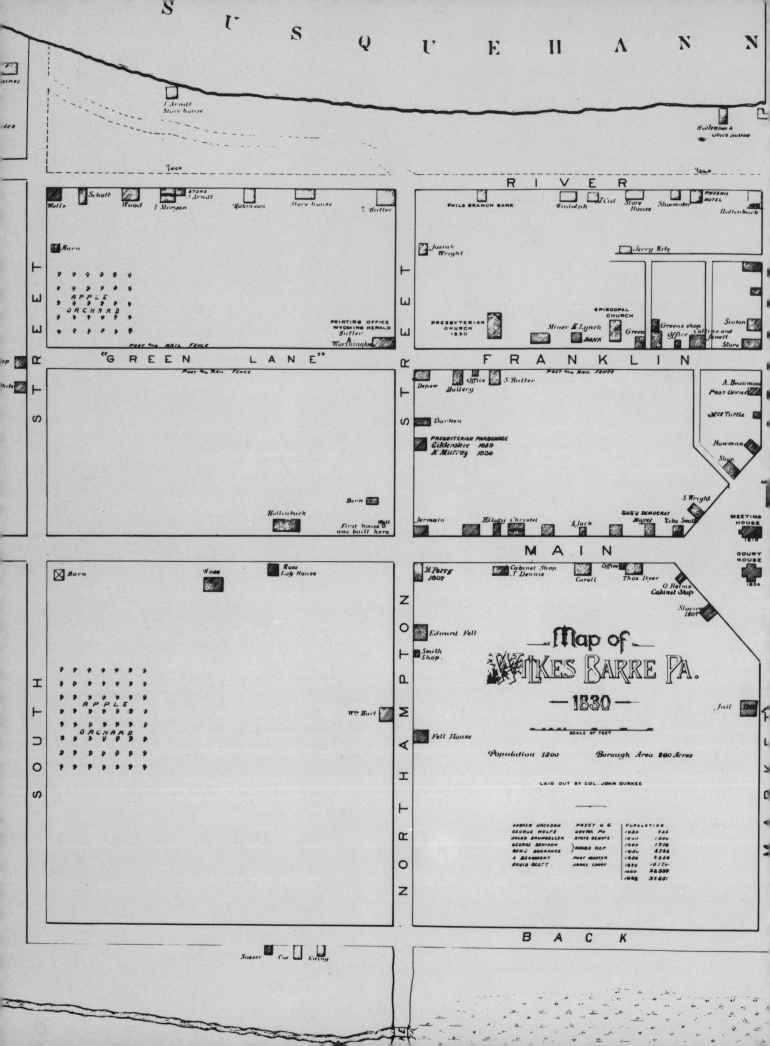

S U S Q U E H A N N

J Arndt
Store house

Hollenback
Store house

R I V E R

Wells *Schott* *Wood* *J Morgan* *STORE* *J Arndt* *Robinson* *Store house* *T. Butler*

PHILS BRANCH BANK *Rudolph* *J Cist* *Store House* *Shoemaker* *PHŒNIX HOTEL* *Hollenback*

Barn

Josiah Wright

Jerry Kitz

APPLE ORCHARD

S T R E E T

PRESSYTERIAN CHURCH 1830

Miner & Lynch *BANK* *Green*

EPISCOPAL CHURCH

Greens shop *Office* *Collins and Jewett Store* *Sinton*

PRINTING OFFICE WYOMING HERALD Butler *Worthington*

POST and RAIL FENCE

"G R E E N   L A N E"

F R A N K L I N   S T R E E T

POST and RAIL FENCE

POST and RAIL FENCE

Depew *Office* *Mallery* *S Butler*

A Beaumont POST OFFICE

Darken

Mil Tuttle

PRESBYTERIAN PARSONAGE
Gildersleve 1829
N. Murray 1830

Bowman Shop

S Wright

MEETING HOUSE

Barn

Jermain *H Cady Chrystel* *A Jack* *Moffet* *SUS'Q DEMOCRAT* *Ziba Smith*

Hollenback *First house 0 was built here* *Well*

M A I N

COURT HOUSE 1804

Barn *Ross* *Ross Log House*

B. Perry 1807 *Cabinet Shop J. Dennis* *Covell* *Office* *Thos Dyer* *O Helme Cabinet Shop*

Slocum 1807

Edward Fell

N O R T H A M P T O N

Smith Shop.

— Map of —
WILKES BARRE PA.
— 1830 —

SCALE OF FEET

APPLE ORCHARD

Wm Hart

Population 1200   Borough Area 800 Acres

Jail

Fell House

LAID OUT BY COL. JOHN DURKEE

S O U T H

M A R K E T

ANDREW JACKSON	PREST U.S.	POPULATION	
GEORGE WOLFE	GOV'N'R Pa	1830	708
JACOB BRUMMELLER	STATE SENATE	1830	1200
GEORGE BENISON	} HOUSE REP	1830	1718
BENJ DORRANCE		1830	2723
A BEAUMONT	POST MASTER	1830	4253
DAVID SCOTT	JUDGE COURT	1830	10174
		1830	23339
		1840	37651

B A C K

Nosser *Cox* *Ewing*